EIN VOLK, EIN REICH, EIN FÜHRER

The Nazi Annexation of Austria 1938

Dieter Wagner

Gerhard Tomkowitz

EIN VOLK, EIN REICH, EIN FÜHRER

The Nazi Annexation of Austria 1938

Translated by Geoffrey Strahan

Longman

LONGMAN GROUP LIMITED
LONDON

Associated companies, branches and representatives
throughout the world

© R. Piper & Co. Verlag München 1968

Originally published in German by R. Piper & Co. Verlag
München 1968 as '*Ein Volk Ein Reich Ein Führer!*' *Der Anschluss
Österreichs 1938.*

The English translation of this abridged version
© The Longman Group Limited 1971

First published 1971

ISBN 0 582 10803 9

Printed in Great Britain by
Western Printing Services Limited, Bristol

CONTENTS

The sources of the photographic illustrations in this book are as follows: Associated Press (1); Foto Hilscher (6); Süddeutscher Verlag (6); Ullstein Bilderdienst (2).

ILLUSTRATIONS

Between pages 144–145

Schuschnigg supporters in Vienna
Arthur Seyss-Inquart in Linz
Chancellor Kurt von Schuschnigg
Wilhelm Miklas, the Austrian President
Engelbert Dollfuss
Cardinal Theodor Innitzer
Guido Zernatto
Guido Schmidt
Odilo Globocznigg
Wilhelm Keppler
Hubert Klausner
Josef Bürckel
Hitler during his first public speech in Austria
Hitler driving through Vienna
Seyss-Inquart presents his Cabinet to the public
Hitler proclaims the *Anschluss*

FOREWORD

The fate of the First Republic of Austria was settled during the course of one week—between 9 March and 15 March 1938. The week began with a desperate attempt on the part of the Austrian Federal Chancellor, Dr Kurt von Schuschnigg, to frustrate the German Reich's lust to annex its neighbour. For the first time in eight years the head of the authoritarian government of this Christian corporate state called upon the citizens of his country to vote. What they were to endorse was his own conception of an Austria, 'free and German, independent and social, Christian and united'. It was intended that this hastily arranged plebiscite should take place four days later, on 13 March 1938. But by 13 March the flags of Nazi Germany were already flying over Austria. And in the Heldenplatz in Vienna on 15 March Adolf Hitler proclaimed 'the greatest act of fulfilment in German history'. He declared Austria to be an integral part of the German Reich.

The annexation of Austria was the first blow struck by Hitler outside the frontiers of Germany. While his Air Force Minister, Hermann Goering, was overthrowing the Austrian government by telephone from Berlin and handing over the helm to a Nazi cabinet, Hitler mobilized the soldiers of the Eighth Army and sent them into Austria. This force of more than 100,000 soldiers and police encountered no resistance. Advancing with the troops as they marched into his homeland, Hitler, an Austrian by birth, saw the rejoicing of his fellow countrymen for himself. Only now did he decide that Austria should be totally absorbed into the German Reich. Just a short time before he had still been thinking in terms of a certain degree of independence.

In March 1938 a centuries-old dream—that of a Greater German Reich—seemed to have been realized. Following the defeat of 1918, politicians in both countries had striven for the union of Germany with Austria. But in the peace treaties the victorious powers had specifically prohibited Austria, the German-speaking rump state of the Austro-Hungarian Empire, from merging with Germany. Nevertheless the idea of union remained alive. And in the years that followed the supporters of almost every political tendency and party came out in favour of an *Anschluss*, that is, a merger with the German Reich. It was only Hitler's assumption of power in Germany that altered this

9

situation. Now the open advocacy of the abolition of the Austrian frontier was confined to Pan-German quarters and the Austrian Nazi Party. Increasingly these groups became Hitler's Fifth Column in Austria.

The National Socialists' first attempt to seize power in Vienna in the summer of 1934 was a failure. They managed to occupy the government building in the Ballhausplatz and to murder Dollfuss, the Austrian Chancellor, but Berlin disowned its fellow ideologues. Hitler still believed he must take account of foreign opinion and hesitated to intervene directly.

The Austrian government appeared to have regained control once more. Dollfuss's successor, Schuschnigg, attempted to build up the national mass movement, the 'Fatherland Front', still further. It was hoped that the maintaining of a clerico-fascist system at home would strengthen Austria's will to resist her National Socialist neighbours. But in the field of foreign affairs the stars were not on Austria's side. England, France and Italy, the countries that had guaranteed the continued existence of the Austrian State, could no longer be regarded as reliable allies. And at the same time, at the beginning of 1938, a Germany grown strong started to increase its pressure. This became overwhelming when at Berchtesgaden in February Hitler compelled the Austrian Chancellor to include 'link-men' from the banned Austrian National Socialist Party in his government.

It was in this situation that Schuschnigg hit upon the idea of a plebiscite. He wanted to put an end to Hitler's increasing blackmail by means of a majority vote of the Austrian people. In the country itself everything seemed at first to go according to plan. Even the Left, which Schuschnigg had himself suppressed, overcame strong misgivings in their desire to support the Chancellor's scheme. On 9 March 1938, making a surprise announcement of the plebiscite, the Chancellor uttered the traditional words: 'Mander, 's ischt Zeit!' ('Men, the time has come!'). Forty-eight hours later he was out of office and the government was in the hands of the Austrian Nazis.

The seven days it took to change the map of Europe are the subject of this book. It presents a detailed picture of what happened hour by hour at the focal points of the action as well as in the secondary theatres. In addition to published books, newspapers and documents, and unpublished documentary sources, use has been made of a great many oral and written interviews with the participants in and witnesses of the events of that time.

Such personal testimonies seemed particularly necessary because in those days of crisis there was much that was never recorded in writing and some documents that were later lost.

A good many lies and errors came to light and a good deal of bluff. Berlin had operated under cover of the assertion to the outside world that Schuschnigg's successor, Seyss-Inquart, had himself sent a telegram calling on the Germans to enter Austria 'to preserve law and order': Seyss-Inquart never sent this. Militarily, the German invasion—although a triumphal procession—is shown by the secret reports of the Eighth Army to have been a fiasco. Resistance during the days of the *Anschluss* was seriously contemplated by scarcely anybody in Austria and practised by no one—either for reasons of self-restraint or out of opportunism or for other motives. It was only a long time afterwards that sporadic resistance began to arise. Nevertheless Himmler's Gestapo[1] and the Austrian brownshirts lost no time in arresting officials and supporters of the Schuschnigg regime, as well as partisans of the banned Left and Jews.

The purpose of this book is to capture both the numerous and diverse facets of a historical event and the many levels at which it takes place. For this reason it seemed necessary to juxtapose the scenes which were played out simultaneously in different places between different sets of characters. It is from such individual fragments that this mosaic of the *Anschluss* has been built up. Every scene and every conversation recorded here is documented by written or oral sources. The authors' thanks are due to all those people whose oral and written evidence has alone made this book possible.

Nothing can be said here of the disenchantment which later overtook many Austrians. Nor of what subsequently befell the people who appear here as actors and observers in the drama. The intention has been to give an objective account of the course of those seven dramatic days when Hitler took what may be seen as his first step along the road to the Second World War. The starting point is 9 March 1938.

DIETER WAGNER

GERHARD TOMKOWITZ

[1] *Geheime Staatspolizei*, the German secret state police. Tr.

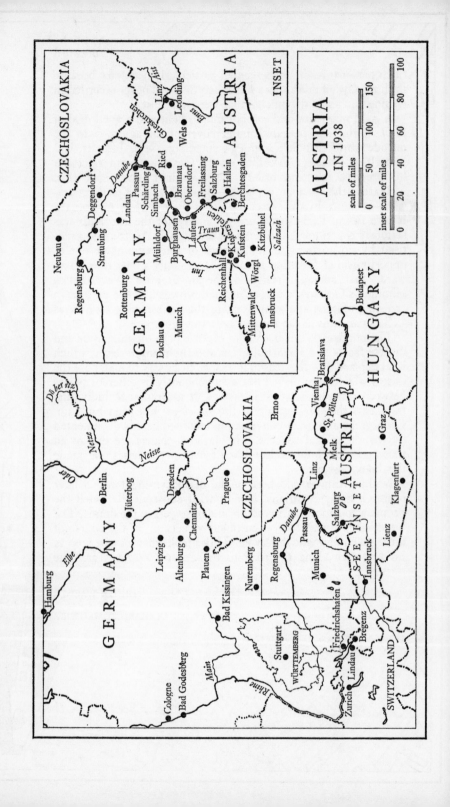

AUSTRIA
IN 1938

scale of miles

inset scale of miles

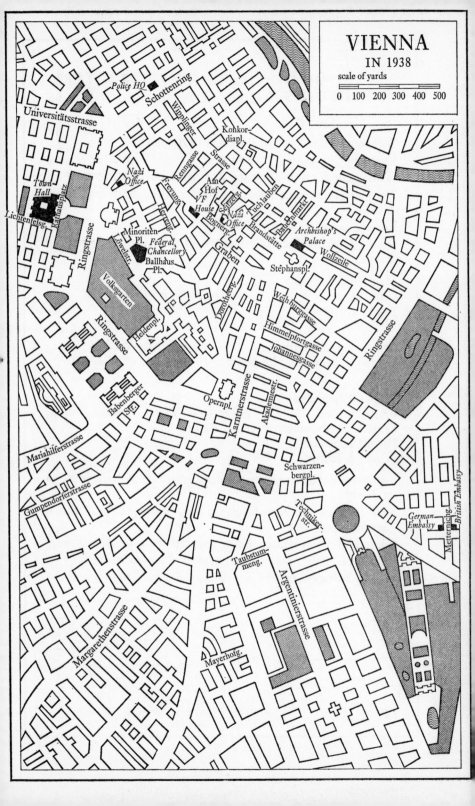

VIENNA
IN 1938

scale of yards

0 100 200 300 400 500

Police HQ

Schottenring

Universitätsstrasse

Wipplinger

Konkor-diapl.

Nazi Office

Strasse

Renngasse

Am Hof

VF House

Freyung

Herreng.

Schreyv.

Nazi Office

Bognerg.

Tuchlauben

Brandstätte

Bauernmarkt

Archbishop's Palace

Wollzeile

Town Hall

Lichtentelsg.

Rathausplatz

Ringstrasse

Minoriten Pl.

Löwelstr.

Federal Chancellory

Ballhaus Pl.

Graben

Stephanspl.

Volksgarten

Dorotheeng.

Weihburggasse

Himmelpfortgasse

Johannesstrasse

Ringstrasse

Ringstrasse

Heldenpl.

Karntnerstrasse

Akademiestr.

Babenberger Str.

Opernpl.

Mariahilferstrasse

Schwarzen-bergpl.

Gumpendorferstrasse

Techniker str.

German Embassy

Metternichg.

British Embassy

Margarethenstrasse

Taubstumm-meng.

Argentinierstrasse

Mayerhofg.

SOME OF THE CHIEF CHARACTERS IN THIS BOOK

Wilhelm Miklas, Federal President of Austria

Kurt von Schuschnigg, the Austrian Federal Chancellor

Guido Schmidt, the influential Austrian Foreign Minister

Theodor Hornbostel, Political Director at the Austrian Foreign Office

Richard Schmitz, Mayor of Vienna

Guido Zernatto, Secretary General of the Austrian Fatherland Front

Manfred Ackermann
Otto Bauer
Josef Buttinger
Alexander Eiffler
leading members of the banned Austrian Socialist Party

Arthur Seyss-Inquart
Edmund Glaise von Horstenau
moderate Nazis in Schuschnigg's Cabinet

Kurt Daluege
Odilo Globocznigg
Franz Hueber
Ernst Kaltenbrunner
Hubert Klausner
Friedrich Rainer
leaders of the illegal Austrian Nazi Party

Fedor von Bock, the German general entrusted with the invasion of Austria

Josef Bürckel, the Nazi Gauleiter who organized the Austrian *Anschluss* campaign

Prince Philip von Hessen, Hitler's special envoy to Mussolini

Wilhelm Keppler, Hitler's specialist on Austrian matters

Franz von Papen, ex-German Ambassador in Vienna

WEDNESDAY, 9 MARCH 1938

The young Foreign Minister of the Austrian Republic, Guido Schmidt, was back in his office on the entresol of the Chancellery. He was the first Foreign Minister Austria had had for a number of years. Until the cabinet reshuffle of February 1938 Chancellor Schuschnigg had himself taken charge of foreign affairs, like many another Austrian Chancellor before him, and Schmidt had been his State Secretary. It was whispered in the tortuous corridors of the Chancellery, not to mention the cafés of Vienna, that Schmidt had always been a good deal more than this—Schuschnigg's evil genius, in fact.

The Chancellor and the Foreign Minister had known one another from their earliest youth. Together they had attended Stella Matutina, the well-known Jesuit school, and their association had continued in later life. Schmidt had been quick to recognize that he complemented the Chancellor excellently in many ways. Where Schuschnigg tended to be shy and withdrawn, Schmidt was outwardly self-confident, fluent and—in the view of many—arrogant. He relieved his friend and chief of many tasks, often very important ones, which the latter found distasteful.

Thus, Schmidt had taken it upon himself the day before to inform President Miklas of the Chancellor's surprising political coup. Just before one o'clock on 8 March the Foreign Minister called at the President's offices. Schmidt told him that the Chancellor now wanted to know whether his policy at home and his attitude towards the German Reich were supported by the majority of the people. For that reason he had decided to announce a plebiscite in a public speech on Wednesday evening. The people would be called upon to vote, 'For an Austria free and German, independent and social, Christian and united.'

When Miklas heard that the vote was to take place the following Sunday he was amazed. He had indeed been urging for years that elections should be held. But in such haste! Nevertheless Miklas promised his support. 'As to the details, there will have to be further consultations with me, for, in accordance with the constitution, the holding of a plebiscite must take place through the President of the Republic.' Schmidt's reply had been brief and abrupt: 'No!' The Chancellor himself would announce the plebiscite. Constitutional lawyers had confirmed that this was provided for in the constitution.

But the President remained unimpressed by the Foreign Minister's polished arguments. The Chancellor would have to oblige him by telling him in person. Moreover, the President had what he believed to be well-founded doubts about whether it was either constitutional or feasible to hold a ballot at such short notice. When he returned to his office after lunch an appointment was arranged with the Chancellor's staff.

And so that same evening of 8 March Chancellor Schuschnigg, who had been busy the whole day with important preparations for the plebiscite, had had no alternative but to see the President. It was only then that Miklas learned how Schuschnigg intended to underwrite the constitutional nature of the plebiscite: by appealing to an article which stated that it was the Chancellor's function to determine the guiding principles of policy. The President expressed reservations and asked for the plebiscite to be postponed. But Schuschnigg had remained firm. It was too late to do this. Their conversation did not end until after midnight. The President had finally resigned himself to the situation: 'Evidently I have become superfluous in this country.'

There were at the most three dozen men in the whole of Austria—politicians from the Chancellor's immediate entourage and officers of the Fatherland Front—who knew of the plan for the plebiscite and the date when it would be held. It was indeed an idea which went back for some years, but the Chancellor had always hesitated to act against his own authoritarian system of government and ask the nation for its opinion. Now the hour seemed to have come. It was the hour of need.

The eyes of Adolf Hitler, the dictator across the border, were greedily fixed upon the land of his birth. Already, long ago, on the first page of his political manifesto, *Mein Kampf*, Hitler had insisted: 'German Austria must return to the great German motherland: not out of economic considerations of any kind. No, no. Even if this union made no difference from the economic point of view—even if it were positively detrimental—it must nevertheless take place. Peoples of one blood belong together in one Reich.'

Ever since Hitler had become the Chancellor and Führer of Germany on 30 January 1933 no year had gone by without him renewing his efforts to realize this demand. Metternich's pale shadows in the Vienna Ballhausplatz had so far tried to resist this pressure from the north by means of a fragile policy of alliances and guarantees.

After their common defeat at the end of the First World War, Germany and the Austrian heartland of the former Habsburg Empire had expressed the wish to be united in a single imperial commonwealth. On 12 November 1918 the Provisional National Assembly in Vienna passed a law with the support of all parties about the form of the state, in the second article of which 'German Austria' was declared to be a part of the Republic of Germany. The Weimar Constitution had also dealt with the *Anschluss* of Austria and Germany. Article Two mentions that other countries could also be incorporated into the Reich if their populations so desired. Article Sixty-one granted German Austria the right, following an *Anschluss*, to be represented in the *Reichsrat*.

But the victorious allies did not allow the defeated powers to come together. In the Treaties of Versailles and Saint-Germain in 1919 Germany and Austria had to forswear all their yearnings for union. However, for many years the issue of an *Anschluss* had been kept alive, particularly in Austria. It was not until Hitler and the National Socialists came to power in Germany that many Austrian supporters of an *Anschluss*—particularly those on the left—lost their enthusiasm.

It was then that the makers of Austrian foreign policy embarked on their desperate search for foreign powers to guarantee the security and continued existence of their republic at the heart of Europe. Finally the independence of Austria was guaranteed by England, France and Fascist Italy in joint declarations on 17 February 1934, and 27 September 1934 and at the Stresa Conference on 13 April 1935.

But at the same time there was a growing impression amongst the western democracies that they would have to find some sacrifice which it would not cost them too much to toss to a hungry Hitler. Moreover, thanks to his adventures in Abyssinia and his aggressive policies in the Mediterranean, Mussolini, who had imperial aspirations for Italy, had come into conflict with the other two powers who were supposed to guarantee Austria's independence.

In this situation Germany and Italy had drawn closer together, although not at the expense of Austria. To avoid upsetting the political situation in Europe and to ensure that he could carry on rearming the German forces in peace, Hitler had proved ready to reach an agreement with Vienna. Relations between Germany and Austria, hitherto extremely tense, had been 'normalized'. Even after this first Berchtesgaden agreement of 11 July 1936, however,

17

the Austrian National Socialist Party had continued to work actively in the underground for an *Anschluss* with the German Reich.

By the beginning of 1938 German-Austrian relations had once again reached a new low. On 12 February 1938 Hitler had invited the Austrian Chancellor and his Foreign Minister, Schmidt, to talks at Berchtesgaden. He received them with threats and insults and then bluntly presented them with an ultimatum. When the two friends returned to Vienna their luggage contained a piece of paper that was to mark the decisive step along the road to ruin. Schuschnigg had given way to Hitler's demand that the banned National Socialists should be represented in his government. In accordance with this agreement, Schuschnigg had appointed the Viennese lawyer, Dr Arthur Seyss-Inquart, to the post of Minister of the Interior. The military historian, Edmund Glaise von Horstenau, who was, like him, a Pan-German, also remained in the cabinet. In spite of this, the pressure had become even stronger. The Austrian Nazis now began to assert themselves in the knowledge that the ultimate head of the police force was on their side. It was in this critical situation that the idea of the plebiscite was born.

In the Fatherland Front building on the morning of 9 March 1938 the staff of two hundred were at work on this major project, intended to guarantee the integrity of the Republic for years to come. But only a very few of them knew what it was all about. The plebiscite was treated as a secret operation by the top officials in the building. Schuschnigg had originally wanted only his personal friend, Zernatto, the Secretary of the Fatherland Front, to be entrusted with the secret of the scheme. But Zernatto had finally convinced him that a poll of this kind, the first in eight years, must be thoroughly prepared for in advance. So Zernatto was granted permission to let a few of the senior party officials in on the secret.

Behind padded doors they were drawing up a kind of battle plan in minute detail, to ensure that every supporter of the Fatherland Front would be mobilized for the plebiscite campaign during the next three days. The men in charge of propaganda, Hans Becker and Dr Fritz Bock, were drafting the campaign literature; the thirty-four-year-old head of the political section,

Maximilian Pammer, was holding talks with the few members of the state police who knew about the scheme, while Dr Albert Hantschk, nearly forty, the administrative head of the General Secretariat, was making contact with the most important members of the Front throughout the country.

These officers of the Front were performing their various tasks with mixed feelings. They were the very people who had put pressure on Zernatto and Schuschnigg himself after Hitler's Berchtesgaden ultimatum: 'Now something must be done. This is the "cold Anschluss".' But this plebiscite was coming too soon for them. They were too unprepared. The electoral lists had not been revised since the 1930 election: the legal basis for the plebiscite seemed to them more than a little dubious; and one argument was repeated over and over again: they had not been given enough time.

Zernatto was considering how to break it to his friend, Seyss-Inquart, that the plebiscite had been fixed for the following Sunday. He knew Seyss to be an ambitious but decent man and a good Catholic besides. He would surely not make any difficulties, thought Zernatto, even if Schuschnigg had in fact bypassed him in this matter. Zernatto, like Schuschnigg, still thought of Seyss as a figure they hoped to use to tame the Nazi extremists in Austria. Zernatto himself had been responsible for bringing the now forty-six-year-old lawyer into politics, when he had observed that Seyss was beginning to play a part in a number of Pan-German orientated groups, such as the Austrian *Volksbund* and the German Club. Seyss, so Zernatto had thought, could gather the moderate Nazis about him and then act as a link man between them and the Fatherland Front and the government.

Seyss did not seem particularly surprised, either by the news or the date. He even prophesied that the government would be sure to emerge from the ballot with a clear majority. The Minister continued in a conversational tone for a further three-quarters of an hour before taking his leave. Zernatto watched him go as Seyss crossed the Platz Am Hof with a slight limp and disappeared into his own office.

Almost as soon as Seyss had returned to his office he began dictating a letter to his secretary. The letter was addressed to 'General Secretary Zernatto' and read as follows:

'Dear Minister, You have informed me today that the Federal Chancellor has decided to hold a kind of plebiscite on the 13th of this month. The Federal Chancellor instructed you to inform me of his decision. I therefore find myself obliged to make known to you my position with regard to this plan, and request that you will inform the Federal Chancellor . . .'

The National Socialists, the letter went on, would now expect

'to be represented in all official and political agencies both of the State and the Fatherland Front. It is unthinkable that the National Socialists should abandon their opposition—not to the State, but to the present situation—until this representation has been granted in all essentials. And, as they are now being called upon unexpectedly and prematurely to vote in a plebiscite in which the voter is bound to give an affirmative answer if he is not to expose himself to the suspicion of holding treasonable views, I am obliged . . . to demand . . . the observance of the following conditions.'

Seyss-Inquart demanded a general secret ballot in all the provinces of the Republic and freedom for all political groups to make campaign propaganda. Special restricted voting arrangements for employees at government offices and factories must be abandoned. On these conditions he could agree to the plebiscite being held and could indeed undertake to guarantee that it passed off without disorder.

But, Seyss continued:

'As the question is not one of fundamental loyalty to the State, but simply of an attitude to the government and to the present situation, an affirmative response from the National Socialists can only be expected if the composition of the government offers the necessary conditions for a positive attitude on the part of the National Socialists.'

After this the Austrian security Minister dictated another letter, this time to the Federal Chancellor. In it he claimed that the plebiscite was unconstitutional and demanded that the ballot be conducted in accordance with the conditions he had laid down in the letter to Zernatto. In addition, he demanded a stronger representation of the 'Austrian National Socialist philosophy' in the government of Austria. Seyss dated his letter to the

20

Chancellor 10 March. Schuschnigg would not be back in Vienna until then.

꧀꧀꧀꧀꧀꧀

Two men emerged from Number 6 Mayerhofgasse in the Fourth District of Vienna, got into a limousine and drove towards the city centre. The car did not belong to them, it was only hired. The hire charge would be paid by the Party, the illegal leadership of the Austrian National Socialist Party. Both occupants of the car were about the same age. In their youth they had fought for the same cause and had both seen the insides of Austrian prisons on a number of occasions. They were Odilo Globocznigg and Dr Friedrich Rainer.

Globocznigg or 'Globus', as his friends in the Party called him, was not quite thirty-four. Born in Trieste and trained as a master builder, he had been granted Austrian citizenship after the defeat of 1918. He had joined the Party at the age of sixteen and he had now been deputy *Stabsleiter* (head of the Party staff) for two years. Rainer, thirty-five, a candidate for a notary's office, who came from the province of Carinthia, had joined the movement eight years previously. He had progressed to become the political adviser of the new head of the Austrian Nazi Party, ex-Major Hubert Klausner.

The banned National Socialists had for some time been able to move about and even to indulge in political activity with relative freedom. It was the Chancellor himself who had granted them the necessary springboard for this. A year previously he had arranged for the setting up of so-called *Volkspolitische Referate* (racial-political councils) within the Fatherland Front, whose sole purpose was to bind the Nazis to the Fatherland Front. These councils, which the National Socialists filled with people of their own choice, provided men like Globocznigg and Rainer with an organization that functioned well and covered the whole country.

At Number 1 Seitzergasse, a street parallel with the long-drawn-out Platz Am Hof, was the office of the real leader of the Racial-Political Council, Walter Pembauer. Seyss-Inquart, the Minister of the Interior, was his nominal superior but the work was done by the fifty-two-year-old former Pan-German Member of Parliament who came from Innsbruck. Pembauer was just sorting the incoming mail when the door was hastily flung open. In stormed Dr Hugo Jury. Jury, an old Party member and a

Wednesday, 9 March 1938

doctor in St Pölten, had achieved the rank of *Staatsrat* (State Councillor) in 1937 when the Schuschnigg regime, under pressure from Berlin, had sought to annex to itself the moderate National Socialists by means of appointments and sinecures. Jury tossed a piece of paper to Pembauer and called out breathlessly: 'Read it!' Pembauer took the sheet, which, as he recognized at once, was torn from a pad of the kind used at the Fatherland Front for taking minutes. It was the announcement of the plebiscite that Schuschnigg planned to proclaim at Innsbruck.

Pembauer read the hurriedly scrawled lines for a second time and looked up at Jury. 'A hoax?' 'Unfortunately not,' replied Jury. 'But how did you get this paper?' Pembauer wanted to know. Then Jury told briefly, in fragmentary sentences, what had happened the previous evening. Schuschnigg had gathered seven loyal colleagues together at the Fatherland Front building, Ministers, political friends, close colleagues. They had discussed the plan for the plebiscite. Zernatto had called in his secretary to take the minutes. But even in the offices of the Front itself the members were no longer safe from the Nazis. The secretary, a member of the banned Nazi Party, had hastily written down the gist of the discussion in the corridors of the Front building on a piece of paper which she had then passed to Jury.

At this moment the car containing Globocznigg and Rainer drew up outside Number 1 Seitzergasse. Jury and the Austrian Nazi Leader, Major Klausner, who had also just arrived, came to the door to meet them. Jury waved the paper like a trophy. They sat down together and discussed what was to be done, but they could not decide how to respond to Schuschnigg's move. Finally one of them concluded: 'We must inform Seyss. He must protest.'

Schuschnigg's Minister of the Interior had just finished dictating his letters to Schuschnigg and Zernatto when the four Nazis, Klausner, Jury, Globocznigg and Rainer, came thundering into his office. They were all talking at the same time and all kept repeating the same word: plebiscite. Seyss-Inquart did not know what attitude to adopt. He had given Schuschnigg his word of honour to say nothing about the plebiscite until the Chancellor had announced it. And Zernatto had made the same point to him an hour ago. Now here were his Party friends and Seyss could see that they knew everything.

Seyss was in a dilemma. As a Minister he felt bound by the

discipline of the cabinet, but as a declared link man with the National Socialists and with Berlin he must pass on his information. He was finally saved by a brainwave. He gave his four Party colleagues the carbon copy of his letter to Schuschnigg. Now they had something in their hands, they could inform Berlin. The four men rushed out of the office in the Platz Am Hof with the letter and ran across to the Seitzergasse.

Once back in the office of the Racial-Political Council, Rainer put through a call to Berlin. The number he asked for was 16 58 61, that of the head of the Central Office for the economic organizations of the National Socialist Party, Wilhelm Keppler. This descendant of the famous astronomer served his Führer in so many different roles simultaneously that even his oldest Party comrades did not always know in what capacity Keppler was acting at any given moment. His most important function was not even formally recognized by means of a regular title or an office. Hitler had made him his special representative for all questions concerning Austria.

He had returned from Vienna only two days previously. He had had talks with the illegal Nazis as well as with members of the government. He had even been to Schuschnigg's house at the Belvedere. In his 'Report on my visit to Vienna from 3 to 6 March 1938' Keppler had written on his return: 'The Austrian Party is now in an excellent state. Klausner has got himself well established and finds loyal support everywhere . . . Dr Seyss-Inquart is working with exceptional skill and has won himself a most influential position, within the Party as well . . . He also intends . . . to attempt to have the SA[1] and SS[2] legalized, for example as disciplinary forces of the Racial-Political Council.' The chief opponents of National Socialism were now the Mayor of Vienna, Richard Schmitz, and the Christian trades unions. But the Movement could no longer be stopped. 'In Austria there is no more bunting and no more brown cloth to be had. The factories have large orders for fresh supplies.'

Keppler had also spoken about this the previous day when he appeared with Ribbentrop, the newly appointed Foreign Minister of the German Reich, to make a report at the Reich Chancellery. Hitler was delighted with both his go-between, Keppler, and with the situation in Austria. Now it would be possible to move at a slower pace. Keppler would visit Vienna at short intervals but

[1] SA, the *Sturmabteilung* or brownshirts, the Nazi militia. Tr.
[2] SS, the *Schutzstaffel* or blackshirts, Hitler's personal elite guard of Nazis, which ran the concentration camps. Tr.

he would not talk about the *Anschluss*. Then Hitler and Ribbentrop had walked over to the window and Keppler had seen Hitler writing something down. When Ribbentrop and Hitler's Austrian emissary left the Reich Chancellery the Minister had said: 'Congratulations. The Führer has just appointed you State Secretary at the Foreign Office.'

On Tuesday morning Keppler had a telephone call from Rainer in Vienna with the news that Schuschnigg was going to hold a plebiscite the following Sunday. The newly minted State Secretary hesitated to believe it. So as to make sure, he telephoned Seyss. The Minister was cryptic. But one thing seemed certain to Keppler: something was up in Vienna. For Seyss had dropped the hint: 'Yes, the situation has become serious.'

Keppler hurried across from the Behrendstrasse to the Reich Chancellery to pass on the news to Hitler. But the Chancellor was himself equally unwilling to accept the information at face value. The State Secretary reported what he had heard from Vienna. Globocznigg was on his way with a letter in which everything was written down. But Hitler wanted to know the exact situation. He leapt up and called to the flight captain who had been in his service for years: 'Baur, clear a plane right away. Keppler must fly to Vienna.'

In Vienna Theodor Hornbostel, the Political Director of the Foreign Office, had a visitor. Colonel Dr Emil Liebitzky, the Military Attaché, was reporting back from Rome. Schuschnigg had sent him to see Mussolini on 7 March with a report about Berchtesgaden and the plans for a plebiscite. The Chancellor had not gone to his Ambassador in Rome, Egon Berger-Waldenegg, with this mission because the latter had no direct access to Mussolini, but would have had to go via the Italian Foreign Minister. Liebitzky, on the other hand, as Military Attaché, could make a direct approach to the Italian dictator and Minister for War.

From Liebitzky's forlorn expression Hornbostel could tell how the mission had fared. 'The Duce calls the plebiscite a bomb,' said the Colonel. Hornbostel had already expressed his own reservations the day before when he learned about the plan. He had been convinced of Hitler's reactions and dubious about Italy's loyalty to the alliance.

Hornbostel told the Foreign Minister on the internal telephone: 'Liebitzky is back.' Then the old-school diplomat (who had already been active in the diplomatic corridors in the days of the Monarchy) went with the Military Attaché to see the young Foreign Minister of the Austrian Republic.

The Duce, Liebitzky reported to the ever immaculate Guido Schmidt, had received him in a friendly fashion and welcomed his report on the events of Berchtesgaden. It was a good thing for Austria to come to an understanding with Germany and to cooperate closely with the Reich. When the conversation had turned to the possibility of a violation of Austrian sovereignty by force of arms Mussolini gave a heated reply: 'That is something they will never do. We have Goering's word of honour.' As for a plebiscite Mussolini had advised against it emphatically. Not only would it provoke a reaction from the Germans: it was also pointless. If it were successful Hitler would not recognize it; if it went badly it would in any case be of no value to Schuschnigg. Furthermore the Duce's attitude was optimistic. In his view there was no immediate threat of danger from Germany.

Guido Schmidt, not normally a patient listener, did not interrupt Liebitzky. When the Attaché had gone Schmidt dialled the switchboard: 'Get me the Chancellor in Innsbruck.' Within a very short time the call came through. Schmidt motioned to Hornbostel to pick up the second receiver and repeated almost word for word what Liebitzky had told him. He added one sentence of his own: 'So Mussolini had advised against it.' The Chancellor's voice sounded a long way off: 'I cannot turn back now.'

At 6.55 p.m., accompanied by Schumacher, the Provincial Governor, Schuschnigg entered the great City Hall at Innsbruck. Every seat in the hall was filled by officers of the Fatherland Front. They rose to their feet and applauded their Chancellor and Front Leader. The hall was decorated with countless Teutonic Crosses and a mass of red-white-red bunting. The platform was framed by banners and flags bearing the national emblem. On both sides stood contingents from the youth organization in white shirts and black trousers as well as guards from the Front militia. The slogans of the Front were chanted in chorus: 'We stand by the Chancellor!' and: 'Red-white-red until we're dead'.

'We Tyrolese,' called Schumacher from the platform, 'rejoice from the bottom of our hearts that you have come to us, to the capital of the Tyrol, amidst our mountains. I am proud of the fact that the first journey you have taken after these difficult weeks has brought you here, to your home. The Tyrol has pledged its loyalty to you, as Chancellor and Leader of the Front. We Tyrolese are loyal, and will always remain loyal.' Tumultuous applause. The military band played: *O Du mein Österreich* ('Oh my Austria') and everyone joined in.

The Federal Chancellor rested both his hands on the speaker's desk:

'I thank you with all my heart for your thunderous outburst of enthusiasm, which is inspired, I know, not by myself but by our Fatherland and, also, I believe, by the road this Fatherland of ours has resolved to take . . . On the occasion ten years ago when I first had the opportunity to make a political speech, standing on this very spot, in this hall, in my home town of Innsbruck, my theme was a call to unity and to peace, though I well knew that only the strong can utter such a call. And now at this hour my message to you is the same . . .'

Schuschnigg promised school places for 30,000 young people in the near future. Thanks to the Labour Service 'further battalions of willing youngsters' would be 'snatched away from idleness and poverty' and would 'learn how to work'. The Front members cheered. Schuschnigg promised new roads for the Tyrol and social improvements: 'Bread and peace for all.' For an hour the Chancellor spoke about a free and German Austria, about an independent and social Austria, about a Christian and united Austria, about bread and peace throughout the country and about the equal rights of all who stood by nation and homeland. Then Schuschnigg adopted a solemn tone: now he needed to know whether all this was what the nation wanted. And therefore: 'Next Sunday, 13 March of this year, we shall consult the people.' This announcement was followed by a roar of applause and shouts of 'Heil Schuschnigg' which lasted for minutes on end. The band played Andreas Hofer's song *Zu Mantua in Banden*. The Front members stood and sang. And Schuschnigg himself evoked the memory of the Tyrolese hero of freedom, against Napoleon, Andreas Hofer, and his battle cry of 1809: 'Mander, 'is ischt Zeit' ('Men, the time has come'). And once again there was tumultuous applause.

The Café Meteor at Number 30 Fasangasse in the Third District was a typical Viennese coffee-house with plenty of plush. Regular customers came here to read the paper, to drink a *Schwarzer* (black coffee), a *Mélange* (white coffee) or an *Einspänner* (black coffee with whipped cream). And on Friday evenings a glee club rehearsed there. For a long time past, however, the tranquillity had been disturbed. Men who had never been seen there before would enter quickly and disappear down the stairs that led to the cellar bar. An aura of conspiracy hung over the place. The waiters knew who belonged and who did not. Inquisitive people were politely but firmly kept out: 'A private gathering, Sir.'

For the cellar at the Meteor, alongside a skittle-alley, was the rendezvous of the political leaders whose movement at the last elections, eight years previously, had succeeded in uniting behind it some forty per cent of all voters. Then in 1934 the strongest political party in Austria—like all other political organizations—had been banned. This was the Austrian Left.

If anything happened in Vienna it generally happened in a coffee-house. Seyss and his circle had the Herrenhof; the 'Legitimists', supporters of the monarchy, met at a café in the Wollzeile; the extreme Nazis at the Café Central. The Meteor had become the headquarters of the illegal Left because it was near Kurt Mantler's home. The former secretary of the Central Union of Provisions Workers and now the chairman of the banned left-wing trade-union movement used to meet his friends in the Fasangasse and for several months past the number of these friends had been increasing all the time.

In the dictatorial 'corporate state' set up by Dollfuss and led by Schuschnigg after his death, there was no place for parties. Everyone had to find a political home within the Fatherland Front, the official organization for unity. But as the National Socialists became more active, the pressure from Berlin grew stronger and Schuschnigg had to yield to this blackmail more and more often, and it became increasingly clear to the Chancellor and his allies that they needed the support of the old Left. Since the setting up of Racial-Political Councils had granted the National Socialists a status which was at least semi-legal, Schuschnigg had attempted an opening to the Left. The first talks had already taken place shortly after Berchtesgaden. Schuschnigg had wanted to appoint one of the spokesmen of the illegal free trades unions as State Secretary for Labour. But Friedrich Hillegeist, the forty-three-year-old union leader whom he had selected for the post,

27

could not be found on the day of the Cabinet reshuffle. So another man, also a former Socialist, had taken the post.

At the Café Meteor the feeling now was that the wind was blowing from a favourable quarter. Sitting together down below in the cellar at the long tables over coffee and beer—the cheapest drinks, which they could just about afford—the illegal Left no longer tried to camouflage themselves when an unfamiliar tread was heard on the stairs. They had grown accustomed to turning themselves at lightning speed into a skittles club or rapidly dealing out the cards for a game. The guards on the doors, who had formerly maintained an uninterrupted watch at the entrance, had also disappeared. They knew that their hiding-place was no secret to the police; but they also knew that Schuschnigg could no longer afford to send his bloodhounds in pursuit of them.

In the general amnesty on 17 February 1938, five days after Berchtesgaden, those released from prison included the leaders of the left-wing unions and those of the Revolutionary Socialists, the organization which had succeeded the 'Socialist Party'. Another five days later Hillegeist and some of his friends were received by the head of the General Secretariat of the Fatherland Front for a preliminary meeting. Only on 3 March did Schuschnigg himself hear what they had to say. That day the Chancellor had just decided to hold the plebiscite. It therefore seemed to him a shrewd move finally to satisfy the workers' demands for a meeting. Hillegeist and twenty fellow Socialists had walked through the gates of the Chancellery in the Ballhausplatz and the sentries of the Chancellery guard had presented arms. The meeting between the Chancellor of the Austrian corporate state and the representatives of the banned trades-union organization and party had lasted for four and a quarter hours. The delegates had not minced their words.

Hillegeist: 'Herr Chancellor! We have long striven in vain for this meeting, which is now taking place so terribly late in the day. If it is to achieve a result of any kind, there must be complete frankness from the very beginning. We do not stand before you as supporters of your government, of your sham trades-unions or of your Fatherland Front.'

Schuschnigg: 'I know very well who you are and I appreciate your resolute spirit and moral courage, for it has enabled you to come and see me, your former enemy.'

One of the delegation then came to the point.

'Do not believe, Herr Chancellor, that we are indulging in rhetoric or trying to put one across you, if we point out that free men fight, and slaves do not. But free men will only fight if they have something worth fighting for. That is why you must first make us Viennese workers free. Give us back the right of free and unfettered speech that Dollfuss took from us in February 1934, and set us free from the presence of your police spies. Give us the assurance that we shall not all be arrested together as "Bolshevik conspirators" if we talk about socialism and Karl Marx.'

The delegates had demanded satisfaction on four points before they would declare themselves ready to support the Schuschnigg government against the danger from the Right: 1. They should be granted the same freedom of action as the National Socialists. 2. Free elections in the Federation of Trades Unions. 3. The right to a daily newspaper. 4. Guarantees for a social welfare programme. But Schuschnigg was unwilling to give his word right away. These things would have to be clarified in future negotiations with the official union organization. He referred Hillegeist and the delegates to the chairman of the official union, Johann Staud, and his colleagues. There was one concession, however, which Hillegeist was able to come away with when he walked out through the gates of the Chancellery at 10.15 p.m. Schuschnigg had given permission for a meeting of the illegal + Left, the first to take place for four years.

But that same Thursday evening at the Café Meteor there had been differences of opinion when Hillegeist and his companions had reported on the talks to the other representatives of the unions, the Revolutionary Socialists and the Communists. The critics had been sceptical: in their opinion there were no miracles to be expected from Schuschnigg and all many of the former trades-union secretaries were after was their old jobs.

On Monday, 7 March, it had seemed to many of the 350 listeners at the meeting at the Floridsdorf Workers' Club as if they had suddenly been transported back into the good old days. In February 1934 this building, part of the workers' flats, had been under artillery bombardment by the government because the Socialists had dug themselves in there. Now for the first time in four years the speakers there could begin their speeches with the word 'Comrades'. Rising to their feet, the 350 had honoured the sacrifice of the victims of the political struggle four years ago. But this, too, had created no unity: the Communists were in favour of giving Schuschnigg unconditional support; the majority wanted to wait for the outcome of the negotiations before making common cause with their enemy of yesterday.

When the representatives of the Left met together again at the Café Meteor on the evening of 9 March, they knew that the sceptics of Floridsdorf had won their point. There had certainly been further negotiations but the negotiators had had nothing to show for them. All they had to report was the remark of Staud, the President of the government union: 'We can manage without you.' A depressed mood spread through the gathering. The cellar was crowded. Many new faces were there. Many of them were people who thought they had better be there if jobs were being given out. Only the Revolutionary Socialists had stayed away. They had put a kind of ban on the Café Meteor for their supporters. The party was represented by Manfred Ackermann, one of its officers, and he was proof against wishful thinking. It had led too often in the past to his arrest and to a thorough acquaintance with the inside of Woellersdorf, the Schuschnigg government's concentration camp. 'Martin' (Ackermann's cover name in the party) had been released from his last period of detention three weeks previously.

That evening at the Café Meteor, where the banned Left were discussing their chances of political resurrection, the news from Innsbruck came as a bombshell. All the voices of doom seemed to be silenced at a blow. The Socialists pinned their hopes on one particular sentence which seemed, for all the clauses it was hedged about with, to represent Schuschnigg's new conception of politics at home: 'But that does not mean that we shall regard a member of the former Socialist Party, if he dons the badge of the national movement, as a fully-fledged member of the movement, if he comes to the Fatherland Front or speaks of Bolshevization and the Red Front. . . . Everyone who was once a member of a party naturally retains a right today to his political opinions and convictions: and the same must apply to all.' The announcement of the plebiscite itself inspired a new confidence round the tables in the cellar bar. Now the negotiations would continue, it was

said. Now the progress would be quicker. By Sunday, by the day
of the plebiscite, everything must be safely buttoned up. 'Schuschnigg needs us now.'

In the Rue Beaujon at the residence of the Austrian Ambassador in Paris, a cluster of people had formed round the wireless set
on the first floor. Vollgruber, the Ambassador, although he was
passionately concerned to know the exact terms of the speech,
was unable to leave the reception room on the ground floor. He
had to look after the remainder of the guests. But a young
attaché kept running up and down stairs between the two floors,
bringing news of what he had just gleaned from the radio.
Ultimately Schuschnigg's speech became the sole topic of
conversation among the guests at the party. The plan for a
plebiscite was welcomed.

At the German Embassy in London Schuschnigg's announcement was received rather differently. Ribbentrop, until recently
Ambassador in London and the German Foreign Minister, who
had arrived in London only that afternoon in order to take his
leave of the British political leaders, was following the speech on
the radio. He felt himself to be in an awkward situation. The
following day he was to have talks with his British counterpart,
Halifax, and other politicians. But he did not yet know what he
should answer if he were asked about Austria. What course would
Hitler take? It was inconceivable to Ribbentrop that his Führer
would take the plebiscite lying down.

But even in Berlin it was not yet known how the Austrian
Chancellor's challenge was to be answered. While Schuschnigg's
speech was still being broadcast Hitler telephoned the German
Legation in Vienna. State Secretary Keppler was called away
from the radio to the telephone. Hitler wanted to know what was
afoot. Keppler could only answer: 'It is all as we had feared.' The
following day, he told the Reich Chancellor, he would be back in
Berlin to make a full report. When Keppler returned to Rainer,
Klausner and Papen, the Austrian Chancellor's speech was
finished. In the reception room in the Metternichgasse the
various possible ways of reacting were discussed. But Keppler
could not advise his Austrian fellow ideologues what to do.

The city seemed as animated as if it were broad daylight. Groups
of people stood arguing on street corners. Lorries drove past,

Wednesday, 9 March 1938

packed with propaganda posters for the plebiscite. Columns of
Front supporters moved along the streets, leaving trails of paper
behind them. And plastered over the walls of buildings and poster
pillars was the thousandfold imperative: YES!

After the broadcast of Schuschnigg's speech the commander of
the detachment of police responsible for protecting the Opera
House district from processions of demonstrators reported sick.
Some remarkable things had already occurred in his sector.
Sudenly there had been a procession of blond giants coming down
the Kärntner Strasse. When they had reached the corner they had
come to a halt and saluted one another—although they had just
been marching along together. Their salutes were intended as a
provocation. They had raised their right hands and repeated over
and over again at short intervals the two words: 'Heil Hitler!'

Then a group of Austrians from the Fatherland Front had
come marching up from the other direction. Their shouts of
'Heil Schuschnigg!' could already be heard some way off. When
the two groups of demonstrators were standing almost opposite
one another the police had formed into a double file between the
rival political factions. Suddenly the Nazis altered the slogan
they were chanting from 'Heil Hitler!' to 'Heil Wache!' ('Long
live the police!'). Then the police officer had ordered his men to
form up against the Fatherland Front. A hail of blows from
rubber truncheons fell upon Schuschnigg's supporters. The
leader of the Front demonstrators just had time to call out to the
police officer: 'What are you doing? *We* are the Austrians here!'
Then he was struck down.

Now that evening, with the situation threatening to become
even more inflammable, Dr Heinrich Hüttl of the Security
Police had to take over the post of the police chief who had
suddenly fallen sick. His task was clearly defined but hard to
carry out. He could allow the demonstrators to march up and
down the Ringstrasse, but he must ward off any attempt to
penetrate into the City Centre. That evening Hüttl's mission was
carried out successfully.

The Nazis were still unsure of themselves. They still did not
know what view Berlin took of the situation, nor had the Austrian
Party leadership told them how to react to the announcement of
the plebiscite. Rainer and Klausner only knew that their supporters were waiting for them to give a lead. So they decided to
act on their own initiative. They drove to a private apartment in
the centre of the city, where one of their party workers acted as a

communications centre and telephone monitor. Rainer dictated the Party's first instruction to the *Gauleiters*, the regional leaders of the Party. The plebiscite, ran the message, was to be opposed. Further instructions were to be awaited. Then Rainer and Klausner drove home. The next day, they hoped, they would know more. For the next day would see the return from Berlin of 'Globus', their Party colleague, whom they had sent to the Reich Chancellery at noon that day as a kind of political postman.

When the Chancellor's speech had come to an end a great many people in Austria had switched off their radios. The news had come as too much of a surprise—had provided too much matter for argument. So only a part of the nation heard the broadcast by Zernatto and some of his staff, who had spent several hours in a studio, waiting for this moment. Zernatto had called upon his fellow countrymen: '... the whole Austrian nation, which supports the policies and the course taken by our Front leader, including those, who have decided to go along with us only during the last few weeks, to vote with us: Yes! With Schuschnigg for Austria!' Then Becker, the propaganda chief of the Fatherland Front, announced the regulations which would govern the plebiscite. Everyone was entitled to vote who was twenty-four and could produce a Fatherland Front membership card or other identification at the polling booth. This document was to be stamped and the voter would then receive a piece of paper measuring five centimetres by eight, on which was printed the word 'Ja'. There was no provision for negative votes. Anyone who was opposed to the plebiscite formula must bring with him from home a piece of paper the same size and write the word 'Nein' on it.

Then Becker announced the 'Ten Commandments' of the plebiscite. The seventh commandment ran: 'Is the ballot secret or public? It is secret, but as a good Austrian I am free to show everyone that I am putting the "Ja" ballot paper into the urn.' The Ninth Commandment: 'Must I go and vote? Of course! As an Austrian I must naturally discharge my duty to vote.' And the final commandment: 'Why, above all, will I go to vote? Because I know that a free and independent Austria under Schuschnigg's leadership is the best thing for all of us.'

These arrangements left the door wide open—as even well-wishers recognized—to all kinds of deception. Since a whole variety of different identity cards would be accepted by the

33

electoral commission, people would be able to vote as often as they liked. One could even vote without any identification at all if, as it said in the published regulations, one was 'personally known to the electoral commission'. The more far-sighted officials of the Fatherland Front, still at work in the building at Number 4 Am Hof, were aware that herein lay the greatest weakness of the whole plebiscite and that here was something their enemies, the National Socialists could—and would—seize upon.

Those who worked with Hitler were accustomed to their Führer's frequent passionate outbursts but it was a long time since they had seen him as enraged as he was that evening. At first Hitler had refused to believe that Schuschnigg would go through with a plebiscite in Austria. Then in the evening Keppler had confirmed that it was true. And now the text of the speech lay in front of him in black and white. For Hitler there was only one possible course. The plebiscite must be stopped.

There had been a time, not so long before, when Hitler and the National Socialists both in Germany and Austria had been in favour of a plebiscite. For the Nazis it had been a means of blackmailing the Schuschnigg government. But it was clear to Hitler that at the present time and with the question put in the way proposed it could only result in a defeat for the National Socialists.

Hitler telephoned Goering at Karinhall and spent a long time discussing with him the measures Berlin could take. Then he gave the following orders: General Walter von Reichenau, Commander-in-Chief, Army Group Four, Leipzig, who was at that moment attending a meeting of the Olympic Committee in Cairo, must be ordered home without delay; furthermore the following morning in the Reich Chancellery he wished to speak to General von Schobert, the commander of the Seventh Army Corps, which was stationed in Munich.

Hitler's aides were able to contact Schobert immediately but the transmission of the order to Reichenau created difficulties. At that moment the General, together with the entire Olympic Committee, was on a voyage up the Nile.

While Hitler was issuing commands which indicated that he proposed to meet the challenge with military action, Glaise-

34

Horstenau's plane was on the way to Berlin. Keppler, too, was expected back in the German capital in the early hours of the morning. Perhaps there was still a chance of resolving the conflict by peaceful means.

THURSDAY, 10 MARCH 1938

Keppler glanced out of the window. In the Kaerntner Strasse down below he saw the traces of the night before. Leaflets of the Fatherland Front littered the cobbles and the pavements. The wind had blown them into the entrances of the grand shops: 'With Schuschnigg for a free and German, Christian and social Austria'. Keppler did not have much time to look at all this: the return flight to Berlin was scheduled for 6 a.m. Hitler's emissary calculated that the plane ought to get him to Berlin by about nine o'clock. He wanted to speak to Hitler quickly. The picture he had gained of the situation in Vienna was characterized by a certain indecision: the militant Nazi groups in Austria thought the best chance of salvation lay in an immediate strike, for they believed they could not risk a plebiscite. The moderate groups stood fast by the evolutionary theory, which held that the union of Austria with Germany was bound to come in the fullness of time. Both wings asserted that the plebiscite constituted a breach of the Berchtesgaden agreements between Hitler and Schuschnigg.

Keppler was on the side of the moderates but he had never hesitated to give the evolutionary process a powerful helping hand. Only on 4 March he had been to see Guido Schmidt, the Foreign Minister, in Vienna. He had first of all complained about allegations that the Austrian Left was being armed and incorporated into the Fatherland Front. Schmidt had replied that he doubted it and said that such a course would certainly not be approved by the government. Keppler had demanded further concessions to the Nazis: first and foremost the lifting of the ban on the Nazi newspaper, the *Völkischer Beobachter*. Schmidt agreed to this and had made still further concessions. Thus he had held out the prospect of a twenty-million contract for the German firm Knorr-Bremsen AG and had looked forward to plans for the suspension of the manufacture of larger cars in Austria as well as a reduction in the import duty on German goods. But nevertheless Keppler had been dissatisfied with the discussion, for, as Keppler well knew, the Foreign Minister was as slippery as an eel and had never yet been ready to take the responsibility for a decision upon himself. Each time he had made a promise he had then hedged by explaining that this was only his personal opinion.

Keppler had been to see Schmidt again on Saturday, 5 March, and had described the Minister's promises as 'empty phrases'.

The tangible results of his visit were so unsatisfactory that the Reich would be compelled to take certain steps. He would be leaving at 7.00 p.m. Up till that time it would still be possible to modify the outcome of the talks.

Following these threats Keppler had been invited to Schuschnigg's private residence at the Belvedere at 5.45 p.m. the same day. After the conversation he now had with the Chancellor he had written down its substance and put it on file: 'To begin with, more or less philosophical observations about the concepts: "German", "Austria", "*Volkspolitik*" (national politics), "National Socialism". Schuschnigg still very angry about Obersalzburg: claims threats were used. . . . Schuschnigg expressed his annoyance at Goering's speech in which he referred to ten million oppressed Germans. I reminded him of the treatment of the Sudeten Germans and also of the fact that the sacrifices of lives and property made by National Socialists in Austria had been far greater than in Germany.'

Keppler had declared to the Austrian Chancellor that National Socialism in Austria could never be destroyed by banning it: that this had only led in the past to revolution, never to evolution. An illegal situation always forced the extremists to the top so that matters were constantly being brought to crisis pitch. Hitler had on his own initiative and in the most magnanimous way recalled the previous Austrian Party leadership in order to make way for new and more moderate people, who were ready to follow an evolutionary course.

Keppler: 'Schuschnigg declared that he could scarcely have worked with Leopold but that he thought well of Dr Jury and believed he could get on with the new people. Jury was a good National Socialist and he had established with him in conversation that many of the views of National Socialism had much in common with the ideas he had held in the years from 1920 to 1925. Furthermore he asked me to take into consideration the great efforts he had made in the direction of Germanization, especially in the Burgenland. He emphasized his absolute loyalty to all the German people, to a common policy, in which he would never frustrate our expectations and declared, in addition, that in the long term he also believed that a German Reich should be created.'

In his negotiations Keppler had also achieved something which could only hasten the development of National Socialism in Austria: the lifting of the ban on the German Gymnasts' Clubs, the Nazi Party's paramilitary training grounds. And the officials of the clubs rejoiced: 'Comrades, this is the breakthrough!'

ᛋᛋᛋᛋᛋᛋᛋᛋᛋ

On Thursday morning in a small two-roomed flat with kitchen and bath at Number 10 Lammgasse in the eighth district of Vienna, Josef Buttinger, the chairman of the Revolutionary Socialists' Central Committee, was preparing to go out. For months this flat had afforded him a refuge while he carried on his illegal political activities under the cover name of Gustav Richter. Neither of his names was on the door. Nor did he pay any rent. That was done by Muriel E. Gardiner, the holder of both a British and an American passport, who was known to Viennese socialists as 'Mary'.

Muriel Gardiner came from Chicago, where she had been born Muriel Morris, thirty-seven years before. In 1930 she had married Julian Gardiner, an English composer and music teacher. In 1932 the marriage was dissolved. Mary had then come to Vienna with her daughter, who was born in 1931, and—not being short of money—had taken up her medical studies. Later on, through an English acquaintance, Tony Hyndman, she had come into contact with several members of the prohibited Austrian Social Democratic Party. There she had also got to know Josef Buttinger. Mary possessed two homes in Vienna: a five-roomed flat at Number 2, Rummelhardtgasse, where she lived with her daughter and Finni Wodak, the governess, and the apartment in the Lammgasse. These circumstances made it possible for her to help out the socialists, in an emergency, with refuge and money.

Buttinger, the socialist reformer, was a worker's son from St Veit an der Glan. A farmhand, then a glass worker and party secretary, who neither smoked nor drank, he had fascinated the rich American woman. They had met more and more frequently: in Vienna and at Mary's weekend house at Sulz-Stangau in the Vienna Woods. Finally at the beginning of 1938 Mary had broken off most of her contacts with other Socialists in order not to endanger Buttinger's safety, and installed him in the Lammgasse.

Buttinger had appeared in Vienna at the end of August 1935 after previously being imprisoned for three months for illegal activities and expelled from Carinthia. The same year he became the chairman of the Revolutionary Socialists and a leading critic of the 'old party' and the group in exile, centred round Otto Bauer in Brno. Bauer was the grand old man of Austrian socialism. At the cost of much personal agony, like most of the young Left, Buttinger had sought a way out of the misery of Austro-Marxism and had only become plunged still deeper into pessimism and bitterness. He had, however, retained his political perceptiveness.

An article by him had appeared in the illegal journal *Der Kampf* in December 1937:

'Throughout its existence the authoritarian government has at every critical stage adopted the course of compromise with Hitler. Schuschnigg knows of no other remedy for the destruction which threatens him than to evade it by coming to terms with Pan-German Fascism. This is the policy which has made him the perpetual pacemaker of National Socialism. There is a great majority opposed to National Socialism in Austria, but Schuschnigg is unable to make any use of the political potential inherent in this fact. He is obliged to obstruct the mobilization of the masses against brown Fascism because, if he does not, he too, will inevitably succumb. . . .'

Now on 10 March 1938 following the announcement of the plebiscite by Schuschnigg, Buttinger saw little hope of a 'mobilization of the masses'. He had arranged to meet 'little' Otto Bauer (as the chairman of the League of Religious Socialists was called, to distinguish him from the exiled socialist leader) that morning on a bridge, the Hietzinger Bruecke. They both wanted to discuss a pamphlet on the subject of 'The Inevitable Collapse'.

The manuscript had been written by 'little' Otto Bauer. For him the permanent catastrophe had begun as long ago as 12 January 1934. It was then that his namesake had sent him to the Jesuit Seminary in the Platz Am Hof to see Father Bichlmair, the head of the Austrian Jesuits and political delegate of the Vatican, in order to convince him of the need for conciliation between the socialists and Dollfuss. Father Bichlmar had declared to him with brutal frankness that he must take note of the fact that Social Democracy was to be finished off. Bauer had retorted to the Father: 'They will murder, shoot and hang if it will help them to achieve their aim.' Then he had left. And he had been proved correct. Just one month later people had been shot and hanged. The government had found a pretext to smash the party and to take over the wealth of the socialist unions for the 'reconstruction +

† of the state'. The Minister of Justice at that time was Kurt von Schuschnigg.

Before Bauer and Buttinger met on the Hietzinger Bruecke this Thursday morning they took evasive action, as they had learned to do in the underground, in order to shake off anyone who was shadowing them. Their manoeuvres were not strictly necessary now. The State Police were certainly still on the lookout, but since the start of serious negotiations between the Schuschnigg government and the representatives of the Left the surveillance had not been very scrupulously carried out. Nevertheless the old habits of the underground died hard. They had become second nature to Buttinger and Bauer.

Their rendezvous on the bridge was itself an old underground trick. On bridges it is easier to see one's 'shadow': and it looks innocent enough on a bridge if passers-by lean over the parapet and gaze into the water. Buttinger and Bauer stood side by side and looked down over the parapet into the river Wien.

Bauer had come to the meeting despite a bad attack of 'flu. Buttinger saw that he was ill. They did not discuss the pamphlet, 'The Inevitable Collapse', any further. Bauer dismissed it straight away. 'It's too late to publish now.' He saw that the forecasts he had written had already come true. 'There's nothing for it now but to pack our bags,' he said. 'Hitler will make mincemeat of everything.'

The 8.10 a.m. express from Innsbruck arrived punctually at the Westbahnhof in Vienna. A great reception committee had gathered on the platform to greet the Chancellor on his return: Guido Zernatto, President of the Police Skubl, and a host of government officials from the Chancellery and party functionaries from the leader's office at the Fatherland Front. There was also a man in the uniform of a Colonel-General, Wilhelm Zehner, the State Secretary for Defence.

A guard of honour of the Fatherland Front militia, the *Sturmkorps*, was drawn up. Their resemblance to the black battalions across the border could not be denied. With their dark blue uniforms the men of the *Sturmkorps* wore storm caps with straps under their chins. This was the former officer's cap from the Austrian army, 'the same as that worn by Austria's great military leader, Radetzky, in countless battles fought by the Austrian Army'.

The need for an armed militia within the Fatherland Front was justified as follows: 'The Fatherland Front is a movement. Every movement needs the protection of the fighting man, needs a body of men who will make it their task to intervene with total personal commitment, wherever the attempt is made to disrupt peaceful construction and the development of the spirit.'

Chancellor Schuschnigg took the salute from the guard of honour and left the station hurriedly. Outside a wave of cheering from a great crowd of people broke over him. His supporters lined the streets shouting 'Heil Schuschnigg!' and 'Red-white-red until we're dead!' To the strains of the *Kaiserjäger* March the Chancellor climbed into his car to drive off to the Chancellery in the Ballhausplatz.

The first thing Schuschnigg wanted to do was to study reactions to the announcement of the plebiscite. On his table lay the report of the State Police for that morning. It was confined to an enumeration of the demonstrations which had taken place during the previous night. The Austrian newspapers had given great prominence to the reports of Schuschnigg's speech at Innsbruck and the plebiscite. But the Chancellor had no eyes for them. What would the Germans say? That was the only question that interested him at that moment.

Schuschnigg summoned the head of the Austrian press service, ex-Colonel Walter Adam, from the Starhemberg Palace in the Dorotheergasse. Adam had entered government service after holding an editorial position on the Catholic *Reichspost*. Schuschnigg asked Adam about the German reactions to his Innsbruck speech. But the press chief shrugged his shoulders apologetically. Nothing. Berlin was silent.

Nevertheless Schuschnigg was convinced that his plebiscite would be a success. He was counting on some seventy to seventy-five per cent of the population to cast their votes in his favour. He was convinced that he could rely not only on his Unity Party (the Fatherland Front) but also on a proportion of the groups with different political inclinations. He had once had a hand in the suppressing of the Austrian Left, but he had himself now re-opened the door a certain way towards its legalization. They would not, thought Schuschnigg, turn their backs on his formula for independence.

The Chancellor was certain of Legitimist (i.e. monarchist) backing. Before making his speech in Innsbruck he had already discussed this with Baron von Wiesner, the leader of the Austrian

41

supporters of the monarchy. Wiesner promised him all the help he could. Since then the Habsburg loyalists had arranged for the printing of ten million leaflets supporting the plebiscite campaign.

It is true that the Legitimists were splintered into countless factions. But the rejection of Marxism and National Socialism was common to all of them. They were overwhelmingly drawn from the ranks of officers, the aristocracy and Catholic academics. But some workers had also found their way into the Legitimist camp. There even existed a plan of Schuschnigg's to form a Legitimist workers' union within the Fatherland Front on the analogy of the Nazi Racial-Political Councils.

Schuschnigg himself was a monarchist at heart. He maintained close contact with the twenty-six-year-old Archduke Otto of Habsburg, who lived in Ham Castle near the Belgian town of Steenockerzeel and travelled on a passport of the Maltese Order of the Hospital of St John of Jerusalem which bore the name of the Duke of Bar. As long ago as 1935 Schuschnigg had obtained a Cabinet council decision which had to a great extent set aside the Habsburg Law.[1] Now, if the government approved, Otto could return to Austria and claim his own. Since then the Legitimist movement had grown stronger and stronger. By the end of 1936, the Archduke had been made an honorary citizen of 1,456 municipalities in Austria.

Communications between the Viennese government and the exile in Steenockerzeel were never broken off. Otto was often kept better informed about affairs of state than the President of the Republic. Since November 1937 it had been clear to him that the country was heading for disaster. To begin with, Otto had arranged for the Chancellor to be sounded out by means of Austrian go-betweens, whom he met in France and Switzerland, to see whether a broadening of the government's base and a renunciation of the policy pursued hitherto with regard to Germany would be possible. Schuschnigg had signified his disapproval. Following this, the twenty-six-year-old Pretender had approached four Austrian politicians, one after another, in an attempt to recruit a successor to Schuschnigg. In making their overtures Otto's confidants had stipulated two conditions: the inclusion of the illegal Left in the government and active resistance

[1] On 2 April 1919 the Austrian National Assembly had passed a decree banning all Habsburgs from Austria and confiscating the family property. Tr.

to the National Socialists. But nobody wanted to step into Schuschnigg's shoes.

And then Otto—his hand strengthened by the catastrophic outcome of Berchtesgaden—had resolved upon a final step. On 19 February 1938 Baron von Wiesner had brought a letter to Vienna from Steenockerzeel. Otto had written to the Chancellor:

'By means of an unparalleled act of violence the enemy of Austria has succeeded in forcing your Government into a perilous position which dangerously undermines our continued resistance.'

At home Otto had recommended reconciliation with the working class and the strengthening of the Austrian Army: abroad, personal approaches to the Western powers. But Otto had gone further than this:

'If you consider you can no longer withstand the pressure from German or ultra-nationalist quarters then I must ask you, whatever the situation may be, to hand over to me the office of Chancellor. I am firmly resolved to go to the limit in the defence of our nation and our state and I am convinced that in so doing I will find a response in the people. In view of the present position which would not permit of protracted processes of recognition on the part of the European powers, it is not my intention to ask of you the restoration of the monarchy on this occasion. I would simply call upon you to hand over the Chancellorship to me.'

The letter bore the signature: 'Otto in a foreign land.'

On 2 March the Chancellor had sent the Archduke his reply, which contained a refusal of his demand. The time for the dynasty lay in some happier future time, when a new Europe, purged once more by war, was resurrected. 'Any attempt at a restoration, whether in the next few years or in the foreseeable future must with one hundred per cent certainty spell the death of Austria.'

Schuschnigg knew Hitler's view that the restoration of the monarchy in Austria would be grounds for war. He also knew of the Western Powers' opposition. Shortly before his death the French Foreign Minister, Barthou, had warned him: 'Whatever you do, don't bring back the Habsburgs.' And the other states which were descended from the Austro-Hungarian Empire were resolute opponents of a Habsburg restoration.

In his office on the ground floor of the Chancellery in Vienna the Political Director of the Foreign Office, Dr Theodor Hornbostel, could no longer leave the telephone for a moment. Hornbostel was forty-nine. After attending the Imperial Konsular-Akademie from 1907 to 1912 he had been in the Foreign Service in Turkey, Albania, Greece, Russia and Hungary. He was known as a resolute opponent of National Socialism. That morning he was constantly being rung up. Friends were welcoming the announcement of the plebiscite and offering their help. Then Dr Skubl, the most senior security official in Austria, telephoned. He expressed confidence about the likely outcome of the plebiscite and reported on the situation in the country. The news from Graz sounded bad. The National Socialists had already taken to the streets.

The Chancellor had directed him above all to make contact with Italy. Hornbostel tried to get through to the Foreign Minister at the Palazzo Chigi, Galeazzo Ciano, with whom he was on friendly terms. But the only reply he got was that Ciano could not be reached. He tried to reach Mussolini at his country seat, Rocca delle Caminate, but with no more success.

The Hungarian Foreign Office telephoned Hornbostel and asked about the German reaction to the announcement of the plebiscite. Hornbostel himself did not know what Berlin proposed to do. The foreign embassies in Vienna rang. Hornbostel drafted a telegram to all the Austrian missions apart from those in Washington and Rio de Janeiro, to inform them about the plans for a plebiscite.

He put the draft telegram into a pouch labelled 'Immediate to Cipher Office'. A messenger took the pouch up to the third floor of the Chancellery. In the cipher department the pouch was opened and the draft of the telegram was taken out. One of the clerks, Eugen K. Mauler, began to put it into code. He chose cipher-dictionary number nine. Hornbostel's text was translated into four-figure groups and then coded again with a cipher-strip.

That was the whole secret of a process which had once seemed so mysterious to the thirty-four-year-old Mauler. Nowadays he found decoding messages a good deal more interesting than encoding them. This demanded powers of deduction and finesse. Only the previous Saturday Mauler had decoded a message, the contents of which had seemed to him to be dynamite. The Secret Service had brought the message into the office. Mauler had spent hours attempting a wide variety of methods. Finally he had uncovered the plain text. It was a dispatch from the Yugoslav Ambassador in Berlin to Stojadinowitsch, his Prime Minister. The Ambassador was reporting that he had been to see Goering in order to discover what the Field-Marshal had said to Seyss-Inquart, the Austrian Minister of the Interior, on the latter's recent visit to Berlin. Goering had explained the following: Seyss and the Austrian Foreign Minister, Schmidt, had been told to make sure Hitler got a good press in Austria until the autumn. Then both ministers were to pave the way for a plebiscite in which—according to Goering—the majority of Austrians would vote for an Anschluss with the German Reich. The fact that Seyss was referred to in the dispatch as a tool of German policy had come as no surprise to Mauler. But the mention of Schmidt had disturbed him. First thing on Monday he had gone to Hornbostel with the decoded message. The Political Director had glanced at it, looked up at Mauler and merely remarked that what was said about Schmidt was, of course, nonsense, but that he would show the dispatch to the Chancellor at once.

That morning, almost exactly twenty-four hours after his previous visit, Arthur Seyss-Inquart, the Minister of the Interior, was sitting once more in the room of Guido Zernatto, the Secretary General of the Fatherland Front. This time he had brought Dr Hugo Jury, of the Austrian Nazi Party, with him to the building at Number 4 Am Hof. Jury was in a state of indignation. He had been told that leaflets were being produced for the Social Democrats at the former *Vorwärts*[1] printing works. Two million of them. The slogan was 'Freedom!' Above it there was the emblem of Social Democracy, the three arrows. Zernatto knew that this report was false. It was Fatherland Front leaflets that were coming off the presses there. But he simply said that Seyss-Inquart should

[1] Previously a newspaper of the Social Democrats before their party was banned.

look into it himself. After all he was the minister responsible for security and had the authority to do so.

When both his visitors had left, Zernatto was handed the letter which Seyss-Inquart had in fact already signed the previous morning. Zernatto, who assumed that Seyss could only have composed this letter after consultation with his political friends, hurried at once to the Chancellery to see Schuschnigg. But Schuschnigg was already in the picture. He showed Zernatto the other letter, which Seyss had also written the previous day, but which he had inscribed with Thursday's date and had only just sent to Schuschnigg. Neither Schuschnigg nor Zernatto were aware that Hitler had been in possession of a copy of the letter to the Chancellor since the previous afternoon.

Schuschnigg gave Zernatto his opinion on each of the individual points and then dictated his reply:

To Dr Arthur Seyss-Inquart, Vienna. Dear Herr Minister, In reply to your valued letter of the 10th inst. I am venturing to inform you that my views are as follows: ... 3. The constitution is framed with a view to authoritarian leadership and in Article 93 gives the Federal Chancellor the right to determine the guiding principles of policy. 4. The possibility is accordingly open to the Chancellor, and fully provided for by the constitution, to secure support for his policy by means of a plebiscite. In my view there is no legal basis for contesting this on constitutional grounds. To do so contradicts both the spirit and the letter of the agreements we have made. The formation of a coalition government is something that I reject; I cannot recognize parties; there is therefore no question of the formation of a second Front, alongside the Fatherland Front, a status claimed in particular by the leader of the Racial-Political Council in Styria, whom I today charge with high treason; this is expressly contrary to the principles of the Berchtesgaden agreement. 5. I have many times been urged to hold a plebiscite, most recently by the Chancellor of the German Reich himself at Berchtesgaden on 12 February, on which occasion, it is true, he added that he and I should both campaign together in Austria. That I should only hold a plesbiscite at a time when the outcome would probably go against Austria cannot reasonably be expected of me. ... That I should stand by and look on while the country is brought to economic and political ruin by violent means cannot be demanded of me. I am in the fortunate position of being able to call the world to bear witness as to which party is in the right and which wants peace. I am firmly resolved to do this if the need arises. Today, at all events, the Austrian National Socialists' conception of 'German Peace' has been clearly revealed for what it is . . .'

The Chancellor closed his letter with the words:

I am at your service at all times and sign myself, with the expression of the highest regard, Schuschnigg.'

Guido Schmidt, the Foreign Minister, received a note from his secretary announcing a visitor. When Schmidt read the name on the piece of paper he realized that he was without doubt in for an unpleasant interview. But it would perhaps be one that gave some indication of how Berlin was thinking at that moment. The German Chargé d'Affaires in Vienna, Otto von Stein, had presented himself at the Ballhausplatz. He had the reputation in Austrian government circles, as well as amongst his diplomatic colleagues at other embassies, of being a typical Party Man. Many people believed he also spied on his own Legation colleagues.

Stein's conversation with Schmidt was short and vehement. In thundering tones the German diplomat demanded the cancellation of the plebiscite. But Schmidt replied just as fiercely, with an assertion that the Austrian Foreign Office had all too rarely employed in dealings with the German authorities in the past: 'Austria is a sovereign state. We will not permit interference in our internal affairs.' Eventually the argument became so violent that Schmidt found himself obliged to show the German diplomat the door. Nevertheless the incident struck the Foreign Minister as being of no importance: he did not even inform the Chancellor about it. Schuschnigg heard no word of this step taken by the German Reich.

When Stein had left, Papen tried his luck, in spite of all the difficulties of protocol. Hitler had asked him if he would intervene. Since the former German Envoy could no longer call at the Austrian Foreign Office and did not wish to do so, he telephoned Schmidt. Papen first proposed that the plebiscite should be cancelled, then that it should be postponed to a later date and, linked with this, that the plebiscite question should be altered. Schuschnigg, Papen told Schmidt, should ask whether the voter wanted an Austria 'that will be true to her German mission in close association with the Reich'. Then the National Socialists, too, would be able to vote 'Yes'. But Papen's manoeuvre was equally unsuccessful.

Following this, Berlin brought up heavier guns. The German Foreign Office told Seyss-Inquart that he must adopt a harder line. State Secretary Mackensen in Berlin informed his Minister in London about this move: 'On the Führer's instructions Seyss-Inquart has been informed through the Legation in Vienna that he must not engage in any negotiations: most he should do would be to reinforce protest already made against plebiscite.'

That morning the German Foreign Minister, Joachim von Ribbentrop, was meeting Lord Halifax in London for an exchange of views. Developments in Austria had provided them with highly topical subject matter for their conversation which was originally to have been of a purely formal nature. Ribbentrop had spent some years in London as the German Ambassador and knew the attitude of Neville Chamberlain's government to Germany and to Berlin's demands in Central Europe.

Three weeks before that had seen the resignation from the British Cabinet of the Foreign Secretary who was no longer prepared to represent Chamberlain's pro-German policy: Anthony Eden. Now there was no longer any obstacle to a rapprochement between Berlin and London. Only the German attitude to the current situation in Austria could upset this dialogue. But the debates in the House of Commons since Eden's resignation on 21 February had shown how cautiously England was now playing it. It seemed as if Chamberlain was determined to live up to the nickname the French had given him. They had spelled his name 'J'aime Berlin'.

Eden had made clear in his resignation speech that he and Chamberlain differed in their judgement of Austria's position following the Berchtesgaden agreement. This had provided the Labour Opposition in the House of Commons with repeated opportunities during the past few weeks to attack the government. In an allusion to the agreement with Austria one M.P. had asked on 21 February: 'Do I understand from the right honourable gentleman that if we give general guarantees we do not expect to keep our word?' and on 22 February another had jibed: 'Is it really proposed to go on with these negotiations as if nothing had happened in Austria? May I ask the Prime Minister whether Herr Hitler has informed the Government whom he wishes to be appointed as British Foreign Secretary?' But in so far as these jibes had received answers they had been non-committal ones. And when at the beginning of March the Austrian Minister of the Interior, Arthur Seyss-Inquart, had made his listeners at Graz a present of the Nazi salute, the only comment Chamberlain had been prepared to make to the House of Commons had been: 'It is at present impossible for His Majesty's Government to estimate the real effect of the agreement reached between the Austrian and German Chancellors at Berchtesgaden on 12 February.'

It was not only in Parliament but also in the British press that the way was being paved for British capitulation to coincide with Ribbentrop's appearance in London. Lord Beaverbrook wrote in the *Daily Express* that England must reach a settlement with Germany. He considered London's commitments in Central Europe could bring only ridicule and discredit. And any project that might bring England into a war through an unnecessary intervention must be rejected. This issue of the paper was being sold in the streets of London as Ribbentrop sat down opposite the British Foreign Secretary, Lord Halifax, at the Foreign Office.

Both Foreign Ministers, Ribbentrop and Halifax, were at an extreme disadvantage. For they were both of them only imperfectly informed about what had become the number one talking-point for all European diplomats since the previous evening. A telegram had indeed turned up for Ribbentrop from Berlin that morning: in it Mackensen, the State Secretary at the German Foreign Office, had briefly recapitulated the most important passages in Schuschnigg's speech. But as for what Hitler had in mind, how the Reich would react, Ribbentrop did not know. Only from the last sentence of the telegram could the Foreign Minister gather that in Berlin the die had not yet been cast: 'Keppler due Thursday morning ten o'clock to make oral report to Führer.'

Halifax, too, had nothing more in his hands than the telegrams from his Ambassador in Vienna, Palairet. The last dispatch, sent on the previous evening, contained the optimistic comment: 'Speech seems to have been received with great enthusiasm.'

49

Thursday, 10 March 1938

Over and above the general questions they discussed, such as the attitude of the Press in both countries, the colonial demands of the Reich and the Anglo-German relationship, Ribbentrop and Halifax continually returned to a single topic: Austria. The German Foreign Minister roundly declared Schuschnigg's plebiscite to be a fraud, while Halifax gave it to be understood that the British government hoped the plebiscite would be allowed to be carried out without interference or intimidation. Berlin must urge the National Socialists not to start a campaign against it. But Ribbentrop was not prepared to give assurances of this kind. He did not know what steps Berlin was preparing to take and countered Halifax's plea with the demand that London must prevail upon Schuschnigg to call off the plebiscite. Halifax replied that this was impossible: one could not prevent an independent state from carrying out a plebiscite of this kind. To this Ribbentrop retorted that the whole thing was nothing more than an attempt by a minority government, which only had about twenty per cent of the population behind it, to impose an unwelcome solution on the majority of Austrians.

Ribbentrop carried away from the conversation with his English opposite number the impression that London would certainly talk but was unlikely to act. Thus, after the meeting, which had lasted more than two hours, he telegraphed Berlin:

'... to judge by the English aversion to any conflict if it can still somehow be avoided, there is no doubt that the present English government does not want a war and in my view it is not responsible for the situation which has currently arisen in Austria. It is my fundamental conviction that England does not at present intend to take any action on her own initiative, but would tend to have a pacifying influence on the other powers. On the other hand the situation would be quite different if it comes to a major international conflict over Austria, that is, with France.'

Then Ribbentrop gave Hitler an indication which would be of significance with regard to the German reaction later on: 'The form in which a German intervention in the Austrian situation, if the occasion arose, could be underpinned is also important. It would be necessary to find an attractive formula from a legal, as well as an actual point of view. For this Schuschnigg has himself provided us with a rich fund of material. For British public

50

Thursday, 10 March 1938

opinion a plausible justification of this kind is particularly important.'

※※※※※※

The new Chief of the OKW, the High Command of the Armed Forces in Germany, General Wilhelm Keitel, had not yet grown accustomed to dealing with the great ones of the Third Reich. He also felt somewhat unsure of himself when he received the order on Thursday morning to come and see Hitler at once in the Reich Chancellery. He had been given to understand that it was to do with Austria. In order to be on the safe side Keitel informed the head of the Reich Defence Department, Colonel Alfred Jodl, before he left the building in the Bendlerstrasse at ten o'clock with Lieutenant-General von Viebahn.

The Chancellor informed the two officers briefly about the political situation. On the following Sunday Schuschnigg had arranged to hold a plebiscite of which both the purpose and the method were contrary to the Berchtesgaden agreement. He therefore intended, if Schuschnigg did not come to his senses, to plan and carry out a military intervention against Austria. Keitel proposed to Hitler that he should send for the Commander-in-Chief of the Army straight away, so that the Chancellor could give his orders direct to the latter. Then Keitel drew attention to the fact that there must be a General Staff exercise in existence under the title 'Special Case Otto', in which the details for a military invasion of Austria would have been laid down. While the Chief of the OKW continued the discussion with Hitler, Viebahn left the study to call Jodl. He instructed the Chief of the Reich Defence Department to fetch the relevant dossier for 'Special Case Otto' out of the safe and come to the Reich Chancellery.

What Jodl unearthed was no more than scanty. There was only an exercise by the General Staff on theoretically possible cases of military engagements. The document was headed 'Directive for combined war preparations of the Armed Forces'. But the members of the General Staff had not worked out operational plans for all cases. For 'Special Case Otto' only considerations of a general nature had been set down. In these it said: 'Armed intervention against Austria in the event of the latter restoring the monarchy. The purpose of this intervention will be to oblige Austria by force of arms to abandon the restoration. To this end, while exploiting the internal political division within the Austrian nation, an advance

51

is to be made in the general direction of Vienna and all resistance is to be smashed.' The officers in the Bendlerstrasse had been unable to imagine the premise for a German military intervention in Austria. They did not believe that the Vienna government would dare to repossess the Habsburgs. Yet this was the only possible reason for a war given and this alone had furnished the 'Special Case' with its name of 'Otto'.

When Jodl had told Keitel what he had found, Keitel drove back to Bendlerstrasse to seek the advice of the Chief of the General Staff, Beck. For the Commander-in-Chief of the Army, von Brauchitsch, could not be reached.

Keitel rushed into General Beck's office in the Bendlerstrasse: 'The Führer requires you to report to him immediately and give him an account of the preparations which are already in existence for the possible invasion of Austria.' But Beck could only tell him what Keitel had already heard from Jodl. 'We have prepared nothing at all.' As they drove to the Reich Chancellery Keitel was followed by General Beck and his deputy, as Chief of the General Staff, Quartermaster-General (I) Fritz von Manstein.

At eleven o'clock Keitel, Beck and Manstein arrived at Hitler's office. Hitler came straight to the point. He explained to the generals that he found himself forced to intervene in the situation that had developed in Austria. He had not himself intended to solve the *Anschluss* question at that moment and by military means but Schuschnigg's plebiscite forced him to take this step. Resistance, said the Chancellor, was not to be expected, for the majority of the Austrian people were still in favour of the union of Austria with the German Reich. And the other European powers would not find any reason to use the German move as a pretext for war.

For Manstein it was the first time he had heard Adolf Hitler speaking about politics in a small gathering. So far he had only heard him speaking to crowds. Everything Hitler said seemed to the General to be well founded. Only one thing surprised him: the fact that there was one power about whose attitude Hitler seemed to be uncertain. The Chancellor was afraid that Italy—which Manstein had believed to be so closely allied with the German Reich—might intervene on the Austrian side in a military conflict between Berlin and Vienna. There had been one occasion in recent years when Italy had taken a stand hostile to Germany: in July 1934 when the Austrian National Socialists had tried to seize power by means of the attempted July putsch and killed Dollfuss, the Austrian Chancellor, during the course of it, Mussolini's divisions had marched to the Brenner as a warning.

But the Generals were not given much time for such reminiscences. Hitler wanted them to tell him how and with what troops a possible invasion of Austria could be carried out. Beck and Manstein conferred briefly together and then Beck proposed the following to the Chancellor: the Seventh and Thirteenth Bavarian Corps as well as a Panzer Division must be mobilized, but there would naturally be difficulties for 'no preparations at all had been made for such a mobilization, or indeed for any operation of this kind, for the political leadership has never—not even by implication—set us such a task. It must therefore be improvised.' For foreign policy reasons Hitler was first unwilling to authorize a mobilization but finally agreed to do so, as he wanted to send the troops into Austria the following Saturday, 12 March. The day before the proposed plebiscite was the latest date on which an invasion of this kind would make political sense.

Beck and Keitel left the Reich Chancellery at 1.00 p.m. They did not know whether they could accomplish the task in the few hours that were available to them. For by six o'clock that day at the latest the invasion plan must be sufficiently far advanced for the mobilization to be effective in time. As soon as they got back Manstein brought the necessary divisions of the General Staff in on the preparations.

For Ludwig Beck, the Chief of the General Staff, the activity set off in his headquarters by Hitler's order was far from pleasing. He knew the *Wehrmacht's* weak spots. He also knew that it would be difficult for the first time in twenty years to set up an Army GHQ and to mobilize the troops that came under it. But his greatest fear was of a war on several fronts, which seemed to him likely. He had already said this at the Reich Chancellery, but Hitler had not wanted to hear about it.

Beck had originally expressed his opinion on 'Special Case Otto', when the General Staff directive had been laid down. At that time, in 1937, he had said in a written memorandum: 'The occupation of the whole of Austria by force of arms would, however, have as its consequence so many military measures, that even if it were successful there would be a danger that the hallmark of Austro-German relations in the future would not be the sign of the *Anschluss* but the stigma of rape.'

But there were only a few officers who thought like Beck and none of them, not even Beck, felt like being guided by his conscience at this moment. They had not even been ready to revolt a month ago when Hitler had dismissed Generals Blomberg and Fritsch from their posts and himself taken over the Supreme Command of all the services. For Hitler's opponents knew that they could no longer rely on the Officer Corps as a whole.

There had already been an occasion, almost exactly a month previously, when it had looked as if Hitler intended to solve the Austrian problem by military means. At that time, during the course of Hitler's meeting with Schuschnigg at Berchtesgaden, when Austria was forced to accede to the German demand for the inclusion of Nazis in the government and an amnesty for the arrested Party members, a military display had been put on. Hitler had had Generals Keitel, Sperrle and Reichenau march into Berchtesgaden so as to convince Schuschnigg that if he did not accede to Hitler's demands, Berlin would march into Austria.

In order to strengthen this impression Hitler had staged a further military charade. The scenario had been compiled at Keitel's house by Admiral Canaris, the head of Military Intelligence, Jodl and Keitel on the afternoon of 13 February. They had sent the text to the Reich Chancellery.

'High Command requests a decision from the Führer on the following proposals: commands will be given on immediate receipt of an indication from the Führer of the letters and numbers to be carried out. 1. No actual preparations to be made in Army and Air Force. No troop movements and switches. 2. False but credible information to be given out which suggests that military preparations are being made against Austria: (a) through Party contacts in Austria; (b) through our customs personnel at the frontier; (c) through travelling agents. 3. Such information could be: (a) all leave cancelled in the Seventh Army Command Zone; (b) rolling stock is being assembled in Munich, Augsburg and Regensburg; (c) the Military Attaché in Vienna, Lieutenant-General Muff, has been summoned to Berlin for talks (actually true); (d) the police posts along the Austrian frontier have taken on reinforcements; (e) customs officials report impending exercises of the Mountain Rifles Brigade near Freilassing, Reichenhall and Berchtesgaden. 4. Lively radio traffic to be laid on in defence region seven and between Berlin and Munich. 5. Actual peace-time exercises to be stepped up (practice flights and winter training). . . .'

Hitler's approval had come in in the night of 14 February but only two days later the simulated manoeuvre had been called off. The Austrian government had agreed to everything Hitler had demanded of it at Berchtesgaden. The Austrians had not, in fact, done this because they had been impressed by the military charade. The Austrian intelligence service had seen through the fictitious invasion.

But this time the preparations were genuine. If Vienna felt safe this time, when it was serious, then the false manoeuvre of February might still have served some purpose in retrospect.

Schuschnigg's announcement of Wednesday evening had been received in Paris and London with marked apprehension. The plan for the plebiscite did not, indeed, take the French unawares but it came at an awkward time. The French Third Republic was once again undergoing an internal political crisis. Some hours before Schuschnigg's speech at Innsbruck the French Prime Minister, Camille Gabriel Chautemps, had put the existence of his government at risk over a minor issue. Now, at midday on 10 March the worst had happened. The third Chautemps cabinet was coming to an end. At once rumours arose in Paris, linking Schuschnigg's plebiscite with Chautemps's resignation. The Prime Minister, it was said, was simply evading his responsibilities. His aim had been to avoid the complications which could be foreseen on account of Austria.

Alois Vollgruber, the Austrian Ambassador in Paris, had nothing very encouraging to report to Theodor Hornbostel at the Foreign Office in Vienna:

'The integrity of Czechoslovakia and the independence of Austria can be counted amongst those issues in Europe which the French government considers to be of vital importance to French interests. Those in authority in France are absolutely convinced that sooner or later Germany will make a new coup of one kind or another against the independence of Austria and that, in the event of Austria being successfully subjugated, Czechoslovakia's turn will follow. At present France seems ready in principle to draw her sword in defence of both of these issues if need be. In practice, however, she must see to it that such an extreme step takes place in the most favourable possible circumstances, which naturally means securing the participation of England. Should England, too, prove ready to defend Austria's independence by force of arms, if need be, then France would certainly go to war to preserve Austrian independence: but if this is not the case then—unless there is some alteration in Italy's attitude meanwhile—France will wait for the violation of Czechoslovakia and only strike then, for then, in the opinion of those in authority in France, England would be drawn into the war too. . . .

'In either case, however, France will only be able to draw her sword if the act of violation is clear, that is if the Austrian government regards itself as violated, if the Austrian people reacts against the violation and if German propaganda has not by then succeeded in convincing French public opinion that in Austria only the government and a few diplomats think of themselves as Austrians.'

In Muriel (Mary) Gardiner's flat at Number 2 Rummelhardtgasse in the Ninth District of Vienna they were sitting down to their midday meal. Following his encounter that morning on the Hietzinger Bruecke, with 'little' Otto Bauer, Buttinger, the Revolutionary Socialist, was still in a pensive mood. He did not know whether and how he could carry out the task the Party had given him of drawing up by that evening an appeal to the workers to vote in the plebiscite. Finni Wodak, the governess who looked after Connie, the child of Mary's dissolved marriage, asked Buttinger how she should vote on Sunday. Buttinger: 'I've just been racking my brains over that for hours.' Little Connie interrupted. Surely it was simple. 'You don't want to vote for Hitler; you can't vote for yourself so the only thing left is to vote for Schuschnigg.'

Buttinger took an hour to write his appeal:

'Workers, comrades. The form in which Schuschnigg has dictated the plebiscite gives you the alternative of either voting "Yes" or helping Hitler-Fascism to power. A victory for Hitler means not only the bloody suppression and unlimited exploitation of the Austrian workers, it also means a defeat for the workers' movement throughout the world and the strengthening of the inhuman dictatorship exercised by German

National Socialism over the workers in Germany. The workers of Austria cannot therefore answer "No" on Sunday to Schuschnigg's question, for this would strengthen Hitler-Fascism. Next Sunday is not the day on which we can settle our accounts with Austrian Fascism by voting against Schuschnigg and pay back the authoritarian regime for all the crimes that have been committed against the Austrian working class since February 1934. Next Sunday we must manifest our burning hatred of Hitler-Fascism. On this day, therefore, the whole working class must vote "Yes" ... With the help of the workers Schuschnigg can win; nevertheless Austria would ultimately be lost if the workers ceased to fight on with undiminished strength for complete political and trade-union freedom. A plebiscite cannot secure the lasting independence of Austria. This can only be won by waging a successful struggle against National Socialism. Down with Hitler-Fascism! Long live freedom!'

By now State Secretary Keppler had been in the Reich Chancellery in Berlin for over three hours. He had remained on Hitler's orders. But he was puzzled to know what this could mean. He had taken lunch, together with a small company, in Hitler's dining room at the Reich Chancellery. Shortly afterwards, while waiting in the ante-room, he had observed Odilo Globocznigg, the Austrian Nazi Party's representative, being shown in to see Hitler. 'Globus' had been kept in Berlin for twenty-four hours. Only now could Hitler make use of him again as a tool in the furtherance of his plans.

After the failure of the approaches made by his diplomatic representatives, Papen and Stein, to the Vienna government, Hitler had decided to give the Austrian Nazi Party a free hand. He directed Globocznigg to give Seyss-Inquart the message that a special express messenger would soon bring a letter in which detailed instructions were set down. When Globocznigg left Hitler's study Keppler saw that the Austrian had a paper in his hand. This, though he did not know it, was Hitler's letter giving the party in Austria carte blanche to prepare for a militant showdown with the Schuschnigg regime.

Every time Keppler saw one of Hitler's adjutants he would ask the same question: could he not now be spared—or were there any further instructions for him? Each time he was told to stay where he was. Gradually the significance of it all began to dawn on him. Perhaps he was being kept a prisoner in the Reich Chancellery to prevent him coming into contact with people and government departments in the city who must know nothing about the military preparations against Austria. This view was confirmed when a telephone call from Edmund von Glaise-Horstenau, the Austrian Minister, was put through to him. The Minister, whom Hitler had summoned to Berlin the previous night from Buerckel's Hotel in Landau, had been kept waiting at Hermann Goering's town villa under virtual house arrest since the early hours of the morning. Hitler had indeed seen him briefly, but he had then put him off until eleven o'clock the same morning. Now, however, eleven o'clock had come and gone and no further meeting had taken place.

When Keppler came back from the telephone he was handed a letter. The sender was the 'Head of the Central Security Office of the Reichsführer SS'. It was addressed to Keppler not as 'State Secretary' but as 'SS Gruppenführer Wilhelm Keppler'. For nine years the former manufacturer had been a member of the National Socialist Party. For three years he had also held a rank in the SS. Keppler opened the letter and read:

'Secret III 224/1 Az. 1790/38
Subject: Organization plan for the Movement in Austria and situation report
    Priority: None
    The attached organization plan for the movement in Austria and situation report is sent with the request that the contents be noted. Signed by the Head of the Central Security Office for Chief of Military Intelligence by order of Dr Filbert, SS-Hauptsturmführer.'

The enclosure contained the following: 'At the head stands the Leader of the Austrian National Socialists, Major Hubert Klausner. Directly subordinate to him as organizational head with the official title, "For questions of the Movement", Globocznigg. Friedl Rainer ranks equally with him as political head of the movement. Subordinate to this compact leadership council are the *Führerstämme* (Führer Clans). These are: the farmers, led by Engineer Reinthaller; the Workers under Sepp Nemetz, the *Mannschaft* (other ranks) under First Lieutenant Lukesch; the Youth under Schoas; the SS under Kaltenbrunner; the *Volkshilfe* (People's auxiliaries) under Langoth ... Diagrammatically the Movement looks as follows: At the centre stands Klausner with the leadership group. In the next ring stands Jury in his capacity as official head of the *Volksdeutsche Arbeitstelle* (German-national labour authority). A further circle outside finds Jury once again in his functions as Councillor for racial-political and constitutional matters. In the outermost circle, which nevertheless from a security point of view envelops the whole like a mantle, is located the Minister of Security and the Interior, Dr Arthur Seyss-Inquart.'

From this communication Keppler could only conclude that his mission in Austria was not yet at an end.

The most powerful organization in Austria was on Schuschnigg's side. At 3.00 p.m. the Roman Catholic Clergy met in conference, called together by a man whom the National Socialists had once been able to rejoice in as one of their own, Cardinal Theodor Innitzer. For almost five years Innitzer, with his stern, ascetic manner, had been the Chief Prelate in Vienna. In the course of his career he had frequently been involved in party politics, or at least he had taken sides politically. Thus in 1929 he had been a Minister in the Christian Social Chancellor Schober's third cabinet.

Innitzer carried within himself the dichotomy that was common to many Austrians in the years following 1918. They had the desire to be united with Germany but they wanted to know that Austrian independence would be protected against the Prussian spirit, which was not loved on the Danube. After Hitler's seizure of power attitudes had changed. The Cardinal was no exception. And so for the Nazis who had formerly called him a 'German Prince of the Church' he ceased in his new guise to be a model for the faithful and became a symbol of those tainted with the alleged blemish of friendship with the Jews. Instead of calling him *Unser Innitzer* (our Innitzer) they called him *Inser Unnützer* (the hindrance).

On this Thursday afternoon the Cardinal saw clearly enough what was now at stake in Austria. He and the conference of Clergy took an unambiguous stand in support of the government and the independence of the Austrian state. Only in this way could Austria be saved from the National Socialists.

Thursday, 10 March 1938

The Austrian Protestant Church, too, composed an appeal that was to be read over the radio that same evening. The message was clear and unambiguous: Yes to Schuschnigg, Yes to the plebiscite question.

꒛꒛꒛꒛꒛

That afternoon in Vienna expressions of opinion about the plebiscite were in increasing evidence in the streets. The front pages of the newspapers were devoted almost exclusively to news about the plebiscite. The Heldenplatz was piled high with pamphlets and leaflets of the Fatherland Front. The Front was distributing a news sheet of its own especially for the campaign, the *Volkswille*. The Inner City looked as if it were covered with artificial snow. The campaign literature of the Fatherland Front lay scattered in the streets and on the pavements. New leaflets rained down from the sky—where the Front's propaganda planes were circling round.

On leaflets, scrolls and banners there was always the same sentence: 'Yes! With Schuschnigg for a free Austria!' Processions of Front supporters marched through the city using stencils to paint portraits of Schuschnigg and Teutonic Crosses on the walls of houses, and on streets and pavements. The radio was almost entirely given over to propaganda for the plebiscite. After the Chancellor's speech had once more been broadcast that morning the Ravag radio station alternated 'Voices from the people'— statements by groups and individuals—with patriotic songs and marches. In the radio's music studio in Vienna the man putting on the records was the Chancellor's brother, Arthur Schuschnigg. The head of the sound recording department had himself been surprised by the turn of events: he had not seen his brother for some weeks.

Youth columns of the Fatherland Front marched through Vienna with placards. The official manifesto was distributed everywhere. 'We can breathe freely. A load has been lifted from our shoulders—which it has taken us all our strength to bear, but which we have borne. But enough is enough. Even Austria's self-discipline has its limits. We are embarking on a three-day struggle for the Fatherland. At the end of it our vision is only of the figure of our dead Leader, Dollfuss, towering in triumph. We must embark on this struggle because freedom and peace for our home-land demand it . . .' And: 'Let the Austrian achieve this highest expression of humanity only so that he may be the better German!' In front of the Fatherland Front building at Number 4 Am Hof the Viennese gathered to demonstrate their sympathy with the government. Inside they left their visiting cards in a silver bowl, handed in bunches of flowers to decorate the portrait of the Front Leader or gave money. A specially instituted bureau entered sums ranging from one to a hundred thousand schillings in the list of donations.

But observers of the Austrian scene that afternoon did not only record sympathetic demonstrations. National Socialists, who still did not know how Berlin would decide and what line their own Party leadership would adopt, took to the streets. They demonstrated, in order to show that they were still there. The police were repeatedly compelled to intervene so as to keep order: at the Opera crossroads, in the Karlsplatz and in the Michaelerplatz. Nazi students from the University of Vienna set out on a walk through the city. Nazi columns marched to the German Railways Tourist Office, opposite the Opera House. In one of the windows there was a giant portrait of Hitler on display. This now became slowly smothered in the flowers handed in at the office by National Socialists.

As the Front expected further incidents, the Mayor of Vienna, Richard Schmitz, who was also the Leader of the Front for the Province, asked the Chancellor for armed protection for the propaganda columns. The previous night these parties had already been attacked by Nazis. On this Thursday, 10 March 1938, the police were constantly kept busy. The alertness of the police force of 7,000 men kept all the principal ways into the city centre under control. Their dark grey uniforms dominated the street scene.

What worried the Front was the prospect of an organized reaction from the National Socialists. For the moment the Nazis were demonstrating off their own bat: neither their own Austrian leadership nor Berlin had given any clear instruction. In order to orchestrate their activities Seyss-Inquart had called in the Racial-Political Councillors, and all supporters of the Pan-German and Nazi lines to a meeting. Leaders from the other provinces had also appeared. Their conclusion was afterwards announced by Dr Hugo Jury: 'We are instructing our supporters not to vote in the plebiscite on Sunday.' The reason given was the arrangements for the plebiscite. The government had by now realized for themselves that their proposed method of voting was open to criticism. A new statement was issued by the Front: naturally ballot papers marked 'No' would also be provided for the ballot on Sunday.

In Graz the 'capital of revolt', in the province of Styria, the criticism was strongest. The Racial-Political Councillor there, Dr Armin Dadieu, sent telegrams to President Miklas and Seyss-Inquart, which were immediately branded as treasonable in government circles: 'The Racial-Political Councillor of the Fatherland Front in Styria protests against the plebiscite, which is contrary to the May Constitution, draws attention to Articles 65 and 172 of the May Constitution, gives notice of the relevant measures to be taken and demands that the Federal President maintain the Constitution.'

Armin Dadieu, a thirty-seven-year-old professor of physical chemistry, launched his attack on the government without consulting either the Vienna leadership of the Nazi Party or Berlin. He could be certain of support in Styria. Only a fortnight previously a petition signed by local government officials there had revealed that ninety per cent of them supported National Socialism. The Party authorities calculated that eighty per cent of the total population of the province sympathized with the Nazis although only 6751 were signed-up members of the illegal Nazi Party—0.6 per cent of 1,140,000.

In Graz, where the Nazis were meeting in the Hauptplatz and the Fatherland Front in the Franzensplatz, there were clashes which came near to civil war. Demonstrators there were already demanding the resignation of the Schuschnigg government at a point in time when Seyss-Inquart in Vienna still believed he could reach his goal by means of negotiations.

Late in the afternoon on 10 March Friedl Rainer of the Austrian Nazi Party was informing Seyss-Inquart about the mood in the provinces. Large groups of the old Republican *Schutzbund* were already armed. The Left were on the streets. In Vienna even the members of the once 'red' Town Hall guard were being armed. The National Socialists were lagging behind. Something must now be done. Scarcely had the Minister of the Interior put down the receiver when his State Secretary, Dr Skubl, called to discuss the situation. Skubl spoke of an increase in the political tension. But so far there had been no serious clashes with the government forces. The police were sufficiently experienced to prevent clashes taking place. Then he outlined his plan of campaign to the Minister of the Interior. The Inner City and the Chancellery could be cordoned off. Seyss-Inquart approved all his State Secretary's plans. Then the following exchange took place. Seyss: 'At the first clash between the executive and the National Socialists I shall have to resign.' Skubl: 'I understand that to mean that you wish to know that such clashes have been avoided. But that if they occur I have a free hand.' He did not expect an answer.

After Skubl had left the room Seyss-Inquart was telephoned by Guido Schmidt, the Foreign Minister. Schmidt declared that he considered the situation to be politically critical. 'Won't you talk things over with the Chancellor?' That was precisely what Seyss had in mind. He agreed. Thereupon Schmidt promised to arrange a conversation with Schuschnigg.

At 4.00 p.m. in Berlin a whole series of senior officers were reporting for orders. They had been summoned to Berlin at midday, once it was settled which units were to march into Austria under the command of the Eighth Army. Fedor von Bock, Commander-in-Chief of Third Army Group H.Q. in Dresden and now designated as the head of the army of invasion; Bock's Chief of Staff, Major-General Richard Ruoff and his 'Ia' (General Officer I) Colonel Hauffe. To Berlin from the Thirteenth Army Corps in Nuremberg had come Colonel Wilhelm Stemmermann; for the Panzer troops Lieutenant-General Guderian; the Commanding officer of the Seventh Army Corps, Eugen von Schobert, had already hurried up from Munich during the night.

Fedor von Bock was a classic example of the Prussian officer type. Aristocratic, tall, slim and elegant in appearance, a monocle permanently fixed in one eye and with a taste for elegant cars and grand attitudes. He was received by the Commander-in-Chief of the Army, Brauchitsch, who had meanwhile got back to the War Ministry, and Beck, the Chief of the General Staff. They told him of Hitler's intention: the Eighth Army was to march into Austria at midday on 12 March to restore order. Bock accepted the task without hesitation. He reckoned only on sporadic resistance, possibly at the frontier and in a few of Austria's industrial centres. The main thing, whatever happened, he observed, was to occupy the capital as quickly as possible.

By this time it was six o'clock. In the five hours he had had at his disposal General Manstein, together with a number of colleagues, had prepared an invasion plan. But Hitler's mobilization order, which was expected at this time, had still not come in. As the minutes ticked by the Head of the Organization Division in the General Staff, Colonel Stapff, became nervous: it was impossible now for the mobilization operation to begin on schedule. But Manstein, who had just proved his ability to improvise, took a more sober view of the situation: when they already had so little time, half an hour more or less made little difference.

Meanwhile all the officers who had been summoned to Berlin were being briefed about the purpose, scale, and tactics of the move against Austria. Only one adjustment had to be made. When Beck told Guderian, the fifty-year-old Panzer General, that he must take over his former command of the Second Panzer Division, the latter broke in to say that in that case his successor, Veiel, might justifiably feel slighted. But as the General Staff did not want to be deprived of Guderian's abilities they put him in command of a joint force consisting of both the Second Panzer Division and the Waffen SS Division, the SS Leibstandarte *Adolf Hitler*. Thus a slight to General Veiel was avoided.

Helmuth Laegler, captain at the General Staff, was not short of work that afternoon. It was in his department that the mobilization of all combatant groups not belonging to the army was set in motion: the police, the SS, and the VGAD (the *Verstärkter Grenzaufsichtsdienst*—reinforced frontier guards). Laegeler had to adapt their peacetime dispositions for the mobilization operation. On his desk lay a great red book which gave him the individual instructions that applied to this particular emergency: the mobilization plan. One of Laegeler's tasks was to convert the customs men into the reinforced frontier guards. The VGAD was to take over responsibility for security and observation tasks on the frontier. As the customs service came under the Finance Ministry, Laegeler had to arrange the detailed instructions with Hoffmann, the official there. In the case of the customs preparations for this eventuality had been made: collar patches and military insignia could be fixed on to the customs officers' uniforms by means of press studs. It was thus a matter of minutes to transform the men on the frontier into combatants.

Then Laegeler contacted the SS auxiliary forces. Here the co-operation would not go so smoothly, he thought. For this reason he telephoned an SS-officer in the War Ministry: 'You must come over. A Führer-Directive has been issued, in accordance with which you must be ready to march within a few hours. I hope you can manage this.' On the other hand the operation for the police was a simple one. They already had plans to hold exercises and parades in south Germany in March. So it was merely a matter of implementing the transport instructions which had already been prepared. The police could then assemble in their quarters in Dachau, Regensburg, Rottenburg and Deggendorf.

At 6.55 p.m., almost an hour after the expected time, Hitler's directive for the partial mobilization of the Eighth Army came in. It was immediately passed on by means of prearranged code words by the High Command of the Armed Forces. The wording was as follows: '1. Setting up of march-readiness of all command authorities and troops capable of swift deployment. 2. First trial-X-Day: 11.3.38 (without frontier guard, engineers etc.). Order effective from 10.3.38, 1900 hours . . .' At 7.05 p.m., this order was received by the Seventh Army Corps in Munich. Thirteen minutes later the Thirteenth Army Corps Nuremberg, was similarly informed, and at 7.30 p.m., the command of the Panzer troops also had the order in their hands. The Air Force received a separate mobilization order. The most junior arm of the German Forces was to make ready 300 JU52 planes for propaganda flights and the dropping of propaganda material.

The Austrian Army had meanwhile not been idle. But emergency orders issued were of a purely defensive character. Individual units were to prepare to defend their own barracks. The reason given was that a Nazi putsch and disturbances throughout the country were expected. More far-reaching efforts were still at the preparatory stage. The thirty-three officers of the General Staff training course in the Universitätsstrasse in Vienna were told by their senior officer that their time in the classroom was now at an end. They were moved to individual Staffs or to the Ministry. In this distribution of posts First Lieutenant Kodré was sent to the Austrian Defence Ministry in the Stubenring. But there, at first, there was no special job for him. So he moved into the office reserved for him and studied the regulations which applied in the case of a mobilization. It was the first time he had held such papers in his hands. While he was still reading them the Chief of the Mobilization Division, Colonel Sohn, put his head round the door

65

briefly. But he had no orders for Kodré. What surprised the First Lieutenant was Sohn's agitation. He cursed the Nazis and Hitler, then he disappeared again. When Kodré got to the end of his day's work at the Ministry he packed up the secret documents and went, as he always did at this time, to the Café Alserhof near his home.

That evening the streets of Vienna were taken over by the demonstrators. More and more columns of them came marching into the centre from the outer districts. Fatherland Front supporters, Legitimists, Socialists and National Socialists all gave their views, marching and shouting, on the plebiscite.

National Socialists tore down two red-white-red flags from a Legitimist bar in the Wollzeile. A fight began which was finally broken up by the police. A Nazi bar in the Thaliastrasse had its windows broken. Crowds of demonstrators blocked the streets and squares. In the Himmelpfortgasse there was a clash between Nazis and police. The Nazis were finally driven back into the Neuer Markt. In the Karlsplatz there was a demonstration by several thousand National Socialists, chanting 'Withhold the vote'.

At 7.00 p.m., the Nazi leader, Dr Friedl Rainer, received a message to say that a Nazi had been stabbed. Rainer at once told Lukesch, the SA leader, to send out detachments marching in close order. Then he telephoned to Berlin: the situation was tense to the point of disintegration. There was a threat of civil war.

The Opera House became a focus for the demonstrations. The Fatherland Front had set up loudspeakers in the Opernplatz over which campaign slogans and march music could be transmitted. And in between came the chanting choruses of the detachments of Fatherland Front and Christian trades unionists: 'Red-white-red until we're dead'. The demonstrators supporting the government stood tightly packed together on the pavements and road-ways. From outside the square Nazis thronged towards the Deutsche Eck where the offices of the German Railways were situated.

Dr Heinrich Hüttl was the police officer in charge of the police operations in the sector bounded by the Ringstrasse, the Akademiestrasse and the Operngasse. His brief was to protect the Inner City from Nazi demonstrators. So far things had passed off successfully, for the most part without any trouble. Hüttl had told his policemen to ward off demonstrators trying to break through, in the first instance by telling them that the Minister of the Interior, Seyss-Inquart, had approved the order for the cordoning off of the Inner City and that outside this area demonstrations were freely permitted.

Suddenly Hüttl saw a huge column of Nazis marching towards him from the Schwarzenbergerplatz. A strong force of Fatherland Front supporters was marching to meet them. He feared an ugly clash. He hurried out to meet the Nazis himself. At the head of the procession marched a man who had become a familiar figure at brownshirt demonstrations. The police referred to him mysteriously as 'the man in the Inverness cloak'. Hüttl knew him by his real name: Kögel. He argued forcefully with Kögel and the Nazis turned away. But then even larger crowds came marching back again. Hüttl sent in mounted police against them. The police were supposed to threaten the crowd twice with their rubber truncheons before using them. But this instruction remained purely theoretical. The police struck out immediately for they could no longer make themselves heard. Singing and yelling, the demonstrators crowded in on them, clapping their hands rhythmically to frighten the horses. Finally the police charged the Nazis with drawn swords. The crowd was driven back with the result that they broke through further along. Soon shouting demonstrators were pressing against the police barrier which closed off the Kärntner Strasse near the Opera House.

While the battles with the demonstrators raged all around there was a further outbreak of the rumours that had already cropped up in the early afternoon: the plebiscite was said to have been postponed. The office of the Front leader countered with a statement: 'As was to be expected, today has seen countless questions raised and countless rumours begotten. It is necessary to confirm that no news is correct unless it is transmitted officially. The only valid sources of information are official communiqués and the decrees of Provincial Governors and the Mayor of Vienna. The plebiscite takes place on Sunday, 13 March. All rumours about postponements or alterations are incorrect. Naturally everyone has the right to vote in complete freedom and secrecy. Everyone can make up his mind freely. Ballot papers printed with the word "No" will also be available . . .' There were already leaflets on the streets: 'Do not believe the rumours! The plebiscite will take place! Your answer is clear! Austria, Yes!'

Thursday, 10 March 1938

In the evening Seyss-Inquart, the Minister of the Interior, explained all his objections to the plebiscite plan orally to the Chancellor, in the presence of the Foreign Minister, who had arranged the meeting. The voting was not going to take place on the basis of the public electoral rolls, following the correct procedure, nor would it take place in the presence of the public electoral commissions. It seemed probable that the constitution would be flouted. In particular Seyss objected to the fact that government servants were to vote at their offices. And in the private sector there was also to be voting in the larger factories. In these cases there was no guarantee of a free and secret ballot. It was Seyss's belief that such tricks were intended to outmanoeuvre the Nazis.

The Austrian Minister of the Interior had received orders from Berlin not to negotiate. He did so nevertheless. The ambitious Catholic attempted to obtain from the Chancellor greater Nazi representation in the cabinet. Becoming more specific about his ideas for the nomination of further fellow-Nazis to posts in the national and provincial governments, he named three names: Dr Hans Fischböck, Dr Hugo Jury and Anton Reinthaller. If the Chancellor would agree to his proposal he would call upon the National Socialists to vote 'Yes'.

As an alternative, Seyss proposed that the plebiscite should be postponed and the plebiscite question extended in a way that would enable the Nazis to find in it an expression of their own political ideology. Schuschnigg's reaction was cool. As regards an immediate licence for National Socialist activity within the Fatherland Front, he would have nothing to do with it. At the end of their conversation, which had lasted over two hours, the Chancellor agreed that consideration would be given to some of Seyss-Inquart's objections to the actual voting method.

Edmund von Glaise-Horstenau, the Austrian Minister, who had been flown to Berlin on Goering's command, while on a visit in Southern Germany, had spent more than twelve hours a virtual prisoner in Goering's Berlin villa in the Air Ministry complex. At 8.00 p.m., he was finally summoned to the Central government offices of the German Reich.

Calmly and with an almost genial air the Austrian General and military historian confronted a Hitler who seemed to have lost all self-control. Perhaps, the German Chancellor shouted and stormed, he should simply attack Austria with bombs and grenades. At all events he was resolved to invade Austria on 12 March on the eve of the day allotted for the plebiscite. Glaise had the feeling that matters were taking 'an ugly turn' but he still clung to the hope that if Schuschnigg would cancel the plebiscite the affair could be resolved.

When Hitler had calmed down again he attempted to use the Austrian Minister as his messenger. He asked him to take two letters to Vienna. One envelope contained the draft for a letter of resignation Seyss-Inquart was to present to Schuschnigg. The second was the outline for a broadcast explaining why the Austrian Minister of the Interior had resigned. But Glaise stood firm. The letters could be sent by means of a normal messenger.

Goering, whom Glaise met shortly after his talk with Hitler, also attempted to use the Austrian as a postman. He tried to press into his hand a letter, the contents of which were to play a significant role in Berlin's tactics during the next twenty-four hours: it contained the draft of a telegram in which Seyss-Inquart was to ask for the despatch of German troops to restore order. But Glaise-Horstenau was equally adamant with Goering and refused to take charge of the telegram. There was a brief but violent exchange between the German and the Austrian Minister. As it was now late, Glaise-Horstenau decided to wait until the following morning before flying back to Vienna.

On Thursday evening Joachim von Ribbentrop, the outgoing German Ambassador in London and Berlin's new Foreign Minister, gave a farewell reception at the German Embassy. The list of guests published in the press included some well-known names, those of Lady Chamberlain; Halifax, the Foreign Secretary; Duff Cooper and Lady Diana Cooper; Hore-Belisha, the Secretary of State for War; Sir Robert Vansittart and other prominent people. Halifax availed himself of the opportunity to ask his German opposite number if they could have a further conversation the following day. Their meeting was to take place after the lunch with the Prime Minister which was already planned. Halifax was concerned about the way the Austrian situation was developing.

Thursday, 10 March 1938

Nevertheless the British government had a good deal of sympathy for the increasingly hard line being taken by the German Reich. This had also been shown at question time in the Commons late that afternoon. When Henderson, the Labour Opposition member, had asked the Prime Minister whether he had no statement to make concerning the question of Austrian independence, Chamberlain had replied: 'No, sir. I have no statement to make.' Henderson then asked:'In view of the special position of Austria will the Prime Minister not, at least, express the hope of His Majesty's Government that this plebiscite will at any rate be carried through without any external interference or pressure so as to permit the Austrian people to exercise their full right of self-determination?' Chamberlain had said nothing. But his claque had given an answer that was music for German ears: 'No, no, no' came the shouts from the Conservative benches. And when, following this, another Labour M.P., Will Thorne, had made a further thrust: 'Does not the Prime Minister realize that the cheers from behind him are from those in favour of Germany going into Austria?' Chamberlain made no reply. German observers of these exchanges could certainly infer that England would not interfere, provided no clashes were provoked by the invasion.

While Bock's subordinates at the Dresden headquarters of the Third Army Group Command Dresden were already making preparations for the ceremony held on the German Heroes' Day, there was a long-distance telephone call from Captain Laegeler in the second division of the Army General Staff in Berlin. At 8.15 p.m., he passed on the following order by telephone to Dresden: 'To Third Army Group Command. 1. Establishment of planning staffs envisaged for command organization in accordance with draft command 4 for Mobilization plan (Army), in the peacetime headquarters of the mustering commands to be carried out for Eighth Army GHQ. Further instructions will be given orally in Berlin to the Chief of the General Staff. 2. First trial-X-day 11.3.38 only for the staff troops of Eighth Army GHQ.'

A short time after this telephone call the officers at the Army General Staff passed on to the Commander-in-Chief of the invasion army two documents which bore the stamp 'Top Secret'. In the first paper, the invasion order, was the following:

'1. Eighth Army invades Austria on 12.3.1938 to restore conditions of order. The instruction to cross the frontier will be given by myself. Instruction is to be transmitted through Eighth Army GHQ: 11.3.38 2200 hours. 2. Objective of the Eighth Army is in the first place the occupation of Upper and Lower Austria, Salzburg, in particular the swift occupation of Vienna. . . . The march on Vienna is to be carried out on the north side of the Danube. In the event of a Czech intervention the provision of further forces is envisaged. . . .' Signature: Commander-in-Chief of the Army, von Brauchitsch.

From the second paper General von Bock could see which Army Corps and units were at his disposal for the invasion. He had supreme command over the Seventh Army Corps, Munich (under General von Schobert); the Thirteenth Army Corps, Nuremberg (under General von Weichs); the command of the Panzer troops (under Lieutenant-General Guderian); Tenth Army Depot (under Lieutenant-General Doehla).

With these papers General von Bock went back to Dresden together with his Chief of Staff and his 'Ia' (GSO I). Bock knew what difficulties this military adventure would raise. He later noted in his war diary:

'Partial mobilization and invasion took both troops and commands by surprise and presented them with a completely new situation. The troops were still undergoing individual training: the military commands and recruiting offices had not received any notice of the mobilization—nor were they prepared for this "offensive" advance. The advance was to take place in the area between Freilassing and Passau which offers unfavourable railway and communications facilities. Railway transport, communications network and supply arrangements for six divisions with any number of Army and GHQ troops could not be made ready in advance. SS formations were called in which in peace time did not come under the Army either from the point of view of organization or as regards mobilization. The unit headquarters and the mass of the troops had only thirty-six hours, which included two nights, at their disposal from the announcement of mobilization to action stations at the frontier, and some of them had less.'

Lieutenant-General Guderian had experience of some of the unforeseen obstacles which the mobilization encountered. The staff officers of General Veiel's Second Panzer Division, who had to form a joint command together with the SS Leibstandarte *Adolf Hitler*, were at that time on a training trip in the Moselle district and had first to be brought back by car.

The Air Force was also making preparations for the Austrian engagement. When General Ehrhard Milch, the State Secretary at the Air Ministry, who had been summoned back from Switzerland, had touched down at Tempelhof airport shortly before 5.00 p.m., he had been driven at once to Goering's town villa in order to take part in a discussion there between the senior officers of the Luftwaffe. The Chief Adjutant to the Commander-in-Chief, General Karl Bodenschatz; the head of the Air Force Personnel Office, General Hans Jürgen Stumpff; and a number of other officers had been already waiting when Milch arrived. Goering had begun by briefly informing Milch about the political situation. When Milch learned that the planes that were to be brought into action were to carry bombs on board he had said: 'If we need bombs we can always come back and fetch them.' Goering had agreed. But in order to be armed in case of any incidents it had been arranged that the JU52 planes were to be equipped with machine guns, which would be ready loaded before the flight. Otherwise the motto was to be: *Blumen statt Bomben* (Flowers not bombs). Now that evening, General Milch was with Goebbels at the Ministry of Propaganda discussing the Air Force preparations for the dropping of leaflets over Austria.

Other sections of the armed forces were also preparing for an unwarlike invasion. Lieutenant-General Guderian asked Sepp Dietrich, the commander of the SS Leibstandarte, who had once again been summoned to the Reich Chancellery, to obtain Hitler's leave for the advancing tanks to be decorated with foliage. And Jodl, the head of the Reich Defence Division at the General Staff, advised his colleagues of the Organization Division: 'Put the bands at the head of the troops and make all your drivers wear goggles—otherwise they will be blinded by the bombardment of flowers.'

But there were other officers—including the Commander-in-Chief of the Eighth Army—who did not view the enterprise so lightly. They knew how shaky the force was that had just been conjured up. Though it was perhaps not possible to look upon Austria as a dangerous enemy, nevertheless the reactions of France, England and Italy remained uncertain. Czechoslovakia too, which possessed a well-equipped army and a good defence system, would not be unconcerned, as a neighbouring country, about events in Austria. The politicians in Prague must be bound to calculate that if Austria fell then Czechoslovakia would be the second victim of Hitler's policy of conquest in Europe.

During these hours of the evening the cellar bar at the Café Meteor in the Fasanengasse was crowded to overflowing. Many socialists and trades-unionists wanted to know how the negotiations between the committee of the illegal Left and the government had fared. The outcome was not exactly encouraging. The Christian Social functionaries of the official trades-union organization had certainly made a few concessions; but on one important question—free elections for all union officials—they had remained unyielding. Everybody round the tables at the Café Meteor knew the reason: the men who were now in power did not want to lose their jobs. It had, however, been agreed that thirty-eight-year-old Hans Sailer, a central committee member of the Revolutionary Socialists, should be entrusted with the leadership of the official Social Trades Union (SAG, the *Soziale Arbeitsgemeinschaft*). The Left were also to be permitted to publish a daily newspaper. Sailer's appointment showed how greatly government circles had changed their tune under pressure from outside. For the man who was now to take over an official post had only a few years before been the chief defendant in a big trial of socialists.

The regulars of the Café Meteor were not entirely agreed as to the course they should adopt. The Communists were unreservedly in favour of supporting the Schuschnigg government in the struggle against the National Socialists. Others asserted that they should first wait until all their demands had been fulfilled. It was finally decided by a majority vote to hold a big demonstration in the Ringstrasse on Friday evening. In order to fix this up with the authorities Franz Olah, a young socialist of twenty-eight, who had been arrested three times on account of his political activities during the past few years, and Alois Koehler, a representative of the metal workers, were sent to see the head of the Vienna State Police, Dr Ludwig Weiser. But Weiser refused permission. No more demonstrations were to be allowed. The Nazi demos had also been forbidden.

While they were waiting at the Meteor for a decision, the former trades-union secretaries and illegal labour leaders, the

73

Thursday, 10 March 1938

Revolutionary Socialists and the Communists continued to argue about what was to be done. Some were in favour of armed resistance to the National Socialists. Their spokesman was the First World War Major, Alexander Eifler. The former Chief of Staff of the Republican *Schutzbund*, the socialist private army which had been formed in opposition to the right-wing *Heimwehr* militia, Eifler came from a family with a military tradition. He had been a titled nobleman (von Lobenstedt) until the collapse of the monarchy but he felt at home among the workers.

On this Thursday evening Eifler was able to tell his listeners in the Café Meteor that a few hours previously he had been talking to Zehner, the State Secretary for Defence, and Schmitz, the Mayor of Vienna. Eifler explained to them that there was a plan to arm the workers, under the leadership of men from the Fatherland Front militia, the *Schutzkorps*.

It was not only at the Café Meteor but all over Vienna and in the provinces that meetings of workers were taking place that evening. Thus the delegates of the workers in the metal, chemicals, glass and paper, and textile industries and the transport and hotel workers were all meeting. The metal workers decided to down tools on Friday morning as a demonstration against the machinations of the Nazis and in favour of their own rights.

By this time the broad outlines of Major Eifler's discussion with the authorities on the subject of armed resistance to National Socialism by the workers were already known in Berlin. The head security office of the SS had a report from Vienna which summed up the situation as follows: 'There are growing indications that our enemy in the near future will be the Popular Front in all its political shades. Orders have already gone out to various militant formations that stand closest to the Popular Front, to hold themselves ready. The distribution of weapons and rubber truncheons is reported from all parts of Austria. This evening the Popular Front and the *Schutzkorps*, probably reinforced by Communists, began tearing swastika badges off National Socialists in the Inner City. Measures against this street terror were taken by the Movement.'

Such reports originated from the ever well-informed SS intelligence office which was located on the first floor of the Vienna *Hochhaus* in the Herrengasse. The intelligence office was well camouflaged. Three plates by the front door proclaimed the fact that here were the offices of the Dunkel canned-fish firm, the Henschel locomotive works and the administration of the Leipzig

Fair. Inside the building Dr Wilhelm Hottl acted as head of the intelligence service. He and his three colleagues strove to gather together everything that might be of interest to Berlin. The material was then photographed with a Leica and sent to Berlin the same evening by post or by special messenger, so that there were no written documents on the premises to give away the true character of the office in the event of a police raid. Even the reports from Austrian embassies abroad to the Vienna Foreign Office very often ended up taking this route.

The stirrings of a Popular Front thus reported to Berlin did in fact exist. During the past weeks attempts had been made through a wide variety of channels to establish contact between government circles and the Fatherland Front on the one side and the prohibited organizations of the Left on the other. In this process personal contacts from the past often played an important part. Former Socialist members of municipal councils, provincial assemblies and the national assembly became aware that they were being wooed by their erstwhile Christian-Social colleagues throughout the country. In Vienna the Café Reichsrat was the meeting place of former deputies of differing political colours. And here the renaissance of parliamentary Austria was already being celebrated over black and white coffees. Nevertheless this coalition of Black and Red had little chance of success. Many members of the government could not adjust their ideas swiftly enough and on both sides the hatred and the past sacrifices could not quickly be forgotten. At all events National Socialism was not prepared to give the various political factions enough time to overcome the tensions between them.

After Seyss-Inquart had left Schuschnigg he received a message that his Party colleagues were meeting at the Hotel Regina. It was late in the evening when he drove over to Number 16 Dollfuss-Platz to report on his negotiations. In a room in the first-class hotel about a dozen members of the Nazi Party were sitting together, members of the national leadership and some of the *Gauleiters*. Near by the national leader, Major Klausner, and his two political advisers, Dr Friedl Rainer and Odilo Globocznigg, were conferring together. Globocznigg had just arrived from Berlin on a special flight. Rainer had driven to meet him at Aspern and brought him to the hotel. Globocznigg reported that Hitler had granted the Austrian Party complete freedom of action.

Three Party leaders, who were known—because of their origins and their careers—as the 'Carinthian Mafia', considered it inopportune to inform their official link-man with the government of this development. So Seyss was only able to note that his Party colleagues betrayed little interest when he told them he had been discussing the possibilities of a Black–Brown coalition with Schuschnigg. They answered him by indicating that Berlin rejected the plebiscite and telling him that the following morning a messenger would be coming who would hand Seyss the necessary instructions.

It was now that the Minister of the Interior was forced to realize that the most important men in the Party were no longer operating with him but against him. Now that there was a prospect of holding office a struggle for power between the various groups became discernible. The radical supporters of Leopold were as good as eliminated, thanks to the enforced exile of their leader. The moderates, amongst whom Seyss counted himself, had missed the chance of an *Anschluss* by evolutionary means. Now the Carinthian triumvirate was in command and Rainer was already issuing orders for the next day.

In the name of Klausner, the national leader, he briefed the *Gauleiters* as follows:

'Three things may happen in the next few days:
1 Cancellation of the plebiscite: in this case the instruction is to hold the most massive demonstrations possible.
2 Schuschnigg resigns: in this case the instruction is for demonstrations to lead to the seizure of power.
3 Schuschnigg takes up the fight: in this case all Party leaders are ordered to act independently by all available methods in order to achieve positions of power.'

Seyss-Inquart took note of this and drove home.

The formations of the Party, the SS and the SA, whose leaders Rainer had addressed, had already that afternoon been instructed to prepare for major engagements. The Head of the Austrian SS, Ernst Kaltenbrunner, a thirty-five-year-old lawyer from Linz, had turned up in Vienna a few hours before. In the Party the SS *Standartenführer*, whose face was furrowed with scars, had the reputation of a gay dog. His affairs were the subject of many stories: he was said to have a lady friend wherever he went. Now, too, he had taken up residence with a lady, the daughter of a coffee-house owner in the Stephansplatz. This hiding place was known to the Party, so that Kaltenbrunner could wait there till it was time to act.

The operations of the illegal formations of the SS in Austria were well camouflaged. The members were for the most part organized into German Gymnasts' Clubs. Here, without attracting attention, the men could receive para-military training: in their training rooms they could gather for Party operations relatively unobtrusively. In the Nazi putsch of July 1934 the starting point for the operation had been a gymnasium. In those days it was still necessary to meet under conditions of the greatest secrecy. Now the SS-gymnasts were much more easy-going about their security precautions, and with good reason. They knew how many friends they had amongst Schuschnigg's police.

In the night of 10 March 1938 the clashes between the National Socialists and the supporters of an independent Austria came to a head once more both in Vienna and in the individual provincial capitals. In Linz, the capital of Upper Austria, the Nazis gave a demonstration of their strength. While thousands, standing in the broad square in front of the Town Hall, chanted: 'We will not vote', a number of activists climbed on to the Town Hall balcony and hoisted the swastika flag. While the forbidden emblem of the illegal Nazi Movement was fluttering over the town on the Danube, another troop of Nazis marched into the Urfahr quarter of Linz. There, in front of the Fatherland Front building in the Urfahrer Hauptstrasse, there was a bloody clash between National Socialists on the one side and Fatherland Front *Sturmkorps* men and *Jungvolk* on the other side. In the heat of the battle the Nazis finally drew pistols and three government supporters were wounded with shots, while five others were so badly beaten up that they, too, had to be taken to hospital by ambulance. Although the injuries were only on the Fatherland Front side, the Nazis at once put it about that they had been attacked. Wild rumours of a full-scale street battle began to spread and the exaggerated stories aggravated the hostility between the camps still further.

In Vienna at about midnight the old Austria was on the march once more. Workers, people from the suburbs and Viennese walked through the city streets. What the Fatherland Front had always striven to do but had never accomplished had now been achieved by National Socialist pressure. The demonstrators marched along the Graben, the broad street that leads to St Stephen's Cathedral, past a landmark which in these hours once again took on a symbolic significance, the Trinity Column. In accordance with a vow made in 1679, the year of the plague, the Emperor Leopold I had had it erected, on the site of the town moat of the former Roman camp. Artists had worked for years on the three-sided pyramid which rose up from the baroque figures and had crowned it with the figures of the Holy Trinity. The stones of the monument bore witness to the fact that on one occasion the city had survived a great peril. . . .

At midnight the home of the illegal Socialist party official Josef Strabl, at Number 14 Wassergasse, in the Third District of Vienna, resembled a party headquarters. All the notable Revolutionary Socialists were there.

That night's meeting of the Central Committee of the Revolutionary Socialists was a decisive one. A Fatherland Front lorry had found the house some hours before and unloaded ten thousand Front badges, intended for distribution to the workers. After the Party Committee had approved the appeal which Buttinger had composed early that afternoon, someone was typing it out: 'On this day, therefore, the whole working class must vote "Yes" . . .'

But Buttinger's pessimism again got the upper hand. Hitler, he professed, would threaten to invade and Schuschnigg would surrender without a fight. For the Fatherland Front was already long since fragmented; the police force was for the most part riddled with Nazis; the workers had no arms to defend the state and even if they had had them the outside world would not come to Austria's aid. But there were optimists, too, at Strabl's flat. One of them had already brought with him the keys to the offices of *Arbeiter-Zeitung* which had been banned years before by the government, so as to get into the editorial offices as quickly as possible the following morning.

While a member of the Revolutionary Socialist Party executive was in the Strabls' kitchen preparing something for the Central

Committee to eat, the Socialists continued to discuss their party's dilemma. Most of them believed it was necessary to fight Hitler. But this very fight could again give the Nazis the pretext they needed to intervene. And so they prepared, too, for the possibility of an emergency: they worked out the guidelines for the continued organization of the Party if Austria fell.

FRIDAY, 11 MARCH 1938

At four o'clock in the morning the head of the German Department at the Austrian Foreign Office, Max Hoffinger, was woken by a telephone call. The clerk at the other end reported to his chief that a telegram had just come in from Munich, which no one could make head or tail of. The text read: 'Leo ready to travel.' Hoffinger, however, knew what it was all about. Over two years ago, when he moved into his job at the Ballhausplatz, he and his colleague, Theodor Hornbostel, had agreed with the Austrian Consul General in Munich on the text of the signal which was to be sent to Vienna if Germany were poised for a military strike against Austria. Now the moment had arrived. Leo was ready to travel.

Hoffinger immediately rang up his Minister, Dr Guido Schmidt, and set off for the office. The telegram was not the only indication of an imminent German invasion. Before leaving his office in the Ballhausplatz late on the previous evening the Political Director of the Foreign Office, Theodor Hornbostel, had asked various offices to keep him informed during the night. The extraordinary silence from Berlin on the subject of the plebiscite had struck him as dangerous. Now the intelligence section of the Austrian Army passed on to him what they had heard from their own sources on the frontier and in Germany. Their reports spoke of road blocks, concentrations of heavy lorries and tank transports.

In Germany the preparations for the invasion continued on into the early hours of the morning of 11 March. Hitler's 'Directive Number One for Operation Otto' was issued at 2.00 a.m., at first without his signature. Thirty copies were prepared. This top-secret military document, issued by the Supreme Commander of the Armed Forces, bore the reference: OKW. L1 a Nr 420/38:

'1 If other measures prove unsuccessful, I intend to invade Austria with armed forces to establish constitutional conditions and to prevent further outrages against the pro-German population.
2 The whole operation will be directed by myself. Subject to my orders, the operations on land will be directed by the

Commander-in-Chief of the Army with the Eighth Army, in the formation and strength recommended to me, and the units shown in the attached documents from the Air Force, the SS and the Police: the operations in the air will be directed by the Commander-in-Chief of the Air Force with the forces recommended to me.

3 Operational duties:

(a) Army

The invasion of Austria must take place in the manner explained by me. The Army's initial target is the occupation of Upper Austria, Salzburg, Lower Austria and the Tyrol, the swift occupation of Vienna and the securing of the Austro-Czech frontier.

(b) Air Force

The Air Force must demonstrate and drop propaganda material; occupy Austrian airfields for the use of further possible reinforcements; assist the Army upon demand as necessary and in addition hold bomber units in readiness for special tasks.

4 The forces of the Army and Air Force detailed for this operation must be ready for invasion and/or ready for action from 12 March 1938 at the latest by 12.00 hours.

I reserve the right to give the order for the crossing of the frontier on land and in the air and to decide the time for this.

5 The conduct of the troops must give the impression that we have no desire to wage war against our brother nation. It is in our interests that the whole operation shall be carried out without the use of force in the form of a peaceful entry, welcomed by the population. Therefore any provocation is to be avoided. If, however, resistance is offered it must be broken ruthlessly by force of arms.

Austrian units that come over to us will immediately pass under German command.

6 On the remaining German frontiers no security measures of any kind are to be taken for the time being.'

The Eighth Army, which Hitler had designated for the invasion, formed up during the course of the night. The officers assigned by the mobilization plan to the staff of the Army GHQ were alerted at their units.

Friday, 11 March 1938

From 3.00 a.m. onwards at the Vienna Law Courts a number of officials were engaged in reading the morning papers. This was part of their job. For in Schuschnigg's authoritarian state the papers were not permitted to appear uncensored. As they read the *Wiener Neueste Nachrichten*, a paper with Pan-German and Nazi sympathies, the readers came upon an article about Sunday's plebiscite. It came from the pen of Dr Hugo Jury, the National Socialist *Staatsrat* (State Councillor) and 'Racial-Political Councillor'.

As soon as they had read it the officials woke the Public Prosecutor for press matters, who had official rooms in the court building. This was the procedure laid down if the night service came upon passages in the newspapers that flouted the criminal law or were politically undesirable. After the Prosecutor had glanced through the article he reported it to the State Secretary for Security, Dr Michael Skubl. He in his turn, with the paper in his hand, informed his Minister, Arthur Seyss-Inquart. Seyss had the whole text read out to him over the telephone. Then he gave his opinion: Jury's article was not treasonable in character, it was simply highly polemical. He saw no reason to intervene on security grounds. But if the Chancellor considered the article to be politically unacceptable, then Skubl should have the paper seized.

Schuschnigg was woken at 5.30 a.m. at his house in the grounds of the Belvedere. Skubl first reported to him the news he had just heard: 'The German frontier at Salzburg completely closed for the past hour. German customs officials have been withdrawn. Rail Traffic stopped.' After this laconic police report Schuschnigg was wide awake. Skubl then told him of the *Wiener Neueste Nachrichten* business. Schuschnigg agreed to the seizure of the paper.

The action went according to plan. The police sent telegrams to all the railway and police stations in all the towns to which the *WNN* was delivered. The police stations in Vienna were also informed. It proved possible to secure the greater part of the 48,000 copies.

The crucial sentence in the incriminating article was the following:

'We Austrian National Socialists are fighting for the indivisibility of the basic principles of the Austrian Constitution and we cannot and will not tolerate the fact that, through the omission from the plebiscite question of two of the most important basic principles of the new Austria—those of the authoritarian leadership and the corporate structure of our state—the way is being opened to a democratic form of state and hence to a Popular Front and the spread of Bolshevism in the Fatherland which is so dear to us . . .'

Jury gave three reasons for the Nazis' rejection of the ballot:

'Because of the unconstitutional implications of the plebiscite question, because of the threat to peace and industry presented by the illegal nature of the form of consultation and because of the lack of equal rights in the way it has been organized, we Austrian National Socialists must refuse to participate in this "plebiscite", which is not provided for in the Austrian Constitution and which is therefore a purely private initiative, the outcome of which it is impossible to calculate.'

In Linz, too, papers were seized. The Linz *Tagespost* had also printed Jury's article. The paper managed to appear, however, with blank spaces. Its local competitor, the *Volksblatt*, also got into trouble because of Jury. It had summarized the *Tagespost* article in a news story. Nevertheless the police measures failed to achieve their object. For the Nazis published a special edition of 200,000 copies of the Vienna weekly news-sheet, the *Volkspresse*. Its content: Jury's article. By the time the police arrived the copies had been distributed.

The day that was now beginning was to prove decisive both for the Chancellor, Kurt Von Schuschnigg, and for the Minister of the Interior, Arthur Seyss-Inquart. Although Seyss had only been asleep for a few hours, he decided to stay up after Skubl's telephone call and went for a walk through the streets of the Dornbach district of Vienna, which were still empty. Glaise-Hortenau was due back from Berlin soon. Then Seyss would know more. But he already had something on his mind. He realized that he had twice been passed over by his colleagues in the Party during the past five hours. The scene at the Regina Hotel the previous evening had shown him that the group round Rainer, Globocznigg and Klausner was acting against him and without him. Jury's article, too, had come as a surprise to him. Schuschnigg, for his part, was disturbed by the news about the frontier. He therefore sent for his driver to take him to the office as quickly as possible.

The Austrian Foreign Minister, Guido Schmidt, wanted to know the exact situation. Shortly after 5.00 a.m., he rang up Franz von Papen at the German Legation. But Papen had no information and he was also in a hurry. He told Schmidt that he had received a call from the Reich Chancellery the previous evening, telling him to come at once to Berlin. He advised Schmidt not to attach too much importance to the closing of the frontier.

Just as Hornbostel was about to leave his home at Number 4 Mayerhofgasse Schmidt telephoned him to say that Papen was on his way to Berlin. Then the Foreign Minister told his colleague to make contact at once with the diplomatic missions in Vienna and the foreign governments. Particularly with Paris, London and Rome.

It was still dark outside when Hornbostel began dialling the British Embassy from his office on the entresol floor of the Chancellery. He wanted first to inform the British Ambassador and the French Minister of the events of the night. For Michael Palairet and Gabriel Puaux were known to be friends of Austria. By 6.15 a.m., both diplomats were in the picture. They at once passed on the news to their governments. And Palairet was in such a hurry that he forgot to number his telegram. He wrote to his Foreign Secretary, Halifax: 'Political Director has just telephoned me to say that Austrian Government learn that German-Austrian frontier has been closed, no trains have been allowed to pass Salzburg since early this morning, and there are reports of troop movements and closing of roads on German side.' Puaux reported in similar terms to the Quai d'Orsay. For the past two days, since the resignation of the Chautemps cabinet, the man in charge there, one of Vienna's staunchest allies in Paris, had been no more than a Foreign Minister subject to recall, Yvon Delbos.

At 6.15 a.m. Schuschnigg left his house in the grounds of the Belvedere. On his desk in the Ballhausplatz he found the report of the State Police for the previous night. Demonstrations everywhere. During the previous night outside Number 8 Florianigasse there had been a severe clash between Nazis and students. Members of the SA *Bund Oberland* had attacked the students with steel bars. Fifteen people had been injured in the fighting, nine students and six members of the SA.

The Chancellor's first visitor was announced. Dr Skubl appeared. He enlarged on the police report. Schuschnigg told him to have the government quarter sealed off with barriers. Guido Schmidt came in with the telegram that Hoffinger had received from the Austrian Consul-General in Munich: 'Leo ready to travel'. But this only confirmed what the Chancellor already knew. The Germans were on the march.

Through the window in the Chancellor's office came the sound of music. It grew louder and louder. One of the Fatherland Front's loudspeaker vans was playing the march *O Du mein Österreich*. When the music finished another record was put on: 'For a free, German, Christian Austria'. Schuschnigg listened for a moment. Then he instructed his secretary to ask Dr Seyss-Inquart and Dr Hugo Jury to come to the Chancellery.

Jury was soon there. He knew what it was all about. For this reason the thickset man with the deep scars in his furrowed face took the initiative at once and thundered:

'Who on earth advised you to do it, Herr Chancellor? Everything was going well and now with this plebiscite all is lost. Believe me they have given you bad advice, Mayor Schmitz and the rest of them.' Schuschnigg retorted that nobody had advised him. He alone bore the responsibility. It was Jury's own people who had brought things to this pass.

Schuschnigg: 'I have resolved to take you at your word. What is at stake is nothing other than a public pledge of support for the Constitution as contained in the Berchtesgaden agreement and as you and your people have repeatedly been telling me yourselves. What do you object to in the plebiscite question?'

Jury: 'For example, the fact that there is no mention of the authoritarian state. We have expressly insisted that the leadership must be authoritarian.'

The Chancellor observed that the authoritarian aspect of his state went without saying. No one who was familiar with the Constitution could have any doubt about it. 'However, if you wish I am perfectly ready to add the word "authoritarian" to the plebiscite question already announced.'

Jury: 'It is too late for that now. The die is already cast.'

Schuschnigg asked Jury where Seyss-Inquart, the Minister of the Interior, was. 'We could discuss the situation with him.' Until then he asked Jury to exercise a mediating influence so as to avert a disaster. 'Herr *Staatsrat*, I ask you to help me.' Jury shrugged his shoulders. 'I will see what can be done.' At this time Seyss-Inquart was at the Aspern airport, Vienna, to meet his cabinet colleague Glaise-Horstenau on his return from Berlin. With Glaise was Dr Franz Hueber, a lawyer who had been Minister of Justice in the Vougoin cabinet in 1930. A former member of the *Heimwehr*, who came from Upper Austria, Hueber was married to Goering's sister, Paula. He worked as a notary and attorney in Wels. He belonged to the inner circle of the Austrian Nazi Party's evolutionary wing.

Seyss learned that a messenger from Berlin had handed in a letter to him from Hitler at the German Legation. He asked Hueber to fetch the letter. While Goering's brother-in-law drove to the Metternichgasse, Glaise remained with his fellow Minister at the airport restaurant and told him of his conversations with Hitler in Berlin. The mood in the Reich Chancellery was agitated and explosive. It was possible that Hitler would solve the problem of Austria by force.

When Hueber returned with the letter, Glaise and Seyss drove together to the Chancellery. On the way Seyss opened the envelope. The two Ministers read what Hitler demanded: the postponement of the plebiscite for several weeks and the holding of a regularized ballot. If this demand was not fulfilled by twelve noon there would be demonstrations by the Party and possibly an invasion. Enclosed with the letter was the draft of a telegram which Seyss was to send to Berlin in case of need. It contained a request for German troops to enter Austria.

卐卐卐卐卐卐

In Germany, meanwhile, the military preparations continued. The first units of the Tenth Division from Regensburg arrived at their operational quarters in the region of Passau. Units of the Seventh Division, the Mountain Rifle Brigade, the Second Panzer Division and other Eighth Army troops were being loaded on to transports or were already on the march to the Austrian frontier, particularly in the area between Freilassing and Passau. They were the first-wave divisions 'capable of swift deployment'—peace-time formations which were made mobile in a limited area. Theoretically they lacked a sixth of their fighting strength: in practice far more, for their supplementary units were only just being mobilized at the garrisons.

In the divisions of the second wave—the Seventeenth Division, the Twenty-Seventh Division and the Ninety-Seventh Division of militia—partial mobilization was beginning. Since six o'clock an advance party of the Eighth Army GHQ, consisting of an officer and two N.C.O.s, were on their way by car from Dresden to Mühldorf, to establish quarters for the Eighth Army GHQ at the Bavarian town on the Inn. At seven o'clock it was reported from Dresden to Army Supreme Headquarters in Berlin that the planning staff of the Eighth Army GHQ was ready to leave. But even by nine o'clock the officers of the General Staff and assistant adjutants due to be transferred from other bases in the mobilization were still missing.

At nine o'clock in the Chancellor's office in the Ballhausplatz in Vienna Guido Zernatto, the General Secretary of the Fatherland Front, was presenting a report to his friend, Kurt Schuschnigg:

1 It is reported from Burgenland that groups of the SS have assembled to demonstrate in the Eisenstadt and Oberwarth districts.
2 Towns on the Bavarian frontier report the arrival of comparatively large contingents of German troops.
3 On the roads leading from Munich to the Austrian frontier troop transport lorries have been observed since the day before yesterday.
4 Our Munich intelligence reports relatively large gatherings of troops in the city where schools are being used as temporary barracks.
5 Motorized units have appeared in Passau. It is reliably reported that in the course of the coming day and night 40,000 military transports will assemble.
6 In various parts of Vienna and Lower Austria SA and SS men have been assembling with rucksacks since the early hours of the morning. Our informants report that these people are prepared for an action lasting three to four days. Reports on similar movements in the other provinces have been called for but have not yet come in.
7 Our members report from all the provinces that there is great tension but a mood of confidence prevails. Interference with the preparatory work and with the plebiscite is expected in isolated parts of Styria and in the larger towns in Upper Austria.

8 Our propaganda is functioning well. We have reports from all parts of the country that the technical preparations for the ballot are proceeding smoothly.'

A part of this information was already known to the Chancellor, thanks to the report already received from the State Police. As for the German troop movements, he referred to them in conversation with Zernatto as bluff. He considered it highly unlikely that Hitler would embark on anything that could cause him international difficulties. In reply to one of Zernatto's questions he described the police security measures as quite adequate.

The Chancellor still urgently wanted to see Seyss-Inquart, his Minister of the Interior. But the latter was nowhere to be found. Schuschnigg asked Zernatto if he knew where Seyss-Inquart was. Zernatto had no idea.

While the General Secretary was reporting to the Chancellor and Front Leader, at the Front building itself, in the Platz Am Hof, bunches of flowers were being handed in for the great portrait of the Chancellor in the hall and laid there as if on a grave. Dr Hantschk, the administrative head of the Fatherland Front, deposited a cheque for 300,000 schillings in his safe. It was a contribution from the chairman of the Jewish cultural community, Dr Desider Friedmann, to the Fatherland Front's campaign fund. The fund quickly grew. Sums large and small were constantly being paid in at the counters of the Front. Hantschk was responsible for the campaign fund. But it was not only money and flowers that were brought to the Front building. Since the early hours of the morning arms from a *Schutzkorps* barracks were also being stored there. In addition to rifles and pistols, machine guns were being distributed to important strategic points in the building. The building was made ready for defence. But Hantschk was doubtful. 'Things will look quite different by this evening.' On his desk before him lay the latest product of the propaganda machine that was now running flat out, small leaflets bearing the words printed in red: 'If you want freedom, peace and bread, support the flag that's red-white-red! The swastika brings want and hate, the swastika brings war and death.'

At ten o'clock in the Chancellery Schuschnigg's doorman opened the door of the Chancellor's office to Dr Arthur Seyss-

Inquart, Minister of the Interior, and Edmund Glaise-Horstenau, Minister without Portfolio. 'I have just been to the airport to meet Minister Glaise-Horstenau. That is why I am late,' said Seyss-Inquart. 'Glaise reports what I knew already, that there is great agitation in the Reich about the plebiscite next Sunday. Hitler is said to be beside himself with rage. Everyone is furious.' Schuschnigg found this quite incomprehensible. 'After all, we are only doing what we have every right to do. We are not departing by one iota from what was expressly admitted in the Berchtesgaden Agreement.'

'No, no,' said Glaise, the Pan-German ex-General. 'This plebiscite is really the limit. It was bound to annoy the Führer. It should have never been started.' Excitedly he continued: 'Look, if we don't stop the plebiscite Hitler will invade.'

Schuschnigg stuck to his point of view. He could see no affront to Germany in the plebiscite. It was a purely internal matter. Seyss-Inquart, the trained lawyer, adduced all his objections to the plebiscite for the third time in two days. He delivered a warning about the dangers of strife to come: the National Socialists would go out into the streets. There would be severe clashes. Glaise urged the Chancellor again and again to abandon the plebiscite. Coming near to tears he said: 'This plebiscite will unleash a world war.'

Finally Seyss communicated to Schuschnigg the contents of the letter the courier had brought: 'Hitler expects disturbances if the plebiscite is not postponed and the plebiscite question modified. He is ready to invade in answer to a cry for help.' Seyss omitted to mention that Hitler had already cast him in the role of the man who uttered the cry. Schuschnigg asked if he was prepared to mediate and try to calm things down. Seyss: 'Yes, but I see little hope.'

A good deal more than an hour had passed since the start of their conversation. The deadline Adolf Hitler had set the Austrian Chancellor for the fulfilment of his demands was twelve noon. So far Seyss had not mentioned the word ultimatum. Now he brought it into the conversation without mentioning Hitler's time-limit. The ultimatum which Austria's Minister of the Interior presented to his Chancellor ran out two hours later. Seyss: 'I must ask for a decision by two o'clock this afternoon.'

Friday, 11 March 1938

At the same time Austria was attempting to meet Germany's armed threat. At 10 a.m., the Vienna radio broadcast the following:

'Here is an announcement from the Ministry of Defence: the Chancellor of Austria has issued the following statement: in order to ensure the complete maintenance of law and order on the day of the plebiscite, in accordance with paragraph 9 clause 2 of the second regulation of the Military Service Law, all unmarried reservists of the 1915 class who have completed at least ten months' service are called up for military duties. They must report at once to their units. Where the State Railways are used by men reporting to their units travel expenses will be credited to them on presentation of their military documents.'

After this the same announcement was broadcast repeatedly. A confidential report which arrived at the intelligence section of the Army GHQ in Berlin at 10.20 a.m., seemed to confirm the seriousness of Austria's efforts: 'Austria has ordered mobilization.'

First Lieutenant Kodré had been sitting at his desk in Mobilization Division of the Ministry of Defence in Vienna since eight o'clock. He had been given no special job to do and he was leafing, as he had been the previous day, through the regulations. 'If we don't mobilize now', he observed to a colleague, 'then it will no longer be possible.' But the colleague replied simply: 'No order has come in yet.' Impatiently Kodré went to his superior officer who snapped at him: 'Kindly remember that in the Army you do not ask questions.' A sort of mobilization had taken place in the reserve division. Apart from a general alert and the cancellation of leave, individual measures had also been ordered. Thus the Dornbirn radio station had already been occupied in the night by thirty-five men with six heavy machine guns. So had Salzburg telegraph office. But the difficulties the Austrian army had to reckon with became evident as soon as the first reservists began reporting to the barracks following the announcement on the radio. Some of them came already wearing swastika badges and giving the German salute as they passed through the main gate.

Before Stephan Tauschitz, the Austrian Ambassador in Berlin, made his way to the Wilhelmstrasse in order to explain the plebiscite, as he had been instructed to do the previous day, he telephoned his opposite number from London, Nevile Henderson. The British Ambassador was already well informed. He told Tauschitz that he had heard reports of a partial mobilization by Germany in Bavaria. The situation was serious. And Hitler would doubtless have difficulty in curbing his extremists.

At the Foreign Office Tauschitz was received by the Political Director, von Weizsaecker. Tauschitz began the conversation by saying that he understood Berlin was upset but that the plebiscite was nevertheless also in the interests of Germany. Weizsaecker disagreed. Hitler considered it to be a flagrant breach of the Berchtesgaden Agreement. The plebiscite was a 'pure charade'. The whole of the Austrian cabinet had not been informed in advance and neither had the Berlin government. He then told Tauschitz that he should pass on these criticisms unadorned to Vienna 'where they seem to cherish some extraordinary illusions about what they can expect of us'. In taking his leave Tauschitz told Weizsaecker that he would very likely have to trouble him a number of times during the course of the day.

Meanwhile Henderson had heard some more news. His French opposite number, François-Poncet, had reported to him that three columns of German troops were marching towards the frontier. Henderson had also learned something from Munich, Nuremburg and Dresden. An Englishman had reported to him from Nuremberg that troops could be seen assembling there, that activity in the air had increased sharply and the sale of petrol to private persons was forbidden. Henderson now sent his Military Attaché to the German War Ministry. But the attaché was told there that all this was rumour. The notion of a march to the frontier was 'ridiculous'. In order to get to the bottom of the affair Henderson sent the attaché to Leipzig by car. He was to make observations on the way.

The British diplomat, having just expressed his 'deep sympathy with Dr Schuschnigg's difficult situation' to his Austrian colleague on the telephone, now cabled to Halifax, the Foreign Secretary, that Schuschnigg's move had been 'precipitous and unwise'. And: 'German methods are indefensible but at the same time I fear Dr Schuschnigg may be risking Austria's independence in an attempt to save his own position.'

Friday, 11 March 1938

That morning a visitor dressed in black called at the prelate's
residence at the Heiligenkreuzer Hof in Vienna. It was Alwine
Dollfuss, the widow of Schuschnigg's murdered predecessor. She
was warmly greated by the occupants, Count Richard Nikolaus
Coudenhove-Kalergi and his wife, a former actress at the Burg-
theater. The forty-four-year-old Count was well known for his
Pan-European ideas. Amidst the baroque magnificence of the
Count's residence Alwine Dollfuss told her friends about a
mission she had just undertaken. She had sought out Benito
Mussolini in Rome. The Italian dictator had been on friendly
terms with her husband.

Alwine Dollfuss had just been to Rome in an attempt to save
the independence of Austria through a personal appeal. She told
Coudenhove of the warm welcome Mussolini had given her. But
she had not achieved her political aim. The Duce had avoided
committing himself. He had confined himself to advising her
personally to take her children to Switzerland.

Outside the lorries of the Fatherland Front drove past. Chanting demonstrators shouted, 'Red-white-red until we're dead!'
Aeroplanes dropped millions of leaflets from the sky which bore
the slogan: 'With Schuschnigg for a free, German, Christian
Austria! Every quarter of an hour election appeals were made on
the radio. The Catholic Action began an appeal:

'Catholic institutions brought German art and culture to this
land. Catholic peoples built German towns and German
villages. For a thousand years the German people of the Ostmark have created a culture of Christian, of Catholic inspiration, which is even today admired by the whole world as one of
the ripest fruits of German creativity. For a thousand years our
fathers have fought and shed their blood for Catholic Austria
and her German mission amongst the nations. Fathers and
Mothers! Young men and women! Catholic Action calls upon
you all! We are fighting for our German, for our Christian
heritage! That is why we vote "Yes"! For a German, Christian,
independent, social Austria!'

The police in Vienna strengthened their cordon round the
Inner City. The Burgtor, the entrance to the Heldenplatz from
the Ringstrasse, was closed to traffic and the approaches to the
Chancellery were barricaded off. Policemen stood at the bridgeheads along the quay. Bus services at the edge of the Inner City

were suspended. In the outer districts fresh crowds of demon-strators were gathering. Their objectives were the Opera House and the Kärntner Strasse, the focus of all Viennese demonstra-tions.

The entire German morning press for 11 March concerned itself with the events in Austria. The silence of the previous day had been broken but a certain restraint in the wording of the reports could still be discerned. Almost all the papers had printed the German News Agency story, but these few lines already left no doubt about the direction the German case was to take. The story included the following: 'One dangerous sign is the fact that the Communist mob masquerading as supporters of the Fatherland Front are trying to gain domination of the Ring-strasse. The slogans of the Red Front alternate with cries of "Heil Austria!"' The *Völkische Beobachter* supplemented this with its own report from Graz. Lorries of the Fatherland Front draped with red banners and filled with Communists were said to have driven through the city. 'The occupants were giving the Com-munist salute and shouting "Heil Moscow!" "Hoch Moscow!"'

But this was only the prelude. Now the newspapers began to attack in unison. The starting signal was given at the German Government's eleven o'clock news conference. The restraint observed so far was to be abandoned. It was time for the press to move into top gear. For this the following ruling was issued: a bolder layout, banner headlines in the popular papers, political news-sheets with the report in two columns.

When copies of the German morning papers reached Vienna it was decided to react. The press officers drafted a statement to the foreign press denying the story that Communists were planning an uprising. But even outside Vienna there were people who knew what interpretation to place upon the German propaganda. The American Chargé d'Affaires in Berlin cabled to Washington that the references to Communist agitation must be considered in the light of Hitler's avowed mission as the opponent of the Comintern. The whole affair, he said, was 'ominous'.

Round about noon at the National Socialists' Vienna headquarters at Number 1 Seitzergasse Seyss-Inquart and Glaise-Horstenau reported the outcome of their long conversation with the Chan-cellor. Their audience were ex-Major Klausner, the Austrian

Friday, 11 March 1938

Party Leader; Rainer, the lawyer; Globocznigg, the timber merchant; State Councillors Jury and Fischböck and Mühlmann, the National Socialist jack-of-all-trades and art critic.

Seyss first read out Hitler's letter. So far Schuschnigg had rejected the demands of the Reich, but he still had until 2.00 p.m. to change his mind. One thing was clear to the Party leaders: Berlin must be told what had happened. This was done at once by telephone.

Then, after a brief discussion, the Party's policy was formulated. If Schuschnigg did not yield to the demands, the two national Ministers must resign. Seyss wrote a letter to the Chancellor in the names of both national Ministers and the national Privy Councillors, Fischböck and Jury, in which the oral ultimatum was confirmed and supplemented with this resignation threat.

In Graz all hell was let loose at noon. While the Fatherland Front was conducting noisy propaganda for the plebiscite and distributing slogans amongst the crowds, thousands were in the streets demonstrating against the plebiscite. The day had begun with a schoolboys' strike. The pupils of the *Handelsakademie* (Trade Academy) had taken to the streets in protest against the dismissal of a National Socialist teacher. Other schoolboys had also played truant and joined the march. The young demonstrators had surged along like a tidal wave. People were demanding Schuschnigg's resignation at every street corner.

Army vehicles of the Vienna Motorized Rifle Battalion drove from one crossroads to the next. Each time men were told to dismount. Then the soldiers lined up in a broad front, fixed their bayonets and marched at a warning pace through streets, squares and bridges, clearing them of demonstrators. Acting on orders, they ignored the shouts hurled at them: 'Jew-protectors!' 'Traitors!' 'Black vermin!' At street intersections soldiers armed with machine guns took up position.

Graz, the capital of Styria, had long been known as the 'capital of revolt'. The Racial-Political Councillor of Styria, thirty-seven-year-old Dr Armin Dadieu, operated openly as a representative of the Nazis. Thanks to the agitation of two illegal activists working at his side, the Nazis were stronger in Graz than in any other Austrian town. This strength was due mostly, however, to

94

opportunists and sympathizers who were not official members of the Party.

The Vienna government could no longer rely on the Graz police force, nor even on the Styrian units of the Army. It was for this reason that the Vienna Motorized Rifle Battalion had been sent to Graz at the beginning of March. While the soldiers from Vienna were taking action against the demonstrators in the city, the members of the Nazi ring within the Army saw their hour approaching. About five per cent of the officers, particularly in western Austria, were members of the ring: amongst the other ranks and N.C.O.s the percentage was somewhat higher. Since 5 March the Nazi organization amongst the ordinary soldiers had been taking orders from the officers' ring.

By midday on 11 March secret orders had already gone out to the soldiers' ring in all the barracks for the plebiscite:

'1 Withhold the vote.
2 Hoist swastika flag over all barracks on the morning of the plebiscite day.
3 To troops designated to help with the plebiscite: disobey orders to fire, and in other ways sympathize with demonstrators, allow the SA free passage through barriers.'

Even the period following a possible seizure of power had already been considered. The ringleader, Colonel Maximilian de Angelis, of the General Staff, who worked in Vienna as an instructor on the Senior Officers' courses, had been asked as long ago as January whether 'in the event of a National Socialist government' he would take on the post of State Secretary for Defence. Angelis, who did not belong to the Party, had at that time expressed the opinion that General Glaise-Horstenau would be more suitable.

At precisely 1.00 p.m. at the Reich Chancellery in Berlin Hitler put his signature to a document, the contents of which had already been transmitted orally to the Commanders-in-Chief of the three services and to the Head of the SS. 'Directive Number One' came into force: 'If other methods prove unsuccessful I intend to invade Austria with armed forces . . .'

The Foreign Office in the Wilhelmstrasse, Berlin, had not been brought in on the preparations for the action against Austria. The government officials there had suffered the disadvantage that their Minister, Joachim von Ribbentrop, was in London for his farewell visit. But even Hitler could see that now things were getting serious he needed the support of the diplomats. For this reason he telephoned Ribbentrop's predecessor, Baron Konstantin von Neurath, at his home, and summoned him to the Reich Chancellery. When Neurath entered the smoking-room a short time later he could see at once from the number of government officials and *Wehrmacht* officers waiting there that something serious must be up. He was particularly struck by the presence of von Papen, whom he had believed to be still in Vienna.

Neurath was at once received by Hitler in his study. Goering was present. The Chancellor informed his ex-Foreign Minister briefly about the plans: he intended to invade Austria that same night. Neurath asked if this was necessary. Hitler explained the reasons and then asked him what measures the Foreign Office must take in the circumstances. Neurath's answer was brief: Ribbentrop must be brought back from London. But Goering was firmly against this, and Hitler shared the view of his Air Force Chief. In that case, said Neurath, the friendly powers must be informed about the proposed step. A formula was agreed on which Neurath noted down on a piece of paper: 'The exclusive purpose of the action is to prevent the shedding of the blood of the German people in Austria, and to guarantee that the Austrian people, in accordance with their right of self-determination, may take their fate into their own hands. Recognition of the Brenner frontier.' Then Neurath gave a short lecture on foreign policy: various states would naturally protest. Notes of this kind would then have to be replied to by the Reich. So that this could function smoothly, Hitler asked his visitor to pass on the agreed form of words to Mackensen, the State Secretary at the Foreign Office.

In the smoking-room Papen was still the focus of the informal gathering. Everyone wanted to know what was really happening in Austria at the moment. Papen had been called in to see Hitler shortly after his arrival at nine o'clock. But Hitler had made no enquiries. He had declared, brooking no argument, 'The situation has become intolerable. Schuschnigg has betrayed the ideal of Greater Germany! By forcing a vote against the *Anschluss* he is simply trying to give himself an alibi *vis-à-vis* the European powers for his un-German policies. He must not succeed. If he believes Mussolini or France will help him he is mistaken. It must not come to that again.' Papen had warned Hitler against over-hasty decisions. But Hitler had remained firm: 'Either the plebiscite is called off or we bring down the government. We cannot go on like this.' Papen had observed that Schuschnigg was still very much open to being persuaded that the plebiscite must be postponed. But it seemed that this suggestion fell upon stony ground.

As the morning had passed the flurry in the smoking-room had grown greater. New faces had appeared. Suddenly Prince Philip of Hessen, the President of the province of Hessen-Nassau and the son-in-law of the Italian King, appeared. He had been summoned to Berlin by Hitler. The Chancellor wanted to send him as a courier to Mussolini. The letter he was to pass on had been composed by Hitler at about noon. Without consulting the Foreign Office, but on the basis of the formula he had agreed with Neurath, Hitler dictated:

'Your Excellency, at a fateful hour I am writing to you, Excellency, to inform you of a decision which appears necessary in the circumstances and which is now irrevocable. During the last months I have observed with increasing concern how an understanding has gradually grown up between Austria and Czechoslovakia. This is hard enough for us to tolerate even in peace-time but in any war which were forced upon Germany, it would be bound to present the gravest possible threat to the security of the Reich. In the wake of this agreement the Austrian state has gradually begun to equip itself along all its frontiers with barriers and fortifications. The object could only be:

1 At a given moment to bring about the Restoration[1] and:
2 If necessary to throw the weight of a mass of at least twenty million men against Germany. ... For years the German Austrians have been oppressed and brutalized by a regime that possesses no legal basis. There is no end to the sufferings of countless tormented people. ... In order to eliminate the tension which was gradually becoming intolerable I made one final attempt with Herr Schuschnigg and decided to make an agreement with the object of finally establishing complete equality before the law. ... The demands I made were more than moderate. ... Herr Schuschnigg gave me solemn

[1] i.e. of the Habsburg monarchy. Tr.

assurances in this direction and an agreement was made accordingly. He did not keep to this agreement from the very first moment. But he is now poised to strike a new blow against the intention of this agreement, by arranging a so-called plebiscite which makes a mockery of all plebiscites. . . .

'Since the day before yesterday this land has been moving closer to a state of anarchy which is still increasing. With my responsibility as Führer and Chancellor of the German Reich and likewise as a son of this soil, I can no longer remain passive in the face of these developments. I am now determined to restore law and order to my homeland and to enable the people to decide their own fate according to their judgement in an unmistakable, clear and open manner.'

Then Hitler made a direct appeal to Mussolini:

'1 Consider this step as no more than one of national self-defence and therefore as an action that any man of character in my position would undertake in the same way. . . .
2 In a critical hour for Italy I proved to you the steadfastness of my sympathy. Do not doubt that in the future there will be no change in this respect.
3 Whatever the consequences of the coming events may be, I have drawn a definite boundary between Germany and France and now draw one just as definite between Italy and us. It is the Brenner. . . .

'I deeply regret not being able to speak to you personally at this moment to tell you everything I feel. Always in friendship, yours, Adolf Hitler.'

After lunch, which the officials and officers had taken in the oval dining-room next to the smoking-room, State Secretary Wilhelm Keppler, Commissioner for Austrian Affairs, saw Hitler handing the letter to Prince Philip of Hessen. They spoke only briefly. Hitler confined himself to generalities. Though he said that the subject was Austria and Schuschnigg's plebiscite he said nothing about his own plans. A short while afterwards Hessen took off for Rome in a special plane. His wife, the Princess Mafalda, was already in Italy. As the morning papers had reported, she had just arrived in Turin.

While the German troops were advancing on the frontier and Hitler's messenger was on his way to see Mussolini, to clear up the vital issue of whether Germany could rely on Italian backing in taking this step, a report came in from the Chargé d'Affaires at the German Legation in Vienna which created the impression that Austria was determined to meet the German pressure with resistance. Von Stein's telegram was military in its brevity:

'Top secret. Copy to Reich War Ministry. The following reported from reliable sources:
1 Trained reservists, 1915 class, are being called up.
2 Staff militia of Vienna city enterprises and of State Railways (former Railway Corps of Lower Austria) have been armed.
3 Fatherland Front militia in Vienna alerted.
4 Vacuum oil ordered by Defence Ministry to supply fuel for vehicles.'

Between twelve and one in the Chancellor's room the situation had been discussed. The Ministers, Perntner, Raab, Schmidt, and Zernatto, the State Secretaries, Skubl and Zehner, and other advisers were arguing about the demands which the two Ministers, Seyss and Glaise, had put to the Chancellor orally that morning. In the midst of this Schuschnigg enquired of Skubl whether his instruction to seal off the government quarter had been carried out. The Police President confirmed that it had.

The long debate led only to the conclusion that a compromise must be negotiated: the terms of the plebiscite should be altered but there should be no postponement. While Schuschnigg was making notes in order to present this in writing to Seyss, his secretary brought in a letter: the ultimatum delivered that morning had been confirmed in writing 'in the name of the National Ministers and Privy Councillors'.

The letter once again claimed that the plebiscite was unconstitutional but considered it possible that it should be held in a constitutional manner after a lapse of four weeks. The arrangements for this were to be entrusted to Seyss-Inquart, the Minister of the Interior. Representatives of the National Socialists were to sit on every electoral commission. Facilities for campaign propaganda were to be granted to all political groups.

If these proposals were rejected the national Ministers and Privy Councillors threatened to resign. Schuschnigg and his two friends were agreed about one thing: their resignation would certainly be construed by Hitler as a breach of the Berchtesgaden

Agreement and used as a pretext for an invasion. The discussion continued.

ꌅꌅꌅꌅꌅꌅ

Round about noon the Revolutionary Socialists' leaflet, which Buttinger had written the day before and which had been approved by the Central Committee during the night, was rushed out on to the streets: 'Workers, Comrades. ... Down with Hitler-Fascism! Long live freedom!' The Communist Party also called upon its supporters to vote 'Yes' in the plebiscite the following Sunday. Their leaflet read: 'We extend our hand to you, workers, without distinction of party, to you, farmers, to you, Catholics, to you, men and women of the intellect, technicians and scientists. ... Your "Yes" will guarantee a free, independent and social Austria which must be a bulwark of peace, progress and freedom against the militant fire-raisers of Fascism.'

The Communists supported the government without speculating on what this might bring them. The Socialists, on the other hand, were still hoping that their demands, placed before Schuschnigg and his link-men, would be met in full. This was also the purpose of a conversation which had taken place that morning between Friedrich Hillegeist, the chairman of the illegal trades unions, Karl Hans Sailer, the Revolutionary Socialist, and Rott, the relevant Minister. Schuschnigg's Minister had shown himself to be optimistic in his judgement of the situation and had put off the workers' representatives until after one o'clock. For until that time he was due to be at Schuschnigg's office for a meeting. Hillegeist and Sailer had been insistent. The seriousness of the situation would brook no further postponement. But Rott had revealed himself confident of victory. 'The plebiscite is assured. ... What else can the workers do but vote "Yes", whether you tell them to or not?' The Left had already been given a similar answer the day before by Staud, the Front trades union president.

It was now one o'clock. At the Café Meteor, the illegal trades-unionist headquarters for some days now, the Left waited in vain for the news that would clarify the whole position. At another coffee-house, in Wieden, in the Fourth District of Vienna, another socialist group was meeting: the so-called Wednesday Circle. They were a loose association gathered round the former First Secretary of the Austrian Social Democratic Party, fifty-three-year-old Dr Robert Danneberg. In the banned Party he was regarded as representing a link between the older socialists who had emigrated and the young ones who had stayed in the country. Danneberg, who had been the real organizer of the Party after 1918, had spent eight months in prison in 1934. The meeting in the Wieden coffee-house was also attended by representatives of the Socialist International. By now they had reached a clear conclusion: every chance, however small, to preserve Austrian independence must be grasped.

Other meetings were being held on the morning of 11 March with the same end in view. Representatives of the Left had been in negotiation with General Zehner, the State Secretary for Defence, on the lines of the ideas for armed resistance worked out by Major Eifler, the former Chief of Staff of the Republican *Schutzbund*. With Zehner had been Schmitz, the Mayor, who, as leader of the Fatherland Front in Vienna, had for some time been trying to bring the workers into Schuschnigg's state. But it was very late in the day now for a combined operation between the Army, the Front militia and the workers. And the objections of many officials of the regime were still too great. They did not think they could risk putting arms into the hands of the workers who had been mown down by government bullets in 1934. And the Left no longer possessed an arsenal of its own, such as that with which it had gone into battle four years before. And so only a few detachments, supplemented with Fatherland Front men and *Schutzkorps* militiamen, were armed at this time.

Theodor Hornbostel, the Political Director of the Foreign Office, had no time to go to lunch. He had so far had little success with the task the Foreign Minister had given him in the early hours of the morning. From London and Paris he had received scant encouragement. And from Rome nothing at all. In these hours the help that Austria relied on seemed very uncertain. Then the Austrian Military Attaché, Major General Justus Jahn, arrived from Paris with a report from Vollgruber, the Austrian Ambassador, on the talks he had had at the Quai d'Orsay. Hornbostel glanced quickly through the long text and read: '. . . France seems at present ready in principle . . . to draw her sword.' But this would only apply if England did likewise. Hornbostel had already established this from his talks on the telephone that morning. He filed the report (reference 52283-13/38) and went back to his telephone.

Friday, 11 March 1938

In London the German Foreign Minister, Joachim von Ribbentrop, was making his calls. He had been to see Sir Thomas Inskip, the Minister for the coordination of defence. Ribbentrop knew Inskip to be a man who had always had an understanding of the German position. This time, too, he had not been disappointed. The Englishman told him that, if Germany showed patience, the Austrian question would sooner or later be settled in Germany's favour. In the history of nations it made no difference whether something of this kind was achieved in two or three months or in two or three years. And he then assured Ribbentrop that the British cabinet would not resolve on any military intervention if Germany settled the Austrian question in this way. But it would be a different matter if Germany began a military action to intervene in Austria. England might well be drawn into a conflict of this kind.

At this time Paris was still hamstrung by the cabinet crisis which had lasted for two days. The politician who was attempting to form a government, Léon Blum, and the Foreign Minister of the previous cabinet who was still exercising office, Delbos, each invited the German Ambassador, Count Johannes Welczeck, to separate meetings. The Foreign Minister expressed his serious concern at the crisis reports coming out of London which spoke of a partial mobilization by the Germans. But he at once qualified this: perhaps these reports were incorrect or exaggerated. Welczeck for his part was able to say with a clear conscience that he knew nothing about the matter. He furthermore affirmed '. . . that we regard Austria and Germany as members of one big family and it is our wish that both relatively minor and relatively major family quarrels should be settled amongst ourselves.'

Chancellor Schuschnigg had called a cabinet meeting for two o'clock. But this was now forgotten. The Chancellor and his closest confidants continued to discuss the situation created by the ultimatum demanding the postponement of the plebiscite and the alteration of the form it was to take. Schuschnigg sketched out his own opinion:

'1 It would be possible to reject the ultimatum presented to us, and to abrogate the Berchtesgaden Agreement, while making known to world opinion our reasons for this. This

would inevitably mean a bloody struggle both internally and with the German Reich, which must be expected to intervene.
'2 It would be possible to accept the conditions put to us. In these circumstances it would be necessary for a completely new government to be formed and for the present Chancellor to resign from the government.
'3 It would be possible to propose a compromise in which the conditions of the letter are accepted with the exception of the postponement.'

There was a long argument back and forth about how the foreign powers would react, whether Austria could count on any support in resisting the blackmail. Mussolini had from the very first described the plebiscite as a 'bomb, which could blow up in our own hand', and as 'Un errore', a mistake. Since then it had not been possible to make contact with the Duce. He was, without doubt, simply refusing to communicate. Italy, in Schmidt's opinion, could certainly not be relied on. France was more trustworthy but was at present undergoing a government crisis. Would England risk its own neck for Austria? Schuschnigg would not rule England out. At the very least he was counting on diplomatic action by London in consort with Italy and France.

Finally the Chancellor came back to his original resolve: to accept the demands of the Nazi Ministers (behind whom stood Berlin) almost in full and simply to refuse to postpone the date of the plebiscite. On reflection Schuschnigg could foresee that the postponement of the date would make it possible for the Nazis to create a massive wave of propaganda. He closed the discussion and asked his colleagues to remain in the building. Schmidt and Zernatto were given the task of communicating the Chancellor's decision to Seyss-Inquart and Glaise-Horstenau, who had meanwhile come to the Chancellery. The Chancellor himself wanted to go and see the President to report on the situation to him.

In the cabinet room at the Chancellery Schmidt and Zernatto informed the Nazi Ministers of the Chancellor's decision: their technical demands would be met but the ballot would still take place on Sunday. Seyss-Inquart declared that he could not take note of this. He was only empowered to accept all or nothing. His friend, Zernatto, tried to pin Seyss down by appealing to his honour: his attitude now was a complete contradiction of his previous conduct. Seyss: 'The situation is no longer in my hands.'

Friday, 11 March 1938

The onus of decision lay with the Party. Zernatto observed that it was an 'impossible situation' for a member of the government to make himself the spokesman for an illegal party which took its orders from Germany. But Seyss was able to point out in reply that ultimately the Chancellor had himself appointed him as a spokesman for the 'National Opposition' and a link-man with the German Reich.

At about 2.30 p.m. Chancellor Schuschnigg went to the President's state apartments. He told Miklas about the Nazi Ministers' demands and about the letter he had received at 1.00 p.m. The foreign political situation had become exceptionally critical. Only now did Schuschnigg tell the President about the German advance on the frontier. And then he communicated to Miklas a sudden decision: 'I am ready to cancel the plebiscite.' Their conversation lasted only a few minutes.

When Schuschnigg got back from seeing the President, Schmidt and Zernatto were waiting for him and told him of Seyss-Inquart's negative answer. Now only two of the three possibilities which the Chancellor had enumerated an hour previously remained open. Schuschnigg had already told the President he was ready to call off the plebiscite. He now gave his friend, Zernatto, the task of bringing a halt to the campaign. The General Secretary knew how hard it must be for the Chancellor to make this decision. Schuschnigg had taken personal responsibility for the plebiscite. In his speech on 24 February he had roundly declared that he would not yield to any further National Socialist demands. Yet once again he was trimming his sails. Schuschnigg indicated to Zernatto the reasons he was to give for the cancellation: for the outside world it was the technical difficulties which made a postponement of the date necessary, within the Front it was Hitler's unambiguous ultimatum.

Shortly before 2.45 p.m., the Chancellor walked out into the Hall of Columns, which adjoined his study, with a poker face. Seyss-Inquart and Glaise-Horstenau were waiting for him. 'The plebiscite is cancelled.' At these words a stone fell from Glaise's heart. The demands of the ultimatum were fulfilled. Berlin and the Party had cause to be satisfied.

Then Seyss was called to the telephone. A call from Berlin. Goering was on the line:

'Hello, Herr Doktor, is my brother-in-law with you?' Seyss replied that he was not, for he knew Dr Franz Hueber was at

the offices of the Racial-Political Council at Number 1 Seitzergasse. Then Goering came to the real point:

'How are things with you? Have you resigned, or have you
anything else to tell me?'

Seyss: 'The Chancellor has called off the plebiscite for
Sunday. This puts myself and the others in a somewhat
difficult position. Together with the postponement of the
plebiscite, extensive security measures have also been taken,
including a curfew for 8.00 p.m.'

Without a moment's hesitation Goering outlined further
demands. In his view the measures taken by Chancellor Schuschnigg were in no way satisfactory. He could not comment officially
at that moment since he was not entitled to do so alone. But he
would inform the Führer within the shortest possible time. Speaking for himself, he saw the calling off of the plebiscite as merely a
postponement but in no way an alteration of the present situation,
which had been brought about by Chancellor Schuschnigg's
attitude and by the breach of the Berchtesgaden Agreement.

Seyss had scarcely laid down the receiver when the whole substance of the conversation was passed on to Zernatto, the General
Secretary of the Fatherland Front, by the Austrian intelligence
service. Monitors were also at work in the research department of
the Berlin Air Ministry and every word of the conversation was
noted down.

Now the Austrian Chancellor had agreed to call off the plebiscite, Goering felt that the point had been reached at which the
Reich must take a hand. Goering: 'The long-desired opportunity is there to carry out a clear and complete solution.' In his
luxurious villa at Karinhall he already possessed a great map on
which the frontiers of Germany were drawn to include Austria.
He now planned to achieve this in reality. His ultimate aim was
total annexation of the rump state of the former Austro-Hungarian
empire. His first goal along this road was the overthrow of
Schuschnigg.

Goering hurried off to see Adolf Hitler. In the Reich Chancellor's study he reported that the plebiscite had been called off. Now
Schuschnigg too must be got rid of. The time for the *Anschluss*
had come. Goering proposed that a reliable man should be sent to
Vienna who could take the whole situation in hand. Hitler's
special representative for Austria, Keppler, seemed to him too
soft. But Hitler decided: 'If anyone goes it will be Keppler.'

Friday, 11 March 1938

While the Field Marshal went back to the telephone to speak once more to Seyss, Keppler was summoned to see Hitler. 'You must fly to Vienna at once,' said Hitler, 'to resolve a grave conflict at the eleventh hour.' Military measures were being prepared against Austria. Schuschnigg had broken the Berchtesgaden Agreement. He must resign. A government must be formed in Vienna which would return within the bounds of the agreement. The Chancellor he would prefer would be Seyss-Inquart.

At five past three the telephone rang again for Seyss-Inquart at the Vienna Chancellery. And Goering delivered the second ultimatum of the day: in Berlin's view the Austrian Chancellor's decision did not go far enough. Because he had broken the Berchtesgaden Agreement Schuschnigg no longer enjoyed their confidence. Nor could they have any confidence in his future dealings. The Nazi Ministers must hand in their resignations immediately and demand the resignation of the Chancellor as well. It was understood that Schuschnigg's resignation must be coupled with an immediate invitation to Seyss from the President to form a new cabinet.

If Berlin did not hear back from him within one hour—that is by 4.00 p.m.—it would be assumed that Seyss was prevented from telephoning. In conclusion Goering called upon the Austrian Minister of the Interior to send off the telegram, the text of which had been brought to Vienna by courier. Seyss was to call for German troops to enter the country.

After his conversation with Goering an agitated Seyss appeared in the Hall of Columns, next to the Chancellor's office, a scrap of paper in his hand on which he had jotted a few notes. He met with Zernatto and Schmidt and read out Berlin's demands to them. Zernatto asked Seyss if there was nothing he could do to alter them. The Minister of the Interior shrugged his shoulders: 'I am nothing more than a historic telephone girl. All I can do is pass on the news. I have no influence.'

Then Seyss told Glaise-Horstenau, his fellow Minister, what Goering had said. He asked Glaise to come with him, to report the news to the Chancellor. But the latter refused, for 'reasons of delicacy'. Seyss went along to see Schuschnigg. Their conversation lasted only a few minutes. When the Minister of the Interior returned to the Hall of Columns he told Glaise he thought the Chancellor's office would be his.

At the Reich Chancellery in Berlin they had already gone a stage further. Hitler's deputy, Rudolf Hess, and Hermann Goering, too, were considering the composition of a new Austrian government. Goering impressed on Keppler the names of those he would definitely want to see in the cabinet. Then Keppler hurried off to the Tempelhof airport with his assistant. At 3.30 p.m. his plane took off for Vienna.

᯼᯼᯼᯼᯼

After the negotiators of the Left had waited in vain at the Café Meteor for the word that would indicate to them the result of their negotiations with the government, they moved to the Inner City, so as to be more available in case they were needed. Thus from three o'clock onwards the entire leadership of the illegal left-wing unions was sitting together in the Augustinerkeller.

Sailer, who had gone with Hillegeist that morning to see Rott, had remained at home. It was to be his task, as agreed with the government, to make a broadcast that evening, to persuade the workers to vote 'Yes' in the plebiscite on Sunday. But so far there were only two words written on the piece of paper that lay on the table in front of him: 'Dear comrades!' Sailer had not managed to get any further. The telephone would not stop ringing. He had had a stream of calls from newspapers, foreign correspondents. All of them wanted to know how things stood with the negotiations.

In his office across the street from the Opera House Dr Friedrich Scheu, a lawyer who was also a correspondent of the *Daily Herald*, was rung up by a friend. Consul Urbas, a man from the left wing of the Christian Social Party, who now worked as foreign political correspondent for the *Reichspost* newspaper, had heard something he urgently wanted to pass on to Scheu: 'I just wanted to tell you that all is lost. Hitler has delivered an ultimatum and the Germans are marching in.' Having said this, Urbas hung up.

The information had been given to Scheu for a particular reason. Urbas knew that because of his job the young journalist of the Left was on good terms with both the government and the socialists and trade-unionists.

Now Scheu was in a position to do something in return for all the information the men of the Left had given him as a journalist. First he telephoned Sailer, who was still putting together the text of his radio appeal. Scheu: 'I think it's all over. There is talk of a German ultimatum. The plebiscite is postponed. . . .' Then he tried to warn others.

Friday, 11 March 1938

That morning it had not been so turbulent in the streets of the Austrian capital as it had been on the previous days. The propaganda convoys of the Fatherland Front—lorries, leaflet distributors, billposters and painters of Teutonic Crosses—dominated the scene. There was scarcely any sign of the National Socialists in the Inner City. But the calm was deceptive. Following the previous night's meeting at the Hotel Regina between some of the Nazi Gauleiters and the national leadership of the Austrian party, preparations were being made all over the country for that afternoon's operations. At 2.00 p.m., it had been agreed, an order would be sent out by Dr Friedl Rainer from the Vienna headquarters, according to the political situation at that time.

However, the developments during the morning and at midday had brought about some delay in Rainer's plan. The discussions at the Chancellery continued. Still nothing was decided. At two o'clock the Gauleiters all over Austria and the leaders of the SA and SS formations waited for the word in vain. Rainer had already postponed the deadline for an hour. Until 3.00 p.m., he waited for the news from the Nazi negotiators at the Chancellery, Seyss-Inquart and Glaise-Horstenau: if no message had been received by then he was empowered by the Party:

1 to send the telegram to Berlin calling for German troops;
2 to release the prepared text of an appeal to the Austrian people;
3 to give the word for the Nazis to seize power.

The fighting units of the Party, the SA and the SS, were already gathered in gymnasiums in a wide variety of Districts of Vienna. It was some time ago now that regular para-military units had been set up, which were trained for fighting in internal political clashes. Only in Gymnastics Clubs and gymnasiums was it possible to gather together and train so many men without causing a stir.

The Austrian provinces were not so peaceful at midday as Vienna. In Braunau demonstrators marched across the long square in front of the Town Hall, chanting Nazi slogans. In Graz, the Styrian capital, the main streets and strategic points were now occupied by soldiers: but the demonstrations continued.

In an attempt to keep the temperature below flash-point the head of the Styrian Racial-Political Council, Dr Armin Dadieu, whom Schuschnigg had already branded the day before as a traitor, was negotiating at one corner of the Bismarckplatz with the captain in charge of the military operation in that sector. Dadieu pleaded that direct force should not be used by the government forces, otherwise he could no longer be responsible for the behaviour of the crowds.

In Linz the local leadership of the SA were gathered at the Hotel Wolfinger. They were waiting for the word of command from Vienna and discussing the actions they might take. Then a piece of news came in that was reassuring for the Nazis: 'Fourth Division with Colonel Sinzinger firmly on the side of the Party'. This meant that the National Socialist soldiers' ring had seized the opportunity offered them by the hour. Already in Linz, as in other garrison towns, the most important military guards that day were packed with soldiers who supported the Nazis. The people on duty on the telephone switchboards in the barracks that day were also almost all politically reliable.

Little Austria's armed forces were indeed on the alert all over the country, but the troops, most of whom were loyal to the government, were confined to their barracks. This made things easier for the illegal Nazi formations as well as for the Nazi soldiers' ring. But as Rainer's word of command had still not come through there were only one or two minor skirmishes here and there, mostly set off by local Party leaders who were unwilling to submit to the discipline of the Party.

Rainer was waiting for a call from Seyss-Inquart. The Minister was supposed to ring him at the Seitzergasse to give him news before three o'clock. If no message came through by then 'then the Party will assume that Schuschnigg has rejected the ultimatum and that both Ministers have been taken prisoner'. Seyss had not himself regarded the affair as being quite so fraught with danger as this, but he had nevertheless promised to inform Rainer. At 2.50 p.m. the call came through: plebiscite called off and no new plebiscite announced; stern security measures taken by the government. Now Rainer issued his order: Case Number One of the directive announced the previous night was to be applied. The situation, as Seyss had described it to him, did not exactly correspond to the basic premise envisaged. But it was no longer possible to work out a new directive and to transmit it to all the Party and formation headquarters in the country. For this reason Rainer's one thought was in all circumstances to bring the waiting Party members out on to the streets. In order to cover himself on this question Rainer asked the German Legation to pass on to Berlin a report about the orders he had given and about the situation now developing in Austria. Then Goering, who was growing ever more impatient, telephoned the headquarters of the illegal Nazi Party. He wanted to speak to his brother-in-law. Hueber came to the telephone. Rainer listened in word for word. Goering: 'The Führer has given Schuschnigg every opportunity. But Schuschnigg rejected them all. So now we must take a different tone. Schuschnigg has until four o'clock to resign. A new government must be formed under Seyss, otherwise our troops will march.' Now Rainer knew his own actions were in line with Berlin. But the new demand must be brought urgently to Seyss. Globocznigg undertook this task and with him went Kajetan Mühlmann, who could, in case of need, be used as a courier. Thus at about 3.30 p.m. the first Nazis from the top leadership of the illegal Party entered the Chancellery.

Schmidt and Zernatto were once again negotiating with Seyss-Inquart. Their proposal: Seyss should take the post of Vice-Chancellor, while Schuschnigg remained Chancellor. But again Seyss refused: his hands were tied.

Meanwhile the Chancellor was speaking to Michael Skubl, the State Secretary for Security: 'You know that in his ultimatum Hitler demanded the cancellation of the plebiscite. This I have done but this no longer satisfies him. He now demands my resignation. Personally I am ready to resign, but I cannot expect my people to accept Seyss. Would you be willing to take over the office of Chancellor?'

Skubl replied:

'Herr Chancellor, I do not believe that is a viable course. Anyone who has learned to know Hitler as I have knows that he does not go back on his demands. If Hitler demands Seyss as Chancellor then he would respond to the offer of myself by invading immediately, for as Police President I have the status, for him, of a personal opponent. In the face of the present situation I believe that Seyss is the lesser of the evils from which we have to choose, for he is a moderate man and averse to all violence. I therefore consider he represents the most tolerable solution.'

At three-thirty Schuschnigg went into the President's state apartments for the second time that day. In the presence of Schmitz, the Mayor of Vienna, Reither, the Provincial Governor of Lower Austria, and Schmidt, the Foreign Minister, he

announced the resignation of his cabinet. The reasons he gave
were Goering's ultimatum and his own desire to avoid fighting.
Goering had given four o'clock that afternoon as his deadline.
The President thundered: 'We will not yield to pressure. I want
to know what the guaranteeing powers have to say to this.' He
was told that intervention by England, France and Italy was
unlikely. Miklas took note of the resignations but said that
Schuschnigg must carry on for the moment. Schuschnigg then
reported that he had discussed the question of the succession with
Skubl but that Skubl had refused to accept the office for himself.

A few minutes after Schuschnigg had left the President's room
Miklas sent for Dr Otto Ender, President of the Audit Office, a
former Chancellor and a farmer's son from the Vorarlberg. Otto
Ender, sixty-three, was one of the President's political allies. He
had been Chancellor once before, for six months, from December
1930 to June 1931.

In the Hall of Columns the Austrian Nazis, Globocznigg and
Mühlmann, had appeared on the scene. Mühlmann went up to
Glaise-Horstenau and asked him about all the to-ing and fro-ing
and inquired how things stood.

Glaise: 'He's a dead duck already.' Mühlmann, amazed:
'Who?' Glaise: 'Schuschnigg. He's capitulated already. I kept
saying to him: Don't hold your plebiscite or they'll invade. But
he goes ahead and holds the plebiscite. Now he's a dead duck.'
Globocznigg, who did not know that Seyss had been speaking to
Goering on the telephone at three o'clock that afternoon, reported
Berlin's demands to the Minister of the Interior, as instructed by
Rainer. Globocznigg then hurried to the telephone and told
Rainer that Seyss was already fully informed. His chief gave him
further instructions for transmission to the Minister of the
Interior: 'The SA and SS must be granted legal status. They
must be established as security organs alongside the police.'
Seyss, too, went to the telephone. At 3.55 p.m. he was once more
in contact with Goering at the Reich Chancellery.

Seyss: 'The Chancellor has gone to see President Miklas to
hand in his own resignation and that of the whole cabinet.'
Goering: 'And is there a guarantee that you will be asked to
form a new cabinet?'
Seyss did not reply directly: 'I will report to you fully about
that by half-past five at the latest.' Goering then declared
categorically that in addition to Schuschnigg's resignation it

Friday, 11 March 1938

was an irreversible demand of the Reich that Seyss should be
given the task of forming a new cabinet.

While Goering was conducting the overthrow of the government by telephone, Schmidt, the Foreign Minister, and Hornbostel, the Political Director of the Foreign Office, were ensuring
that the British Ambassador, Palairet, and the French Ambassador, Puaux, were kept informed of every new development.
Puaux had already advised Schuschnigg to play for time. The
German Embassy must first of all be made to confirm the
ultimatum.

Shortly before four o'clock Dr Stubl appeared in President
Miklas's room. Miklas suggested, as Schuschnigg had done, that
he should take the post of Chancellor. But Skubl refused,
repeating the reasons he had already given. He tried to convince
the President that at that moment the most acceptable course
would still be for Seyss to become Chancellor. But Miklas
stormed: 'I shall yield only to force.' Skubl said that force was
already present in the threat of an invasion: they must not allow
things to reach the point where troops marched in. To the
President's remonstrance that resistance must be attempted
Skubl replied: 'Resistance against such unequal odds would
mean an absolutely hopeless struggle. Every sacrifice would be a
vain one.'

The President's room grew fuller. Otto Ender, President of
the Audit Office, came in. Miklas: 'Hitler has threatened that
if I do not install a National Socialist Government by four o'clock
he will invade. I shall not do it. Let him invade. It is now four
o'clock. There is no sign of him yet.'

Then Chancellor Schuschnigg reappeared and formally handed
in his resignation. Miklas found all this incomprehensible. He
could not for the life of him see any connection between the
plebiscite and the Berchtesgaden Agreement, which the Nazis
complained had been broken. Perhaps the whole thing was only a
private annexation move by Goering, a piece of bluff, and not an
official ultimatum from the German Reich at all. Everyone seemed
to clutch at this straw. Miklas demanded that immediate contact
be made with the German Embassy in order to clarify the
question. Then the President's room emptied again.

Meanwhile, amidst arguing groups in the Hall of Columns,
Seyss-Inquart, the Minister of the Interior, was drawing up a
rough list of ministers. His cabinet would include not only Nazis

but also German Nationalists and Catholics. Seyss was acting on the assumption that the current government crisis would only have repercussions within Austria, and would not affect relations between Austria and the German Reich. He wrote down Guido Schmidt's name on his list as his prospective Foreign Minister. Then Zernatto took the paper from his hand and handed it to Schmidt without comment. Schmidt took one look at it and shook his head. 'You must realize that for me there are still such things as loyalty and decency. I have travelled a long road with Schuschnigg: when he resigns I resign.'

By now it was four o'clock. All through the afternoon Dr Hornbostel, at the Vienna Foreign Office, had been trying to make contact with Rome. The only information he had been able to obtain was that the Duce was not there and Count Ciano could not be reached. Now the message came through that the Italian government was not in possession of sufficient facts to form a judgement on the situation. It must first of all inform itself of all points of view. This in turn made the news from Paris and London worse—for Hornbostel had been told that both governments were ready to act provided Italy took action as well. Before Hornbostel finally allowed himself a short break for coffee, after a spell of duty which had lasted ten hours, he went up the spiral staircase to the Chancellor's office on the first floor. There he saw Schuschnigg and President Miklas. As they listened to his report their faces bore the mark of despair. Then Hornbostel went out to the Café Herrenhof.

Hornbostel's colleague, Max Hoffinger, had been equally unsuccessful in his attempts. Apart from the French and British Ambassadors in Vienna, Puaux and Palairet, no important European state seemed to be interested in Austria's plight. The Italian Embassy evinced no sign of life. And there were other diplomatic missions which were well known at the Foreign Office to be on good terms with the German Embassy, such as Poland and Yugoslavia, that did not even bother to make any enquiries. As Hoffinger commented bitterly: 'They must already have written us off as dead.'

Meanwhile Ribbentrop, the German Foreign Minister, had been lunching at Number 10 Downing Street with the British Prime Minister, Neville Chamberlain. During the course of the meal Mrs Churchill had grown accustomed to the fact that her neighbour at table, Sir Alexander Cadogan, Under Secretary of State at the Foreign Office, kept being handed dispatches. Nevertheless the paper which was now given him by a messenger seemed to be something out of the ordinary. Cadogan read it, stood up and went over to Chamberlain, who was sitting on Frau Ribbentrop's right. The Prime Minister and the Secretary of State had a brief conversation. Then Chamberlain signalled to his wife and after a short while, when the meal was finished, she said: 'Let us *all* have coffee in the drawing-room.'

Meanwhile Cadogan had been handed a further paper which clearly contained even more startling news. When Chamberlain had learned the contents of the telegram he went over to Frau von Ribbentrop. He told her he was sorry he must detain Herr von Ribbentrop but something very serious had happened which made it essential for him to have a private word with him. Then Chamberlain accompanied Frau von Ribbentrop to the Embassy Mercedes that was waiting in Downing Street and said goodbye to her. Chamberlain invited the German Foreign Minister, who had remained behind, into his study. Halifax, Cadogan and the German Chargé d'Affaires, Woermann, came with them.

Chamberlain read out the most important passages from both papers. They were telegrams from the British Ambassador in Vienna. The first had been received in London at 1.45 Greenwich Mean Time (in Vienna it was an hour later). The message read: 'The Chancellor was presented this morning with an ultimatum from Minister of the Interior and Glaise-Horstenau demanding abandonment of plebiscite and threatening that in case of refusal Nazis would abstain from voting and could not be restrained from causing serious disturbances during voting. They also demanded positions in provincial governments and other bodies.' Palairet had gone on to report that the Chancellor was inclined to call off the plebiscite and that he had made a compromise proposal. The two Ministers were going to refer this to their supporters in the Party 'but really of course to Herr Hitler'.

But it was only the next telegram, which had come in during the meal, that had caused Chamberlain to ask Ribbentrop for an interview. It had arrived at 3.00 p.m. London time. So that it could be sent off more quickly and passed on more quickly to the Prime Minister Palairet had drawn it up in clear text:

'Under threat of civil war and absolutely certain menace of

military invasion Chancellor gave way rather than risk bloodshed in Austria and perhaps in Europe. He agreed to cancel
Sunday's plebiscite on condition that tranquillity of country
was not disturbed by Nazis. This was referred to Hitler by
Minister of the Interior who was told that it was not enough
and that Dr Schuschnigg must resign and be replaced by
Minister of the Interior. Dr Schuschnigg asks for immediate
advice of His Majesty's Government as to what he should do.
He has been given only an hour to decide.'

When Chamberlain had finished reading out the message he
said that as a result of this threat an exceedingly serious situation
had arisen. But Ribbentrop was able to assert with a clear conscience that no news of this kind was known to him and that he was
therefore unable to give any conclusive explanation. Then he
made the qualifying remark that if there had been any threats they
must have been uttered by Seyss-Inquart in the name of the
Austrian National Socialists. Halifax, the British Foreign Secretary, was very agitated by the news from Vienna. He had so far, he
said, had no opportunity to discuss the new situation with the
Prime Minister; the use of such threats was 'intolerable'. He
proposed that the plebiscite should be held at a later date. But the
Prime Minister interrupted him: that was no longer the question,
the plebiscite had been called off. And Ribbentrop rubbed it in
with the remark that it must now be obvious that Schuschnigg
could no longer be trusted.

The German Foreign Minister was able to conclude from the
Prime Minister's words that Chamberlain was showing a certain
understanding of the German action. But Chamberlain told him
that British public opinion would find it hard to tolerate if the
question were solved by the application of pressure or indeed by
force.

Ribbentrop took his leave in order to speak to Berlin from his
Embassy. Chamberlain urged him to do so quickly for there was
no time to be lost and asked him to point out to Hitler the regret-
table effect such events were bound to have on Anglo-German
relations.

Shortly after 4.30 p.m., Vienna time, Palairet was able to give
Chancellor Schuschnigg the British answer to his plea for advice.
He read over to him the text of the telegram:

'We have spoken strongly to von Ribbentrop on effect that
would be produced in this country by such direct interference

in Austrian affairs as demand for resignation of Chancellor enforced by ultimatum, especially after offer to cancel plebiscite. Ribbentrop's attitude was not encouraging but he has gone off to telephone Berlin. His Majesty's Government cannot take responsibility of advising the Chancellor to take any course of action which might expose his country to dangers against which His Majesty's Government are unable to guarantee protection.'

It was five o'clock. Eight hours had passed since Seyss-Inquart and Glaise-Horstenau had delivered the first ultimatum to the Schuschnigg government. It was almost three hours since the Chancellor had complied with its demands: the plebiscite had been cancelled. An hour and a half previously, following a second ultimatum, he had resigned from office. Now, in the late afternoon of 11 March, the Germans were marching on the frontier while the National Socialists within the country were poised to strike against the government. Crisis reports kept coming in from the provinces. News of clashes, of demonstrations, of defeats.

At the Chancellery in Vienna still no new Chancellor had been found. For more than an hour now Odilo Globocznigg had been back at the Chancellery. He had been sent over by his superior in the Austrian Nazi Party, Dr Friedl Rainer, to act as go-between. Now Globocznigg realized that events had come to a standstill in the Ballhausplatz, so he set off to discuss the next moves with Rainer. As he left the government building reinforcements were just being added to the guard outside. Over the past two hours extra security measures had already been taken. When the news came through that a fairly large crowd of people was moving up from the Ring towards the Chancellery, the guard commander gave orders for the two main gates to be closed. Shortly afterwards the command of the guards battalion had also ordered an alert. The regulation security measures were at once carried out: in each of the inner courtyards of the Chancellery a heavy machine gun was set up, directed towards the outer gate and loaded; the guards of honour and sentries outside the entrance gates and at the corners of the building were called in. The crowd of people in the Ballhausplatz and the side streets, which was getting more and more dense, had been molesting the guards. People had tried to tie armbands with swastikas on them on to the sentries. When youths climbed up the façade of the building over the window grilles to the first-floor balcony, so as to force a way into the Congress Room which lay behind, the guard commander gave the order to post two sentries with loaded rifles and fixed bayonets behind the glass door which led to the balcony.

At 5.00 p.m. the Commandant of the Chancellery guards appeared in the guard room with the C.O. of the Second Company who, as an experienced officer, was to take over the command of the soldiers in the Chancellery. At the same time the strength of the guard was being increased by the addition of units of the Second Company. Preparations were made in case the centre of government had to be defended.

Rainer and Globocznigg, the Nazi leaders, drove to the German Legation in the Metternichgasse. On the way Globocznigg reported on the position at the Ballhausplatz: 'Things at the Chancellery look really bad. Miklas refuses to accept Schuschnigg's resignation.' Globocznigg had been given the job of passing on to Berlin some of Seyss-Inquart's reservations. The Minister of the Interior was particularly concerned, like most National Socialists in civilian life, by the fact that over in Germany thousands of fellow Austrians in the Nazi Austrian Legion, from whom no good could be expected, were waiting in readiness. These were illegal Nazis who had crossed the border and had been built up over the years with financial help from Berlin into a special para-military formation. But they were not only men who had left their country for political reasons. It was known in Vienna that there were many criminals amongst them. 'Everything from matricide upwards,' as one police department official was in the habit of putting it.

At the German Legation Globocznigg telephoned Goering. It was exactly 5.00 p.m. when their conversation began:

'I have to report the following: Seyss-Inquart has been in Conference with the Chancellor until four-thirty. But he is not in a position to dissolve the cabinet until five-thirty because it is technically impossible.'

Goering: 'By seven-thirty the new cabinet must be formed. . . . Is Seyss-Inquart there?'

Globocznigg: 'No, he isn't here. He is in conference. That is why he sent me to the telephone.'

Then Globocznigg began to speak about the Austrian Legion, but Goering interrupted: 'We're not talking about that! I want to know what's happening. Has he told you that he is Chancellor now?'

 Globocznigg: 'Yes, sir.'

 Goering: 'Is he properly in charge now?'

 Globocznigg: 'Yes, sir.'

 Goering: 'Yes, sir! Yes, sir! Speak up, man! When will he have formed the new cabinet?'

 Globocznigg: 'The cabinet . . . perhaps by nine-fifteen . . .'

 Goering: 'The cabinet must be formed by half-past seven.'

Odilo Globocznigg reported that the Party, with all its formations, had been legalized and that for the past half-hour the SA and SS had been functioning as auxiliary police. Then Goering, who believed the victory was already in his pocket, came on to the question of the new cabinet.

 Goering: 'Keppler will bring the names. Oh, I forgot to mention Fischböck. Fischböck must be given Trade and Commerce.'

 Globocznigg: 'Of course. No question!'

 Goering: 'Kaltenbrunner will get Security and Beyer will get the Armed Forces. The Army will be taken by Seyss-Inquart himself, for the moment. There's no doubt about Justice. Do you know who?'

 Globocznigg: 'Yes, yes.'

 Goering: 'Tell me his name.'

 Globocznigg: 'Well, your brother-in-law, isn't it?'

After that Lieutenant-General Muff the Military Attaché spoke to Goering. Keppler would not be coming until 5.40 p.m. Muff also tried to deliver a warning against sending in the Austrian Legion, for reasons of foreign policy. But Goering interrupted him: 'We will take care of that. Foreign policy will be decided exclusively in Germany.' He added a qualification: 'In this matter.'

The group of politicians and Party members in the smoking-room at the Reich Chancellery in Berlin had grown still larger. Apart from Hitler and Goering, the top brass there also included Rudolf Hess, the Führer's deputy; Dr Wilhelm Frick, the

Minister of the Interior; Wilhelm Keitel, the Chief of the High
Command; Walter von Brauchitsch; Franz von Papen; and Dr
Otto Dietrich, the press chief. The chief topic of conversation was
the attitude of the other powers. What would Italy do? A preliminary indication had already been given. Count Massimo
Magistrati, of the Italian Mission, had appeared at the Foreign
Office. He had wanted to know from Weizsaecker what Berlin's
view of the Austrian question was. There was no shortage of
rumours but it was difficult to obtain a true picture. Weizsaecker
had briefly described the German viewpoint and told him that
Keppler had gone to Vienna. 'I hope we shall learn more towards
the evening.' In face of disturbances in Austria, precautionary
measures had been taken in South Germany. Magistrati had
asked in conclusion that his government should be 'quickly
informed' of 'any new developments in the situation or of any
particular decisions which might be taken by the Berlin government'. Weiszaecker had noted: 'Count Magistrati showed himself to be understanding of the fact that the Führer is bound to
feel himself grievously injured by Chancellor Schuschnigg's
action.'

Shortly after his visit to the German Foreign Office in the
Wilhelmstrasse Magistrati had telephoned back there to read out a
telegram from Rome: 'If by any chance it is rumoured that
Mussolini advised Vienna to hold the plebiscite, he wishes it to be
known that although he does not in any way interfere in Austria's
internal affairs, he advised strongly against the plebiscite.' Later
State Secretary Mackensen noted in the margin of the telephone
transcript: 'Evidently there was consultation in advance.' Magistrati had asked for his message to be taken straight to Hitler. But
even this news did not noticeably serve to reduce the tension at
the Reich Chancellery.

Goering's telephone conversation with Globocznigg in Vienna
at 5.00 p.m., on the other hand, did bring about a reversal of
mood. After hearing Globocznigg's false report Goering rushed
into the smoking-room: 'We've done it. Schuschnigg has resigned.
Seyss is forming a cabinet of people acceptable to us.' When
Papen heard this he went over to Hitler: 'Now your demands
have been met. For heaven's sake call off the preparations for the
invasion now. Everything will be resolved by peaceful means.'
Hitler: 'Yes, very well, that can be done.' Brauchitsch was
relieved: 'Thank God we have been spared that.'

Following Hitler's decision to suspend the invasion order the

Friday, 11 March 1938

Army General Staff were informed. The head of the Reich Defence Division, Colonel Alfred Jodl, noted in his diary: 'Schuschnigg resigned; Seyss-Inquart Chancellor; SA and SS serving in uniform'.

At 5.20 p.m. Goering telephoned his brother-in-law, Franz Hueber, in Vienna. Goering: 'Now listen, Franz, you take over Justice. And on the express desire of the Führer, you also take Foreign Affairs for the time being. Later on someone else will get it.' Then the two of them went through the other cabinet names: Fischböck, Kaltenbrunner. . . . The whole thing was to be home and dry by seven-thirty. Then Goering gave further orders: 'Quickest possible disarmament of the reds who were armed yesterday, and no half-measures either, of course.'

꧁꧁꧁꧁꧁꧁

Rainer and Globocznigg made their way to the Chancellery through the streets of Vienna, which were becoming more animated at every moment. Meanwhile Seyss-Inquart had left the government building and gone to his office in the Herrengasse. When Mühlmann who had been searching for him, entered Seyss-Inquart's office the Minister was on the telephone. Seyss beckoned to him and held out the receiver to him: 'Goering is on the line. Tell him what the situation is.' Seyss had just told Berlin that he had still not been asked to form a government. Then Goering had realized that Globocznigg's report had been false. 'Listen. That won't do at all. Under no circumstances. The whole thing is under way now; so listen, someone must tell the President at once that he is to hand over power to you. . . .'

Mühlmann came to the telephone and described an unsuccessful attempt by the National Socialists to get in to see Miklas himself. 'We were not even admitted. It looks, therefore, as if he had no intention of giving in.' Then Seyss came back on the line. Goering: 'Will you please go immediately, together with Lieutenant-General Muff, to the President and inform him that if our demands are not accepted there and then—you know what they are—the invasion will take place tonight . . . and Austria's existence will be finished. . . . I shall give Muff the same orders right away. If Miklas still doesn't understand after four hours, now he'll have to understand in four minutes.' At 5.31 p.m. Seyss-Inquart put down the receiver.

Fourteen minutes later Muff, too, was in the picture. He

informed Seyss-Inquart of the German ultimatum: 'If Field Marshall Goering has not heard by 7.30 p.m. that Seyss-Inquart has been made Chancellor then two hundred thousand men, who are waiting ready at the frontier, will march in.' When Muff had finished Seyss said: 'I know that already. Now you must come over. Come at once.' Then Seyss hurried over to the Chancellery.

In the Fatherland Front building at Number 4 Am Hof everything had been in a state of confusion since three o'clock. Some Front officials had heard about the cancellation of the plebiscite. Others went on working as if nothing had happened. There was a stream of reports and enquiries from the provinces which had to be dealt with or passed on.

The administrative head of the Fatherland Front, Albert Hantschk, had been in constant touch by telephone with Zernatto, at the Chancellery, all day. He had known, as well as if he had been sitting in the Chancellor's ante-room, exactly how the situation was developing at the seat of government. But from five o'clock onwards he was unable to get through to Zernatto. Hantschk became worried and decided to drive round to the Ballhausplatz himself.

The head of the *Neues Leben* division at the Fatherland Front, Dr Rudolf Henz, was responsible, as the head of the division, for the 'cultural word' at the Vienna radio station in the Johannesgasse. That day his job was to organize the Front's propaganda campaign. In the evening all the various Provincial Governors were due to broadcast. Their speeches were to be recorded locally. Only Eisenstadt, the capital of Burgenland, did not have its own studio. For this reason Henz had sent off a crew of technicians at about lunchtime to record the speech on a disc. As a precaution, in case anything went wrong, he had copies of all the speeches in his desk. As telephone communications with the Fatherland Front were steadily deteriorating, Henz sent one of his staff to the Platz Am Hof. He was to act as link-man. Then came the bad tidings that the recording team had been held up. Finally Henz lost contact with his link-man as well.

Albert Hantschk found Zernatto at the Chancellery. The General Secretary was deeply depressed. 'It's all finished. I can't stay here. I'm leaving the country.' Then he told Hantschk to be prepared to disband the Fatherland Front. Hantschk knew what was to be done now. He rang up Pammer, the Director of the Political Section, and told him to burn all the most important of the Front's files. He further ordered him to clear the building of all the arms belonging to the Front militia which had been stored there. At all costs the arms must be removed from the strategic defence posts. When Pammer had passed on these orders and the bundles of documents were burning in all the stoves and fireplaces in the building, he, too, went over to the Ballhausplatz.

In Linz the Fatherland Front's position was even worse than it was in Vienna. The Front militia, the *Schutzkorps*, drew their own conclusions and disbanded. Then the individual men emerged from their barracks, a converted factory, in civilian clothes. They no longer cared to be seen in the streets wearing the uniforms that had been copied from the SS. They trooped out through the main gate, above which stood the proud inscription: 'Loyalty is not for hire.'

The Nazi functionaries, Globocznigg and Rainer, met up with the Ministers, Seyss-Inquart and Glaise-Horstenau, in the Hall of Columns at the Chancellery. The main obstacle on their road to power was still President Wilhelm Miklas. At 6.00 p.m. he summoned the one-time Chancellor, Dr Otto Ender, for the second time that day. When Ender came into the room the President was alone. At first the conversation followed the same lines as two hours previously. Miklas: 'Hitler extended his time limit until half-past five; and once again he has not invaded.' Then Miklas became more specific. 'The situation is as follows: I cannot make Schuschnigg stay and now you must become Chancellor.' Ender: 'That is very nice, but my personal need for the office of Chancellor has already been amply satisfied.' Miklas: 'Then I must choose Schilhawsky.' Ender: 'I wish Schilhawsky luck.'

With a man like Ender, members of the previous government had proposed to form a broadly based cabinet that would include the National Socialists. Seyss-Inquart would be Vice-Chancellor. But the coalition of Black and Brown had collapsed even before this solution to the crisis had been put to Seyss-Inquart. Schilhawsky represented a different idea. The Inspector-General of the Austrian Armed Forces was brought in by Miklas because he still hoped that the German invasion threat could be met with military resistance. But Schilhawsky, too, when interviewed by the President, refused.

In the early evening at a quarter-past six—in London it was 5.15 p.m.—Lord Halifax called upon Ribbentrop for tea at the German Embassy, as had already been arranged the previous day. He brought with him yet another alarming telegram from Vienna, the contents of which Sir Alexander Cadogan had, in fact, already telephoned through to the German Foreign Minister as soon as it had arrived. Palairet had reported: 'Austrian Government wish Foreign Office to know that a *démenti* of ultimatum now published by German news service is totally untrue. Ultimatum is positive fact: Minister of the Interior is now waiting to send Schuschnigg's answer which has to be delivered by 5.30 (English time 4.30) and German troops are to be set in motion at 6 (English time 5) if it is not satisfactory.'

Ribbentrop had telephoned the Berlin Foreign Office. And at 5.05 p.m. after his return from the lunch with Chamberlain, Woermann, the German Ambassador, had described the meeting to von Mackensen, the German State Secretary. Ribbentrop now declared to Halifax that his officials in Berlin had no information about any ultimatum presented by the Reich or about military threats to Austria. When Lord Halifax remarked in reply that perhaps Herr Hitler had acted alone, without consulting the German Foreign Office, Ribbentrop reacted indignantly. At this moment Woermann came into the room and brought Ribbentrop the news that Schuschnigg had resigned and Seyss had now become Chancellor. This information, which was based on Globocznigg's false report to Goering, appeared to alter the whole situation. Ribbentrop expressed the opinion that this was the best thing that could have happened. Halifax must surely concede that it must be the aim of all to find a peaceful solution. Now Ribbentrop had found his tongue again. There were some occasions when nations had to act in a way that others might consider too hard. Had not Britain acted similarly with Ireland from time to time?

But Halifax did not share his view at all. At the moment there were only a few witnesses of this exhibition of naked force. But what would European public opinion say when everything became known? It would inevitably begin to ask how the German government could be prevented from solving other problems by naked force. Halifax did not accept the comparison with Ireland. Whatever might be said about it, Ireland had been a part of the

Friday, 11 March 1938

United Kingdom like London or Yorkshire. But what was happening now was happening between two independent states.

᪣᪢᪣᪢᪣᪢᪣᪢᪣᪢

After 6.00 p.m. Nevile Henderson was brought evidence by two members of his Embassy staff which convinced him that this time Germany was serious. First of all, the Deputy Military Attaché returned from the German War Ministry, where only that morning it had been intimated to his superior that rumours of a military advance were simply 'ridiculous'. An officer on duty there had now apologized for the information given that morning. The concentrations of troops were necessary to prevent the 'spread of Marxist disturbances to Germany'. This was the version agreed on, in conformity with the reports in the German newspapers that morning. At almost the same time the Military Attaché himself returned from his drive along the Berlin-Leipzig autobahn. He could now supply details. He reported to the Ambassador that he had observed 'far more than 300 armed police in convoys making a total of 250 vehicles and 150 motorcycles. Amongst them were many lorries with radio equipment, tanks, petrol tankers and buses from Berlin. Many vehicles left by the roadside, mostly by the SS.'

In London Halifax learned from his Ambassador in Paris that the French Chargé d'Affaires in Rome, Blondel, had been snubbed by the Italian Foreign Minister, Count Ciano. Blondel had asked for an interview but had received a curt message from Ciano stating that if the object of the interview was Austria, that was a subject regarding which the Italian government had no reason to concert with France or Great Britain. During these hours France was the only European power which was prepared to go to the limit and if necessary to take military action. But France knew that on its own it was too weak.

Now when the Foreign Office in London saw that France's initiative in Rome had met with a rebuff, Britain followed the French lead. At 6.40 p.m. Halifax instructed the British Ambassador in Rome to try his luck: 'Please seek immediate interview with Signor Mussolini . . . and invite him to give us his views.'

But the British Ambassador had no luck either. The Italian Foreign Minister noted in his diary: 'After the sanctions, the non-recognition of our Empire and all the other miseries inflicted on us since 1935, do they expect to rebuild Stresa in an hour, with Hannibal at the gates?'

The Austrian Ambassador in Paris, Alois Vollgruber, had been waiting for almost an hour at the Quai d'Orsay for a meeting with Delbos, the acting Foreign Minister. The minutes ticked slowly round to six o'clock. Vollgruber had only known what was happening in his own country for about three hours and he had only discovered it by indirect means. After lunch the Chef de Cabinet at the French Foreign Office, Charles Rochare, had rung him up. Vollgruber and Rochare had been friends since the days when they had both served in their countries' missions in Rome. Rochare: 'There's something up in Vienna.' Vollgruber had driven round to the Quai d'Orsay at once. There Rochare had said to him: 'We still have no exact information but there is talk of an ultimatum. Schuschnigg is to resign and a Nazi government is to be formed.' Vollgruber had then telephoned Hornbostel in Vienna from his own Embassy. Hornbostel had said: 'I have no instructions to give you but do what you consider is right in this situation.'

When Vollgruber had turned up again at the Quai d'Orsay, Rochare had said: 'Things look bad.' Vollgruber had asked for a meeting with the Minister. For an hour Delbos had been busy telephoning London. Finally Vollgruber was admitted. But the French Foreign Minister, who had always seemed to him friendly and well disposed towards Austria, could do nothing for him. 'Rochare has already told you what we know,' said Delbos. 'But we can do nothing on our own.' The telephone conversation with London, Vollgruber concluded, must have made it clear that Britain would not intervene. The Austrian Ambassador's pessimistic forecast, which the Austrian Military Attaché had already passed on to the Ballhausplatz that day, had been confirmed by events. At 6.30 p.m. Vollgruber returned to his apartment. There were preparations to be made, for he was expecting guests that evening.

While the German Military Attaché in Vienna, Lieutenant-General Muff, was driving to the Austrian Chancellery to deliver the German ultimatum officially, as Goering had ordered, Hitler's Austrian representative, Wilhelm Keppler, was landing at Aspern airport. It was already dusk as he and his assistant climbed out of the plane and hurried through the airport building. The airport commandant called after him: 'Herr Staatssekretär!' Keppler turned irritably. 'Herr Staatssekretär! Herr von Stein from the Legation has been here and left a message to say would you please speak to no one and come straight to the Legation.' Keppler merely barked, 'I see,' turned on his heel and disappeared.

Shortly before 6.00 p.m. Keppler reached the Metternichgasse. Before he had even had time to take off his hat and coat he was called to the telephone. Goering wanted to put him in the picture about the latest developments. But he himself was no longer clear as to what was happening in Vienna. Although Seyss-Inquart had contradicted Globocznigg's news about the National Socialists' success, Goering nevertheless repeated the false report to Keppler: 'At our demand Seyss-Inquart has been appointed Chancellor and is to form a National Socialist government at once by seven-thirty. . . . The game has definitely gone that way, hasn't it? Well, Seyss-Inquart wanted to fly here before he takes the thing on, but that's unnecessary and not possible either. The whole thing must be fixed by seven-thirty, the cabinet as well, otherwise things won't run smoothly, right?'

The next topic of conversation was the list of ministers. Seyss, said Goering, must also take over the Ministry of Defence, Kaltenbrunner Security, Fischböck Trade and Commerce, Hueber Justice and 'Foreign Affairs as well, for the time being'. Goering emphasized this point. 'It's been discussed with the Führer. Just now. Important because of the immediate effect.' Klausner was envisaged as Vice-Chancellor and Minister of the Interior. Goering went on: 'And then there's Glaise, Glaise had better be Minister without Portfolio—or what else is there?' Keppler: 'State Secretary for the Army.' Goering: 'Oh no, no, no, we can't have that. Anything but the Army. He mustn't turn up there. . . . We all want to give credit to Horstenau because he's certainly a very decent, fine man, but we don't want—he's become rather nervous these days—to make such heavy demands on him.' He went on: 'You must see to it that the frontiers are closed immediately, because of the flight of money.'

Finally Goering became quite explicit: 'To make things quite clear you can say to Seyss-Inquart that the invasion cannot be delayed. The troops will march in in this strength, they are only waiting for the word. If we have no news by seven-thirty the troops can be held up no longer. So Seyss-Inquart must telephone me before seven-thirty.' When this conversation had finished, at 6.06 p.m., Keppler tried to get hold of Seyss-Inquart on the telephone. He was told by the Ministry of the Interior to try the Chancellery. To be on the safe side Keppler went over there himself. It was now clear to him that at that moment Goering was the man in Berlin who was forcing the pace.

Meanwhile Muff had reached the Chancellery. But Seyss-Inquart was unwilling to go to see Miklas. As an Austrian Minister and future Chancellor he refused to be a party to the German ultimatum. So Muff performed his task alone. As he had been instructed, he gave Miklas the message: a Seyss-Inquart cabinet by 7.30 p.m. or the Germans march in. But the President remained unruffled. He refused. He would not appoint an Austrian Chancellor under the threat of force. Austria was indeed a German country, 'but a sovereign and independent state like Luxembourg, the Netherlands, Denmark or other teutonic countries'. And it appointed its governments freely and independently. Miklas, the historian, found himself thinking about the war of 1866. He found it strange 'that on that occasion we were thrown out of the German confederation and now the attempt is being made to bring us back into the Reich again by force of arms.'

Muff had barged in on a discussion Miklas was having with Schmitz, the Mayor of Vienna, and Kienböck, the President of the National Bank. When he saw he was making no headway with Goering's ultimatum, he adopted a more friendly tone and asked Miklas, with whom he had always been on good terms, whether he might speak to him 'as one German to another'. He then personally urged him to appoint Seyss-Inquart. A moment later the tone of the conversation became harsher again. There were noisy exchanges between Muff and Schmitz. The German Military Attaché left, having achieved no success.

Meanwhile Keppler had also reached the Chancellery. He went up to Seyss-Inquart, Rainer and Globocznigg: 'Hullo, and how are things getting on with Seyss-Inquart's Government?' Rainer: 'We haven't got as far as that, yet.' Seyss then told Keppler that Goering's news was false and had already been contradicted. Keppler began to put to them Goering's proposals for the cabinet. 'Goering's wishes are as follows ...' But Rainer ambiguously repeated his remark: 'We haven't got as far as that, yet.' Keppler asked Seyss-Inquart to go with him to see the President. Once again the Minister of the Interior refused. But he gave Keppler a piece of advice on the way: it was best to speak to Miklas as calmly as possible.

At that moment Muff came up to the waiting National Socialists. From him Keppler learned that his mission had failed.

Muff: 'I've just been to see Miklas on the subject.' While they were in mid-conversation Keppler was called to the telephone. It was 6.28 p.m. Goering wanted to know what was happening. Muff's action, Keppler told him, had been abortive. Goering: 'Well, what does Miklas say?' Keppler: 'Well, that he won't do it.' Goering: 'Then Seyss-Inquart will have to depose him. Go upstairs again now and simply tell him that Seyss-Inquart is to call out the National Socialist guards and that I will give marching orders to the troops in five minutes from now.'

The conversation was cut off for three minutes.

When Goering got through again Keppler was already with Miklas. Goering, who did not know this, asked: 'Is State Secretary Keppler there?'

Keppler's assistant: 'No, he is with the Chancellor.' Goering: 'With the President?' Assistant: 'No . . . They are all together.'

Goering held on until Keppler returned. The latter reported: 'Well, I have been with the President again but he has refused everything.' Then Seyss-Inquart came to the telephone and explained that it might take another five or ten minutes to get a final decision. Goering insisted that Seyss should then make an urgent priority call to him:

'If things don't happen within that time you will have to seize power, you understand?' Seyss: 'Yes, you mean if he threatens?' Goering: 'Yes'. Seyss: 'Yes, all right. We'll manage that all right. . . .'

Both the ultimatums from Berlin, delivered in rapid succession between 6.00 and 6.30 p.m. by Lieutenant-General Muff and State Secretary Keppler, had failed. Keppler had indeed followed Seyss's recommendation and informed the Federal President in a quiet tone of voice that Berlin demanded a Seyss-Inquart government. Finally Keppler left it that he would call in again on Miklas shortly before 8.00 p.m.

Now Keppler's assistant was busy rounding up people to talk to Keppler. When he met Zernatto, the General Secretary of the Front, he bragged about all the forces at present massed on the border. But Zernatto was already fully aware of the danger. Half an hour previously he had been discussing the question of Chancellor Schuschnigg's personal safety with Schmidt and Glaise-Horstenau. Zernatto thought the Chancellor ought to leave the country. But Schuschnigg refused: he had always worked for the good of the country. Austria was his home. He had done nothing wrong. Nobody could require him to leave his homeland.

Shortly after 6.00 p.m. Dr Alphons Ubelhör burst into the announcers' room at the Vienna radio station. A good hour before that he had gone over to the Fatherland Front building because their telephone no longer seemed to be working. Excitedly he blurted out: 'The plebiscite is cancelled.' When he had composed himself he went to the microphone and read over the air the news that he had just brought with him: 'After making a report to the President, the Chancellor and Leader of the Front has decided to postpone the plebiscite arranged for 13 March. At the moment no further news is available.' The duty officer sent word of a change of programme to the head of the Music Department: switch to solemn music.

The picture in the streets of Vienna changed as abruptly as the radio programme. In the Inner City the Nazis appeared in crowds. Swastika flags were unrolled. The sound of slogans chanted in time with the tread of the marching demonstrators became louder and louder. The supporters of the government became fewer and fewer. Soon there was a rumour circulating in Vienna that Hitler was going to speak on the radio at 7.00 p.m.—but this proved to be false.

Towards 7.00 p.m. the thronging of the crowds in the Ballhausplatz in front of the Chancellery became greater and greater. Otto Huber, the head of the President's office staff, appealed to the commander of the guard. 'Please restore order.' The Guards would not have found this very difficult. At the Hofburg, opposite the Chancellery, there were 300 men waiting in readiness.

Friday, 11 March 1938

In the inner courtyards of the Chancellery there were machine guns. The guard commander asked for permission to shoot. That Huber could not give him.

In Schuschnigg's entourage there was talk of the possibility of resistance. Richard Schmitz, who had unsuccessfully thrown the mobilization of the workers into the debate earlier on, as a means of resisting the growing pressure, asked Skubl, the State Secretary for Security, if he could put down the spreading insurrection. Skubl said he could but at the same time added: 'I cannot, however, stop the Germans marching in as soon as the first clash takes place.' In the State Secretary's view there was no way out of the situation.

Schuschnigg continued to attend to government business. He called a halt to the few military defence measures which were still being undertaken and gave General Sigismund Schilhawsky the order to offer no resistance when the German troops marched in and to withdraw his troops to behind the river Enns. This had been the main line of defence in the plan devised by Field Marshal-Lieutenant Jansa, the only senior officer to give any thought to defence against a German invasion, and whom Schuschnigg had sent out into the cold under pressure from Hitler.

In the Hall of Columns Dr Friedl Rainer was pressing for an immediate seizure of power. He asked Keppler's permission to give the order to all the Nazi Gauleiters. 'The German forces are on the march now,' said Rainer. 'No. They are not on the march.' 'Then,' said Rainer, 'we must take advantage of the moment when the government believes they are on the march. We must act.' Keppler refused: 'You cannot do that.' In that case, Rainer observed, Klausner, the Leader of the Austrian Nazi Party, would soon give his approval. He then spoke to Globocznigg, who was also urging a quick seizure of power. He left the Chancellery and made for the Nazi headquarters in the Seitzergasse.

In the rooms and corridors of the Chancellery the Ministers and officials were still standing about in groups. Guido Zernatto asked Seyss-Inquart: 'How do you picture the future?' Seyss: 'There are two points on which I will not negotiate: the independence of Austria and the right of the conservative-Catholic element to follow their own way of life.' At long last Seyss felt himself to be Chancellor.

Meanwhile at the Chancellery President Miklas was waiting for the German invasion, for at 7.30 p.m. yet another German ultimatum was due to expire. Then State Secretary Skubl appeared in his room with a message he had just received on the telephone: 'German troops are crossing the frontier.' Miklas spoke again with Schuschnigg. Yet again the Chancellor urged him to ask Seyss-Inquart to form a government. But Miklas held to the view that the German troops would in any case take over executive power. He refused to appoint Seyss. In the circumstances the resolution of the cabinet crisis seemed to him immaterial.

The news of the German invasion spread through the Chancellery like wildfire. The tension seemed to give way to a general sigh of: 'At last!' As Schuschnigg came out of the Presidential wing he saw Ender, Schmidt and Hornbostel standing in the great anteroom. He went up to them and said: 'I am announcing my resignation.' At this point in time neither the outgoing government nor the National Socialists knew that the news Skubl had passed on was false.

In the office of Schuschnigg's secretary about thirty people were standing together. The Chancellor's secretary was setting up a microphone. There was a direct link between the office and the Ravag radio station in the Johannesgasse.

The radio sets were switched on in several newspaper offices and also in the foreign missions in Vienna. Even the Austrian pretender, Archduke Otto of Habsburg, had been rung up in Steenockerzeel by his Legitimist friends and told of the impending broadcast. Someone else who knew nothing about all this was once again President Miklas himself. At 7.47 p.m. Schuschnigg walked over to the doorway between his own study and his secretary's office. At this moment Keppler was once more talking to the President. Again Miklas refused to appoint Seyss. In the same wing of the Chancellery, meanwhile, Max Hoffinger, the head of the German Department at the Foreign Office, was talking on the telephone to Dr Erich Bielka at the Austrian Consulate-General in Munich. That afternoon Bielka had driven out from Munich to Kufstein. On the way he had seen long military convoys. He was now describing what he had seen.

Schuschnigg began his last speech. With his back turned towards his colleagues and opponents, he spoke facing his own empty office:

Friday, 11 March 1938

'Men and women of Austria, today has faced us with a difficult and fateful situation. It is my task to tell the Austrian people about the events of this day. The government of the German Reich has presented the Federal President with an ultimatum, subject to a time limit, requiring the President to nominate as Federal Chancellor the candidate proposed to him, and to appoint a government in accordance with the proposals of the German government: failing this, an invasion by German troops will take place at the appointed time.

'I declare before all the world that the reports which have been spread in Austria, that there have been workers' riots, that rivers of blood have flowed and that the government was not in control of the situation and was unable to maintain order on its own are pure invention from A to Z. The Federal President has instructed me to inform the Austrian nation that we are yielding to force.

'Because we are resolved on no account, even at this grave hour, to spill German blood, we have ordered our armed forces, in the event of an invasion, to withdraw without substantial—without any—resistance, and to await the decisions of the next few hours. The Federal President has entrusted the leadership of the armed forces to General Schilhawsky, the Inspector-General. All further instructions to the armed forces will be issued through him. And so I take my leave of the Austrian people at this hour with a German word and a heartfelt wish: God protect Austria!'

After Schuschnigg had finished speaking, those present in his secretary's office witnessed an expression of pent-up rage by one of the Fatherland Front's supporters at the Nazi policy of blackmail. Even the National Socialists seemed shaken. Seyss-Inquart murmured to himself: 'Shall we live to survive our fate?' Then Huber, the President's Chef de Cabinet, attacked him. 'You are supposed to be the Minister of the Interior. It's disgraceful what is happening out there now. You must see that order is restored.' Seyss shrugged his shoulders: 'If Miklas will not appoint me then I can do nothing.' The shouts of the demonstrators in the Ballhausplatz could be heard through the closed shutters.

꾠꾠꾠꾠꾠

When Max Hoffinger came up to the first floor after his telephone conversation with Bielka in Kufstein he found Schuschnigg and

Schmidt arguing with the President. Miklas had finished talking to Keppler and had just come over. Schuschnigg and Schmidt were once more urging the President even now to hand over the Chancellorship to Seyss in order to solve the cabinet crisis. But Miklas refused. He believed it was only a resolute adherence to the rejection of the ultimatum that might still leave open the possibility of 'negotiations on a more peaceful basis'. Then Schmidt asked the ex-Chancellor to go to a place of safety—at the very least to spend the night at the Hungarian Embassy. But Schuschnigg refused.

In the Fatherland Front building shortly before 8.00 p.m. Dr Fritz Bock, the deputy propaganda chief of the Front, had heard a shout: 'Schuschnigg is speaking.' Bock knew nothing about the Chancellor's resignation. He had learned the news neither from the Ballhausplatz nor from the radio. Now Bock and the other Front officials rushed into Zernatto's office and listened to the rest of the speech there. It was clear to all of them that the ultimate catastrophe had occurred. Bock, who was now the senior official present, gave the order to vacate the building as quickly as possible. After making a round of the empty rooms he instructed the four *Schutzkorps* militiamen on duty in the guard room on the ground floor to hand over the Front building to whoever came first, the police or the SA. Then he shut the door.

The detachment of police near the Opera House, who were under the command of Dr Heinrich Hüttl, could no longer withstand the assaults of the National Socialists. When Hüttl learned of Schuschnigg's resignation he withdrew his men from the street and posted them under the arcades of the Opera House. He did not want his men to be saluted as 'German police': nor did he want to expose them to abuse.

That evening trades unionists were gathering together at various different branch meetings in Vienna and the surrounding district to discuss support for the plebiscite. Some of these had only been called at midday that day. At the union building at Number 112 Margarethenstrasse legal and illegal trades unionists sat down harmoniously together. Franz Olah, a unionist of the banned Left, had persuaded Franz Jöstl, a government-recognized union official, to chair the meeting. But it was Olah who addressed his comrades and colleagues. Suddenly Jöstl was called to the telephone. When he came back he broke the news that made the meeting superfluous: the Germans had invaded and Schuschnigg had resigned.

Friday, 11 March 1938

The National Socialists were increasingly in control of the streets. In the provinces the National Socialists became even more active following Schuschnigg's speech. In Linz an extra edition of the Linz *Tagespost* with the banner headline SCHUSCH-NIGG'S DOMINATION ENDS proclaimed the event of the hour. In Graz tens of thousands of people gathered with the SA and SS for a torchlight procession. Already that afternoon, when Rainer had called for the demonstrations to be stepped up, many houses had been hung with swastika flags. There were even some public buildings already flying the Nazi flag. The 'capital of revolt' was doing its best to live up to its name. From the window of the Graz firm of Steirerfunk the Racial-Political Councillor of Styria, Dr Armin Dadieu, delivered a fiery speech: 'At last the National Socialists in our German Austria will achieve their freedom. But our work, fellow-Germans, is not yet finished. There can be no rest and no peace. We must continue working until the final victory is ours.' In conclusion the Nazi formations were called upon to march to their stand-to stations to await further orders.

Inside the Chancellery in Vienna almost all the office-holders in the previous government had given up the game for lost. Outside in the Ballhausplatz the crowds of National Socialists were massing and the leading Nazis had been able to make their way past the sentries into the government offices. But the man in Vienna's Town Hall was not yet ready to throw in the towel. During the past few weeks Richard Schmitz, the fifty-three-year-old Mayor, had been a driving force for union with the workers. He had sought to organize a common front against National Socialism. Shortly after the Berchtesgaden meeting in February Schmitz had had talks with Friedrich Hillegeist, the left-wing trades-unionist, while maintaining contact with friends of Otto of Habsburg, who, like him, considered that only a government which included the illegal Left would be capable of resisting the Nazis.

After his talks at the Chancellery that afternoon Schmitz had returned to the Town Hall. Here the defence preparations he had ordered had been put into effect. A hundred men of the Town Hall guard—normally only a third of this number were on duty—stood at their posts. Late that afternoon the officers of the Town Hall guard had drummed up all the soldiers in the city.

The Town Hall gates were closed off with iron grilles and wooden doors. The windows on the lower storeys were barricaded.

It was true that the soldiers of the Town Hall guard possessed only out-of-date weapons, but they were sufficient for the purpose: rifles, pistols and machine guns from the First World War. The sentries stood at all the gates and some of the windows, beneath the great clock and right up on the battlements of the gothic revival Town Hall.

At the Chancellery, meanwhile, word had got round that the Germans had not yet invaded and that Skubl had been taken in by a false report. Seven minutes after the start of Schuschnigg's broadcast Seyss-Inquart was on the line to Berlin again. He had no idea that Schuschnigg's speech was already known about in the German capital and reported to Goering: 'Dr Schuschnigg is to announce on the radio that an ultimatum was given by the German government.'

Goering: 'Yes, I heard that.'

Seyss: 'And the government has put itself out of office. General Schilhawsky has command over the military here and will withdraw. They now take the attitude here that they are waiting for the invasion.'

Goering: 'So they haven't appointed you?'

Seyss: 'No'.

Goering: 'Removed you from office, then?'

Seyss: 'No. Nobody at all has been removed from office. The government itself has, so to speak, withdrawn from its duties and is simply letting things take their course.'

Goering: 'And you are not nominated, that has been refused?'

Seyss: '. . . They are simply letting it happen, the invasion. The idea is that when the invasion takes place the executive power will in any case pass to other people.'

Goering: 'All right then. I shall give the order to march in and you must see to it that you take over. Make clear to all the leading people what I shall tell you now: Anyone who resists or organizes resistance will be dealt with summarily by our military courts, the military courts of the invading troops. Is that clear?'

Seyss: 'Yes'.

Goering: '. . . the President refused to appoint you and that, too, is resistance.'

Seyss: 'Yes, well . . .'
Goering: 'Right. So now you have your official orders.'
Seyss: 'Yes'.
Goering: 'Well, good luck to you. Heil Hitler!'

When Seyss returned from the telephone the noise of the demonstrators outside had got even louder. Seyss was again urged to restore law and order. Guido Schmidt suggested that he should make an appeal to the people. Seyss agreed to try this. He drafted a short speech and at 8.18 p.m. he went to the microphone:

'Men and women in Austria! Fellow Germans! With reference to the events of today and having particular regard to the events which now face us, I must remind you that, as before, I remain in office as Minister of the Interior and of Security and feel myself to be responsible for the maintenance of law and order in this country. I call upon everyone to uphold this law and order. Particular discipline will be needed during the next few hours and days. If there are to be demonstrations today then they must at no time take on a disorderly character. In particular I call upon the National Socialist formations responsible for order and security to ensure that law and order is preserved everywhere and to exert an influence to this end upon their own fellow National Socialists. I count upon you to support the executive in their task wholeheartedly and to put yourselves at the disposal of the executive. I would issue a particular reminder that resistance of any kind to the German army, which will enter the country in any case, is in all circumstances out of the question, for the executive forces as well: our paramount duty is the maintenance of law and order in this country. Stand by your posts! Unite and help us all to go forward into a happy future!'

Then Seyss summoned the commandant of the Guards detachment at the Chancellery. He was to maintain order and keep out unauthorized persons. The officer declared that he was at Seyss's disposal and returned to his post on the ground floor.

At the Nazi headquarters at Number 1 Seitzergasse Rainer reported to Klausner, the Austrian Nazi leader, at about 8.00 p.m. that the Chancellery was still in turmoil. There was still no prospect of a new government. Klausner then discussed the situation with Jury; Veesenmayer; Lukesch, the SA leader; Kaltenbrunner, the SS leader; and Mohrenschild, from Klagenfurt.

Lukesch offered to have 6,000 SA men on the march within half an hour. Kaltenbrunner offered 500 SS men within the same amount of time. Then Klausner gave his orders: seizure of power throughout the country. In Vienna the formations were to march to the Chancellery and occupy the building with forty men. In addition to this the Fatherland Front building, the larger commercial concerns, the Town Hall and the radio station must be taken. Rainer passed on the order to the Party bosses by telephone. But he first informed Odilo Globocznigg, who was at his post in the Chancellery.

At this time government agencies from all over the country were beginning to ring up to ask the Minister of the Interior how they should act. The man who took these calls was Globocznigg. He was ready with instructions: they were to do nothing. The previous administration would be replaced by new men. In between whiles Globocznigg telephoned Party leaders in the provinces or sent telegrams. He did this almost always in the name of Seyss-Inquart and at the expense of the Austrian government. The Party leader in Linz, August Eigruber, received two telegrams simultaneously. One came from 'Chancellor Seyss-Inquart' and informed Eigruber of his appointment as acting Provincial Governor. The other came from Rainer and made Eigruber acting Leader of the Party in Upper Austria.

At 8.00 p.m. the panic flight from the German and Austrian Nazis began. The Ostbahnhof was full of refugees. In the station hall and on the platforms there was a throng of people with bundles, cases and cardboard boxes. In their anxiety they crowded into the train and stood packed like sardines. Salvation seemed near. It was forty-five minutes to Marchegg, forty-five minutes to the frontier.

When the Bratislava train had left, more and more refugees arrived at the Ostbahnhof. They were waiting for the train for Brno and Prague: time of departure: 11.15 p.m.

The shortest route to the frontier was the road to Bratislava. After 8.00 p.m. it was filled with traffic, as it had rarely been before. While the columns of refugee cars were moving towards the east, Guido Zernatto's black limousine had already reached

137

the frontier crossing at Marchegg. Guido and Riccarda Zernato were cleared through the customs with especial courtesy. The formalities lasted less than five minutes. Over in the distance the lights of Bratislava could be seen.

卐卐卐卐卐卐

In Berlin that evening Goebbels's Ministry of Propaganda was busy hoodwinking public opinion into believing that Germany had put no pressure of any kind on Austria. The German News Agency published a statement 'setting the record straight' on Schuschnigg's resignation speech.

'At 7.50 p.m. this evening the former Austrian Chancellor, Schuschnigg, broadcast a speech on the Vienna radio in which he made a series of untrue statements. Amongst other things Herr Schuschnigg claimed that in an ultimatum to which a time limit was set the Government of the German Reich had demanded that the Austrian Federal President appoint a new government. This assertion of Schuschnigg's is untrue. It was not the German Government that delivered such an ultimatum: it was Austrians and Austrian Ministers who, faced with an increasingly critical situation in Austria, and with Chancellor Schuschnigg's own policy, which was leading to disaster, made these demands themselves.

'Herr Schuschnigg further claimed that the Government of the German Reich had presented the Federal President with an ultimatum insisting that he appoint a government in accordance with the proposals of the German government. This, too, does not correspond to the facts. It was Austrian ruling circles themselves, fully aware of the situation in Austria, who put these demands to the President.

'Thirdly, the former Austrian Chancellor claimed that it was pure invention to say that disorders had broken out in Austria and that the government was no longer in control of the situation. Yet hundreds of reports, coming in all over the world from Austria, prove, on the contrary, that there had already been untold clashes, that in very many places Marxist disorders had taken place. For example, Communist mobs were arming themselves in Wiener Neustadt and countless attacks had already occurred, at the very time when Schuschnigg was uttering these false statements.'

At the Reich Chancellery Goering—when he was not on the telephone to Vienna—was constantly urging Hitler to abandon all hesitation and give the invasion order. Hitler seemed gradually to be setting aside his objections which were based on the effect this would have on foreign opinion. But he still insisted that a request for the troops to march in must come from Austria.

By this time it was clear to both Hitler and Goering that they would suffer a massive loss of prestige if they simply waited for events in Vienna to take their course. The ultimatum, which Muff and Keppler had delivered to the Austrian President, would then have been shown up as nothing but an empty threat. The consequences for future dealings with Austria would probably be far-reaching. It was for this reason that the two of them had grown angry over the Austrian President's steadfast refusal to appoint Seyss-Inquart as Chancellor.

After Goering's call to Seyss-Inquart had ended at 8.03 p.m. Wilhelm von Grolmann, a Lieutenant-Colonel of Police and adjutant to Frick, the Minister of the Interior, saw Hitler and Goering coming out of the call-box by the telephone exchange. Goering had to go there to speak to Vienna because the telephones in the smoking-room were out of order. Grolmann watched the *Luftwaffe* boss urging Hitler on. Suddenly Hitler stopped in his tracks, raised his right leg, slapped his thigh with the flat of his hand and shouted, 'Now for it!'

Goering rushed into the smoking-room yelling for his adjutant: 'Bodenschatz! Bodenschatz!' Then he gave a new invasion order to the armed forces 'in the name of the Führer'. Lieutenant-General Viehbahn, the head of the operations staff branch, put the military in the picture. The position had changed once more. The invasion was taking place. But Hitler would not assign authority over the executive in Austria to the Chief Command of the Eighth Army.

While the invasion order was being passed on orally to the military commands, Goering again telephoned Vienna. He wanted to tell Muff, the Military Attaché, about the new situation:

'Tell Seyss-Inquart the following: In our view the government has now resigned, but he himself has not resigned. He is therefore to continue in office and to take the necessary measures in the name of a government. The invasion is going to take place now and it will be made known that anyone who offers resistance will have to bear the consequences. But the Austrian troops can join us at any time, or march under the protection of the German troops. Seyss must try to ensure things don't get out of hand.'

Muff: 'Yes, Seyss is doing that. He's already broadcast.'

Goering: 'And he is to take over the government now. He must take over the government and finish the job quickly now. The best thing would be for Miklas to resign.'

Muff: 'Well he won't do that. It was very dramatic. I spoke to him for about a quarter of an hour. He declared that under no circumstances will he yield to force and he will not appoint a new government.'

Goering: 'Oh. And he won't yield to force?'

Muff: 'He won't yield to force.'

Goering: 'Well, what does that mean? He just wants to be kicked out then?'

Muff: 'Yes, he is going to stay put.'

Goering: 'Well, with fourteen children maybe you have to stay put. Anyway, tell Seyss. Seyss must take over the government.'

Shortly after that, at 8.45 p.m., Hitler issued the invasion order in writing in his Directive Number Two:

'Top Secret
From the Supreme Commander of the Armed Forces
OKW. LIA Nr 427/38
Subject: Operation Otto

1 The demands of the German ultimatum to the Austrian government have not been fulfilled.

2 The Austrian armed forces have been ordered to withdraw in the face of the advance of German troops and to avoid fighting. The Austrian government has withdrawn from office.

3 To avoid further bloodshed in Austrian towns the German armed forces will march into Austria at dawn on 12.3 in accordance with Directive Number One. I expect no effort to be spared to ensure the aims laid down are achieved as swiftly as possible.

Adolf Hitler.

Goering was already on the telephone to Vienna again. At 8.45 p.m. he got Keppler's assistant, who at this time was at the German Legation, to give him a report on the situation. He was told: 'There are very big demonstrations here. The situation in Wiener Neustadt is somewhat tricky. The SA and SS are just taking up their duties as auxiliary police and will shortly be taking over all official buildings.'

Scarcely had Goering laid down the receiver when Keppler put through a call to him at 8.48 p.m.

'I should like to report to you briefly. President Miklas has refused to do anything. Nevertheless the government has ceased to function. I have spoken to Schuschnigg and he told me they had ceased to exercise their functions and we must do it.'

Goering: 'Say that again.'

Keppler: 'They have ceased to exercise their functions and Schuschnigg himself has said that we must do something. Bouhler has spoken to Seyss-Inquart on the telephone . . . In a short while Landesleiter Klausner is going to speak on the radio and I should like to ask now whether a prominent person in Berlin could also address a few words to the Austrians.'

Goering: 'Yes, well, I don't know yet. Now listen to me: the main thing is that Seyss-Inquart has taken control of the entire government. Radio, everything must be secured . . .'

Keppler: 'We do have the government now.'

Goering: 'All right. You are the government. Now listen: the following telegram is to be sent here by Seyss-Inquart. Write it down: "The provisional Government of Austria which, following the resignation of the Schuschnigg government, sees it as its task to reestablish law and order in Austria, addresses an urgent request to the German government for support in this task and for help in preventing bloodshed. For this purpose it requests the German government to send German troops as soon as possible." '

Keppler: 'Well the SA and SS are marching through the streets, but things are very quiet here . . .'

Goering: 'Well, listen to me: he must close the frontier so that they can't make off with all their valuables.'

Keppler: 'Yes, sir.'

Goering: 'And then—most important—he must take over Foreign Affairs.'

Keppler: 'Yes, we haven't anyone for that yet.'

Goering: 'All right. That doesn't matter. Seyss must take over and bring in some other people. He must bring in those we suggested to him. He must form a provisional government. It doesn't matter a damn what the President says.'

Keppler: 'Yes, they won't do anything.'

Goering: 'Now then, our troops will cross the border tonight.'

Keppler: 'Yes.'

Goering: 'Very well. And will he please send the telegram as soon as possible.'

Keppler: 'I will send the telegram to Seyss-Inquart at the Chancellor's Palace.'

Goering: 'Now look, show him the telegram and tell him all we ask—in fact he doesn't need to send the telegram at all. All he needs to do is to say: "Agreed." '

Keppler: 'Yes, sir.'

Goering: 'Ring me up for this either at the Führer's or at my place. Now get going. Heil Hitler!'

At the *Haus der Flieger*, the *Luftwaffe*'s 'Airmen's House' in Berlin, the traditional Air Force Ball was beginning. Weeks before all the high-ups and celebrities in Berlin had been invited by Goering to this glittering annual social event: the Diplomatic Corps, the Services, the Party—about two thousand guests in all. Each of the round tables in the great hall was laid for eight or ten people. Only at Goering's table there were places for fifteen.

There was a single topic of conversation: Austria. But none of the guests knew of the decision that had just been reached at the Reich Chancellery. Then someone came in who must know more than most: Goering's Number Two, Ehrhard Milch. Bombarded with questions by the diplomats, Milch parried them: he knew nothing. The State Secretary then made a short speech. Goering, he said, was still in conference with the Führer and Reich Chancellor. He sent his apologies, and would be coming on later. The ball began.

Two places remained empty: the Austrian Minister in Berlin, Dr Tauschitz, and the Military and Air Attaché, Major-General Pohl, had not come to the ball. They had spent the whole afternoon and evening at the Austrian Embassy in the Bendlerstrasse in a mood of deep depression. They had waited in vain for information from Vienna. From time to time Tauschitz had rung Vienna but no one had been willing to give any news: 'How should I know? I am only a junior official.'

As the Air Force Ball started Tauschitz received a piece of news from Vienna. It came from his chauffeur. He had heard it on the radio: 'The Chancellor has resigned.'

卐卐卐卐卐卐

At the Zum goldenen Hirschen restaurant in the Argentinier-strasse, Vienna, a celebration had been in progress since 8.00 p.m. A reunion of the former Second Artillery Regiment of the old Imperial Army. Over beer and wine the old soldiers relived battles long past. Among them was Colonel Maximilian de Angelis of the General Staff, lecturer and second-in-command for the senior officers' training courses. But the Colonel, the underground head of the hitherto relatively insignificant Nazi soldiers' ring, was not to remain there for long. At nine o'clock he was called out. A lady standing near him asked him to come away. 'It's happening at last,' she said, excitedly. The Colonel did not need to take a second look. On her coat, bold and clear for all to see, his friend was wearing a swastika.

Embossed metal swastika badges were selling in the Inner City like hot cakes. There were countless people on the streets. In the Ringstrasse there were torchlight processions. People carried posters reading: 'Austria is free.' The police wore swastika armbands. Jewish shops had their windows smashed in. A few brave policemen tried to stop the looting of shop windows, reminding the crowds of Seyss-Inquart's broadcast, in which he had spoken of law and order.

Before the Chancellery itself there was an immense crowd of demonstrators with swastika flags. They were augmented on all sides by troops of the SA and SS. Cars with their lights switched off and Nazi flags in the windows stood ready at strategic points. Soldiers of the guard prevented individual Nazi demonstrators climbing through the windows into the Chancellery. The crowd wanted to see Seyss. They wanted to hear him speak. But the Minister sent word that for the moment he was not available.

Before the Fatherland Front building the Teutonic Crosses were torn down and trampled underfoot by the howling mob.

Friday, 11 March 1938

A swastika flag already hung from the façade of the building. The demonstrators smashed the windows and broke in.

In front of the radio building in the Johannesgasse a troop of the SS marched up in mufti, wearing shorts, white stockings and swastika armbands, and occupied all the entrances. The security guards were sent home. Shortly before that several Nazi radio technicians had assumed power in the building. The Director General's chair had been occupied by one of them. He had appointed other swastika-wearers to keep a watch on the people he did not regard as reliable. The SS made Dr Pesendorfer provisional superintendent. A radio journalist went out in the street in order to capture the mood of jubilation with the microphone.

In Wels there were street processions with torch bearers, drummers and buglers. The bulk of the police went over to the Nazis and put on their own swastika armbands. The Chief of Police was arrested by a Squadron Sergeant-Major. The Mayor refused an invitation to hoist the Nazi flag over the Town Hall. But a few minutes later three flags were already hanging there. There was no sign of resistance. The Front militia remained inside their barracks. And at the Nazis' local in Wels, the Café Markut, the Party leaders were already giving out jobs.

At 9.00 p.m. the planning staff of the Eighth Army designated for the invasion had arrived at the Bavarian town of Mühldorf on the Inn by special train from Dresden. At the stops on the way the Commander-in-Chief, General von Bock, had been in telephone contact with the Army General Staff. At 1.41 p.m. he had telephoned Berlin from Chemnitz and at 4.08 p.m. from Hof.

The fact that Schuschnigg had resigned and that by now the plebiscite had almost been forgotten was still unknown to the C-in-C of the Eighth Army. His staff moved into the school at Mühldorf. The orders worked out on the journey were now to be issued. But the duplicating machine had been damaged in transit. So the copying out of the orders by hand caused a delay. Other difficulties also cropped up. Waiting for them on arrival was the evening report of the Seventh Corps, which had arrived in Mühldorf at 8.00 p.m. In it the commanding officer of the Corps, General von Schobert, proposed: 'With regard to the undermanning of the forces of the Seventh Division which have so far been

144

Supporters of Schuschnigg driving through Vienna after the announcement of the plebiscite on 9 March 1938

Arthur Seyss-Inquart, the Minister of the Interior, is
saluted by Austrian Nazis at Linz

Chancellor Kurt von Schuschnigg

Wilhelm Miklas, the Austrian President

Above left: Engelbert Dolfuss, Schuschnigg's predecessor. Above right: Theodor Innitzer, Cardinal Archbishop of Vienna. Below left: Guido Zernatto, Secretary General of the Fatherland Front. Below right: Guido Schmidt, the Austrian Foreign Minister

Above left: Odilo Globocznigg, deputy *Stabsleiter* of the Austrian NS party. Above right: Wilhelm Keppler, Hitler's specialist for the *Anschluss*. Below left: Herbert Klausner, leader of the Nazis in Austria. Below right: Josef Bürckel, the German *Gauleiter* who organized the *Anschluss* campaign

Hitler makes his first speech in Austria from the balcony of the town hall at Linz

Hitler driving through Vienna, protected by soldiers and SS men in escort vehicles

Seyss-Inquart's ministers show themselves to the waiting crowd on the
balcony of the Chancellery

At the Heldenplatz Hitler proclaims 'the entry of my homeland into the German Reich'

disembarked here, and with regard to the increasing movement of Austrian troops at less than full strength'—that the frontier should not be crossed before midday on the twelfth.

Another armed contingent, too, was growing nervous at the prospect of the invasion. At 9.00 p.m. the long-awaited mobilization order from Berlin arrived at the headquarters of the 'SA Relief Corps North-West' in Bad Godesberg. 'Relief Corps' was a cover name for the 'Legion', the militant troop of Austrian Nazis in exile trained in Germany. To support the 4,000 men who were stationed in eight towns—the size of the troop could be doubled within a short time by calling up reservists—the German Nazi Party paid out 700,000 marks per month. After much pressure their leader, SA Obergruppenführer Hermann Reschny, had been given leave to mobilize. But even German and Austrian Nazi leaders were no strangers to nervous anxiety at the prospect of action.

All that separated the opposing camps in the Chancellery in Vienna was an ante-room five yards wide. Seyss and his National Socialist supporters still occupied the Hall of Columns: Schuschnigg, Miklas, Schmidt and other Fatherland Front politicians were in the Cabinet Room opposite. At 8.00 p.m. the members of the outgoing government had vacated their departmental offices. In the Cabinet Room the ex-Ministers were safer, for the windows only looked out on to the inner courtyard, which was protected by the guards. During the last few hours the National Socialist demonstrators, by whom the Chancellery was now completely hemmed in, had tried to climb up the front of the building, with the intention of hanging a swastika flag on it. Miklas, now in the Cabinet Room, could no longer see what was happening outside in the street and the Ballhausplatz. He had reports brought to him about the situation at regular intervals. But the answers he was given were mostly stereotyped: Everything was under control and the security precautions were good. 'The Chancellery is completely protected internally by guards and police, and the gates are closed', Guido Schmidt told him soothingly.

Still nothing was decided. Still Austria lacked an effective government. After Schuschnigg had publicly announced his resignation at 7.50 p.m., Seyss had broadcast his claim to be the only Minister to have remained in office. But Miklas had signed a document that belied this. It was the acceptance of Chancellor Schuschnigg's resignation. Miklas had written: 'In accordance with Article 86 of the Constitution of 1934, I relieve you, at your own wish, from the office of Federal Chancellor and from your responsibility for the Federal Ministry for Defence. In accordance with Article 86 of the 1934 Constitution, I also relieve from their offices the remaining Ministers of the Federal Government, together with all the State Secretaries. Vienna, 11 March 1938.'

The leadership group of the Austrian Nazi Party had meanwhile returned to the Chancellery. After giving orders for the seizure of power in Vienna and the provinces, Dr Friedrich Rainer had had a call from Globocznigg. His situation report from the Chancellery: 'We are just not getting any further.' Rainer had driven to the Ballhausplatz with Klausner, Jury and Edmund Veesenmayer. They had found the gate locked. In reply to their knocking one of the guards had called out: 'Who goes there?' Rainer had replied that they came on behalf of Seyss-Inquart. But for safety's sake the guard had checked with Seyss. Then the Nazis were led by the guards through the courtyard to the entrance—past the machine guns intended for the defence of the building.

Rainer found the situation in the Hall of Columns exactly as it had been an hour before, when he left the Chancellery. Seyss-Inquart shrugged his shoulders and said: 'There is nothing to be done.' Rainer informed him of the orders he had just given. From out in the provinces the victory reports began coming in to Globocznigg. The few National Socialists in the Chancellery were the only people there taking any action. Rainer sent for a typewriter and asked all round: 'Is there anyone here who knows anything about forming governments?' Then Dr Friedrich Wimmer, the Ministerial Secretary from the Constitutional Department, stepped forward. He revealed himself to be an underground Nazi. So as to be able to give both theoretical and practical help, he carried the 'little blue book' under his arm—the Constitution of 1934.

Rainer sat on a sofa. In front of him, on a table that was too high, the typewriter. Seyss and Keppler peered over his shoulders, one on the right, one on the left. Together they began to draw up a list of ministers, following Goering's suggestions and some ideas of their own. Since Schmidt had refused to remain as Foreign Minister and the Austrian National Socialists were unwilling to give such an important post to Goering's brother-in-law, Dr Hueber, Wimmer finally proposed the name of another illegal Nazi, who had so far had the status of an official of the third rank, *Sektionsrat* (Section Councillor) Dr Wilhelm Wolff, a Catholic Supporter of the *Anschluss*. When the list was ready Rainer proposed that all the politicians and officials who were named on it as Ministers should be summoned at once to the Chancellery.

At the Reich Chancellery in Berlin they were still waiting for the telegram from Vienna requesting help. It was almost an hour since Goering had dictated the text to Keppler. The longer version—which had been sent to Vienna by courier in the early hours of the morning—had thus been superseded. Repeatedly, during the past sixty minutes, the people in Berlin, acting on Goering's behalf, had urged that Seyss-Inquart should send off the telegram: or at least give his agreement.

After his conversation with Goering shortly before 9.00 p.m. Keppler had gone to see Seyss. But the latter had refused to call the German troops into the country by telegram. As Minister of the Interior he could not do such a thing, this did not come into his sphere of responsibility. But then he had added: 'If I am really appointed Chancellor then we must talk about it again.' Now it was almost a quarter to ten. Keppler came to see Seyss again. The latter had meanwhile told Schuschnigg and the other politicians who were present in the Cabinet Room what Goering wanted him to do. He had been called upon 'to ask for military assistance from the Reich', because Communist disorders had broken out and 'the continued shedding of blood could not otherwise be prevented'. But Seyss had at the same time assured them he had no intention of fulfilling Goering's demands, since, thank God, there was complete peace in Austria. Now when Keppler pressed him again Seyss was markedly less resolute. To the State Secretary's question: 'What shall I tell Berlin?' Seyss-Inquart replied: 'Do what you like.'

At 9.54 p.m. Berlin asked again what had happened to the telegram. The press chief, Dr Dietrich, telephoned on behalf of Goering's chief adjutant, General Bodenschatz.

Dietrich: 'I need the telegram urgently.' Keppler: 'Tell the Field Marshal that Seyss-Inquart agrees.' Dietrich: 'That is excellent. Thank you very much.' Keppler: 'Keep in touch with the radio. Some announcements will be coming through.' Dietrich: 'From where?' Keppler: 'From here, from Vienna.' To make doubly sure Dietrich asked again: 'So Seyss-Inquart agrees.' Keppler replied: 'That's correct.'

The text of the telegram was at this moment waiting ready to be transmitted by the teleprinters of the German News Agency. Dr Dietrich arranged for it to be passed on immediately. Thus by ten o'clock sharp the British Ambassador, Nevile Henderson, was already able to inform Lord Halifax in London. He cabled to the Foreign Secretary: 'It is announced here by the Deutsche Nachrichten Bureau that Seyss-Inquart has appealed to German government to send troops to keep order.'

At the Reich Chancellery Hitler was radiant about the news of Seyss-Inquart's alleged agreement. But the foxy diplomats, Papen and Neurath, could also see the danger contained in Keppler's news. The former envoy in Vienna said to the former Foreign Minister: 'This is such an important message from Vienna that we must unquestionably have it in writing.' And added: 'For heaven's sake be careful that it doesn't become a second Ems telegramme.' But Goering had already taken care of such objections. And so a few hours later Neurath had a telegram, in the margin of which he was able to scribble: 'To be added to the files of the F.O. v.N. 12/13.'

The document looked genuine: strips of paper pasted on a telegram form. But the forgers in Berlin had slipped up over the time. Alongside the reference number Z 57966/65 for 11 March on this cry for help addressed 'To the Führer and Reich Chancellor' the time of sending was given as 21.10 hours. It was supposed to have been received in Berlin thirty minutes later, at 9.40 p.m.—fourteen minutes too soon. For if it had been received at 9.40, why was Dr Dietrich still saying on the telephone to Keppler at 9.54 p.m.: 'I need the telegram urgently . . .'? There was one other slip. At a special press conference starting at 8.00 p.m. a government spokesman had already officially declared that a provisional government headed by Seyss-Inquart had called for German troops to be sent into Austria. Finally, too, it should be noted that Berlin had responded prematurely to the cry for help, which had not yet arrived—and which never would arrive. Hitler had signed the invasion order at 8.45 p.m. As a diplomatic fig-leaf, however, the telegram forged in Berlin proved useful. The British government, in particular, needed a document of this kind, which enabled them to prove to British public opinion that they had done all that was humanly possible, but that Austria had herself called in the German invaders.

The fictitious cry for help from Vienna was reported by the German Foreign Office to the German diplomatic missions in the individual capitals the same evening 'for the purposes of information and adjustment to your statements . . . In order to prevent a catastrophically chaotic situation', the German communiqué commented, 'the German government has considered it necessary to give way to the appeal addressed to it.'

When the German News Agency report, which quoted the wording of the telegram, became known in Vienna, members of the previous government took Seyss-Inquart to task. But the 'historic telephone girl', as Seyss had called himself in the course of that afternoon's telephone marathon with Berlin, could state with a clear conscience that he had not sent any appeal for help.

At 10.10 p.m., Berlin time, the British Embassy sent a further cable to the Foreign Secretary in London. It consisted, for the most part, of a summary of Nazi rumours that were being spread in Germany to justify the invasion that was about to take place. The British Consul-General in Munich had collected the reports and passed them on to Berlin. Halifax read: 'Mobilization orders issued at midnight, concentration began 1.00 a.m. this morning. . . . It is said that it is only a demonstration. Following rumours have been spread by National Socialist Party that Czechoslovaks have crossed into Austria, that French Communists have arrived to organize a Communist revolt and that Austrian Government have gone red and are shooting Austrian National Socialists.'

At the Air Force Ball in Berlin the dinner, which had lasted for hours, was finished. The diplomats continued to talk about the Austrian situation. Goering, the organizer of the feast, was still not there. At 10.30 p.m. Ivone Kirkpatrick, of the British Embassy, arrived at the table of the British Ambassador, Sir Nevile Henderson, with a telegram from Lord Halifax, which had been dispatched in London half an hour previously. Many eyes were on the British Ambassador as he read the message. It referred to the telegram from Palairet, the British Ambassador in Vienna, in which the latter had informed his government about the German ultimatum which expired at 7.30. Henderson was familiar with the telegram from Vienna. Now he read his Minister's instructions which resulted from it:

'Please represent immediately to German government that, if this report is correct, His Majesty's Government feel bound to register protest in strongest terms against such use of coercion backed by force against an independent state. . . . As I have already pointed out to German Minister for Foreign Affairs here, such action is bound to produce gravest reactions of which it is impossible to foretell the issue. I am informing the French government that this protest is being made in case they wish to act likewise.'

Henderson instructed Kirkpatrick to send a written protest to Neurath. He drove straight back to the Embassy and wrote a letter which followed the text of Halifax's telegram almost word for word.

Henderson remained at the Air Force building because he wanted to have a word with Goering. The latter soon arrived in his gala uniform. He was nervous and greeted a few guests only fleetingly, Henderson among them. The Field Marshal sat down at his table—the sign for the entry of the dancers of the State Opera. But Goering had no eyes for the ballerinas and no ear for the waltz rhythms. He tore a blank strip off his programme and wrote on it in pencil: 'As soon as the music is over, I should like to speak to you and will then explain everything to you.' The last half-dozen words Goering underlined three times. Then he passed the note to Henderson, via the wife of the American Ambassador.

When the performance was over Goering withdraw with the British Ambassador to his private room in the building. Henderson began by informing Goering of the protest uttered by Halifax against the German ultimatum. Goering declared that he had full authority for the government of the Reich, since Hitler was leaving Berlin for a few days. He rejected the protest on the grounds that the ultimatum had come not from Germans but from Austrians. The German government had simply acceded to Seyss-Inquart's request for help. German troops were at that moment marching into Austria. Schuschnigg had broken the Berchtesgaden Agreement with his call for a plebiscite. For this reason Hitler could no longer trust the ex-Chancellor. The course on which Germany had embarked was the only possible one.

In reply to this Henderson declared that, while he must reluctantly concede that Schuschnigg had acted with precipitate folly over the plebiscite plan, nevertheless Germany was behaving like a bully and was menacing the whole peace of Europe. Goering commented that the reuniting of Germany and Austria was the righting of an ancient wrong which would harm no one. He gave Henderson his assurance that the German troops would be withdrawn as soon as the situation in Austria was stabilized. From this conversation Goering deduced that London would certainly protest but was unlikely to fight.

At the Bendlerstrasse, Berlin, at about 10.30 p.m. Colonel Jodl was making a note of the decision Hitler had given in reply to a question raised by the Army General Staff. The question was one about the behaviour of the troops, which the General Staff, wishing to be prepared for all eventualities, even the unlikeliest, had raised twenty-fours hours previously. The principal point raised was the attitude to be adopted towards Czech and Italian troops. Jodl was now setting down the reply Hitler's adjutant had passed on to him. The Italians, Jodl noted, were to be treated as friends; the Czechs, if they entered Austrian territory, as enemies.

At the German Ministry of Propaganda everything had been made ready for the invasion. Doctor Joseph Goebbels, the Reich Minister for the Enlightenment of the People and Propaganda, had been busy until ten o'clock that evening writing appeals in person and altering the texts every time fresh news came in from Vienna.

But it was not only in Berlin that the impending invasion gave cause for hectic activity. In Prague the Czech Prime Minister had called together all the Ministers who could be contacted to a special meeting at the Kolowrat Palace. The sole subject on the agenda was the events in Austria. The same subject was also discussed at a meeting of the Polish cabinet that night. In both capitals they were certain that Hitler's expansionist urge would not be satisfied with Austria.

Dr Jury had provisionally put Lahr, the Deputy Mayor of Vienna, in charge of the city. Now Lahr had to get past the guards into the Town Hall to give the news to Richard Schmitz. The newly appointed Mayor sent his secretary, Penka, on ahead with fifteen SA men. He himself followed by car. While Penka was marching with the stormtroopers via the Löwelstrasse, the Ring and the Rathausplatz, he was wondering whether the Town

Hall guard would offer resistance. By the time he had reached the entrance in the Lichtenfelsgasse Lahr's car was driving just in front. The guards opened the metal grille and the wooden gate and Penka and the SA men marched into the inner courtyard of the Town Hall behind Lahr's car. Lahr went up to the guard commander and told him he had been appointed Mayor and the officers of the guard were to be informed of this.

Then Penka, some of the remaining Town Hall officials and the SA men moved into the Deputy Mayor's office. Meanwhile Lahr himself sought out the man he was to replace, Richard Schmitz. The Mayor's family were still sitting together discussing what was going to happen. Then Lahr entered and announced in clipped military tones: 'I am taking over.' Even now Schmitz could not make up his mind to leave. He gave his family instructions to destroy all papers and documents which might later cause trouble for city officials or politicians. The papers were burned by the Schmitz children in a kitchen bucket in the lavatory with the ventilation switched on: they included the diary of the eldest daughter, Gertrud (she was just about to finish her dissertation on the Christian Social Party under Professor Srbik), in which she had made a record of all her father's visits and meetings during the past few years.

Down below in the Town Hall courtyard the situation had become serious. So as to have an escape route if the worst came to the worst the Town Hall guard had removed the manhole covers off the sewers in the inner courtyard. There were some fifteen entrance shafts down which they could escape to the outside.

Meanwhile men of the armed Nazi formations had also penetrated at the Chancellery. At 10.00 p.m. First Lieutenant Schulz was on duty just by the back entrance which led to the Mestasiogasse when a man by the name of Felix Rinner presented himself. He claimed to have orders from Seyss-Inquart to protect the safety of the parties engaged in negotiations in the government building. The guards officer sent word to Seyss, but he knew nothing about it. Rainer had arranged this manoeuvre so as to be able to go the whole hog in an emergency. He wanted to exclude from the start the possibility of a fiasco like the failed putsch of 25 July 1934. Seyss said he required no protection and that it was unnecessary. However, he finally agreed. And thus Rinner and his forty SS men of the famous Eighty-Ninth Sturm were admitted to the Chancellery.

Once Rainer's coup with the Eighty-Ninth Sturm had proved

successful, the Nazis knew for certain that the Schuschnigg regime would yield to them without a struggle. Felix Rinner made his men mount guard outside the most important rooms. Only the Cabinet Room, where the Federal President, the ex-Chancellor and some of his Ministers and some officials loyal to the government were still sitting together, was out of bounds to the Nazis— on Seyss's orders.

Though the Federal President might persist in his refusal, the battle had been fought and won. The door of the Hall of Columns opened and in came a towering guardsman. He went over to the group of National Socialists gathered round Rainer's typewriter. He was carrying a tray, on which were beer, mineral water and ham rolls. The new masters had been acknowledged.

It was in Rome that evening that Austria's fate was ultimately decided. Hitler's messenger, Prince Philip of Hessen, had landed a good two hours previously, carrying the German Chancellor's letter to the Duce. The Italian Foreign Minister, Count Ciano, had just finished his evening meal at his office when Hessen was announced at 9.00 p.m. He had taken the emissary to Mussolini at once.

Only shortly before that Ciano had received another German visitor. Plessen, the Chargé d'Affaires, had come to discuss the Austrian situation with the Italian Foreign Minister. Following this visit Plessen had reported to the German Foreign Office:

'According to a summary of a conversation, which Ciano gave me to read, the French Chargé d'Affaires asked on the telephone ... "with regard to Austria's appeal and the German ultimatum which is running out" for a visit to Ciano, already arranged, to be put forward "so as to reach agreement on a concerted action by France, Italy and England." In reply to this he was told point blank that the Italian government rejected any discussions of concerted action. If he had nothing else to propose the bringing forward of the date of his visit was unnecessary ...' Plessen continued: 'Ciano made a gesture with his hands which can perhaps be translated as: "Need I say more?" and added "We neither observe nor take part in anything that is directed against Germany." '

Friday, 11 March 1938

When Ciano had been told at 8.00 p.m. that Schuschnigg had resigned he had quickly taken his leave of the German Chargé d'Affaires. The next couple of hours would be important for the Foreign Minister, for at 10.00 p.m. the Fascist Grand Council was due to meet. The previous day, sitting in its first session in the Year Sixteen by the Fascist calendar, it had adjourned itself until that evening. Mussolini and Ciano were apprehensive of being attacked during the session over the Italian government's attitude to Germany on the Austrian question.

Now, shortly after 10.00 p.m. Mussolini felt reassured as he entered the session of the Grand Council. Hitler's letter, which Philip of Hessen had brought him in the very nick of time, was just what he needed. With Hitler's recognition of the Brenner frontier in his pocket Mussolini could run rings round his critics. Meanwhile the royal messenger had left the Palazzo Venezia and driven back to the German Embassy. Here he put through a call to the Reich Chancellery. At 10.25 p.m., the transcribers at Goering's *Luftwaffe* Research Office noted down: 'Philip of Hessen asks for the Führer. 11.3.38 F1 Zuerich 22.25-22.29'.

Hessen reported:

'I have just come back from the Palazzo Venezia. The Duce has taken the whole thing in a very friendly manner. He sends his very best regards. He said he had heard about the business in advance from Austria. Schuschnigg had told him on Monday. He said it was quite impossible, a piece of bluff, one could not do such a thing. Then he had replied that unfortunately it was already arranged and they could not go back on it now. Then Mussolini said that in that case Austria was a dead letter as far as he was concerned.'

Hitler: 'Then please tell Mussolini I will never forget him for this.'

Hessen: 'Yes, sir.'

Hitler: 'Never, never, never, come what may. I am ready to make quite a different agreement with him.'

Hessen: 'Yes, sir, I have told him that, too.'

Hitler: 'As soon as the Austrian affair is out of the way I am ready to go with him through thick and thin—no matter what happens.'

Hessen: 'Yes, my Führer.'

Hitler: 'Listen—I will make any agreement—I no longer feel myself to be in the terrible position we would have had militarily, if I had come into conflict. You may tell him that I thank him from the bottom of my heart. I will never, never forget him for this.'

Hessen: 'Yes, my Führer.'

Hitler: 'I will never forget him for this, come what may. If he is ever in any kind of danger then he can be certain that I will go to his aid, whatever the odds, and then let come what may, even if the whole world should turn against him.'

Hessen: 'Yes, my Führer.'

Although more than an hour had passed since the first SA men had entered the Vienna Town Hall and the former Deputy Mayor, Major Lahr, had attempted to take over, a formal transfer had not yet been effected. In Lahr's office, meanwhile, discussions were under way about the taking over of the key posts. Then a group of National Socialists had appeared on the scene determined to get things moving. They were Karl Gratzenberger, a printer, Sobolak and Kotzich. Sobolak had led the Vienna Party organization throughout the years when it had been banned. He had built it up so efficiently that the Party now possessed an organization it could rely on in every operation. Its eight or nine hundred political leaders formed the backbone of every demonstration. In addition to these there were some 25,000 illegal Party members and beyond them a great circle of sympathizers. When Sobolak had left his house in the Josefstadt district that morning it had already been clear to him that this would be the day of decision. He had put his pistol in his pocket and said to his wife: 'Either I shall be home by the evening or you will hear what's going on.'

In Richard Schmitz's ante-room the Nazi group argued with the Mayor. But Schmitz remained adamant. He would not hoist the Nazi flag, nor would he hand over the Town Hall. Even now, during the last hour of the day, when Miklas was the only man left at the Chancellery who was still offering resistance—and this was growing steadily weaker, Schmitz would not give in. He said to the National Socialists: 'Chancellor Schuschnigg did not resign of his own free will. He only yielded to force. I, too, will only yield to force.'

At 11.30 p.m. members of the German Gymnasts' Club, armed with rifles, came driving up to the Vienna Town Hall in cars. The Town Hall guards, who were still guarding the gates, abandoned their resistance. They allowed themselves to be persuaded by the National Socialists to open the gates. When Lahr, the Mayor designate, was told that a large crowd of the SA had assembled in the arcade courtyard he sped down the staircase with Gratzenberger in order to make sure the right thing was done. The SA demanded that the Town Hall guard be disarmed. Lahr tried to mediate: the soldiers had only acted out of loyalty to their oath and ought not to be dismissed under dishonourable circumstances. The guard marched into the courtyard in three ranks. After one of the Nazi leaders had made a short speech, assuring the soldiers that nothing would happen to them, they laid down their sword belts and pistols before them on the ground. Then they were sent into the large dormitory on the ground floor of the eighth staircase. Here they were to remain for the night. But eleven of the original hundred were no longer with them. They had continued at their posts outside with swastika badges on their arms. They had for a long time been members of the illegal Party.

At the Chancellery the talks had now reached a decisive stage. The news that sounded as victory music in the ears of the National Socialists in the Hall of Columns represented tidings of defeat for Schuschnigg and his supporters in the Cabinet Room. In Vienna the Nazis were in control in the streets and had occupied the main public buildings. In almost all the provinces and in all important towns the seizure of power was an accomplished fact. In this situation President Miklas declared himself ready to abandon the position he had clung to so stubbornly. But he was only willing to give way partially. Shortly after 11.00 p.m. Seyss-Inquart emerged from the Cabinet Room, crossed the ante-room where the messengers normally sat, and went up to his supporters in the Hall of Columns. He told them that under the 'pressure of the seizure of power which has already been effected by the National Socialist Party throughout Austria', Miklas had entrusted him 'with the carrying out of the business of the Government of the Republic'.

This possibility was provided for in Paragraph 84 of the May Constitution of 1934. The Nazis rejoiced when they heard the news from Seyss-Inquart. But soon they were regarding this development more soberly. Dr Friedrich Wimmer, the official from the Constitutional Department in the Chancellery, the man who had been advising the new masters for some hours now with his 'little blue book' in his hand, consulted the Constitution. There he at once also found the hidden snag: a government thus called into being required the counter-signature of the Federal President in all matters.

Dr Jury, who, like Globocznigg, was manning a telephone in the Hall of Columns, passed on news of the new situation to the already occupied Ravag radio station. For the Nazis were confident that, now they had got this far, there would be no stopping them. At 11.14 p.m. Jury's announcement was transmitted: 'Under the pressure of the political situation in the country, the Federal President has entrusted Minister Seyss-Inquart with the maintenance of law and order and the direction of the Chancellor's office.' Even before this announcement had been made Berlin was already aware of the new situation. At 11.12 p.m. Keppler had rung up Julius Schaub, Hitler's forty-year-old personal adjutant, from the Chancellery in Vienna and reported to him that Seyss-Inquart's legal status had now been established. 'The people who will run the individual ministries have been appointed and will be made known tonight.' Schaub wanted to know the exact position: 'He has not appointed him Chancellor, just to carry on government business?' Keppler: 'Yes. But we'll soon fix it up.'

Rainer and the other Nazi activists at the Chancellery thought differently. 'We can't get anywhere with this government.' They nevertheless took it as a basis for trying to draw up a revised list of Ministers while Seyss was sent back for further negotiations with Miklas in the Cabinet Room.

Throughout the afternoon and evening Berlin had steered and fuelled the situation in Austria, by means of countless telephone calls. Now it was the turn of the radio to be pressed into service as a weapon in the political struggle. The seizure of power was driven home not only by means of news bulletins about the situation in Vienna and the provinces but also with mood pieces. With music too. Seyss-Inquart's speech was repeated, sandwiched between Mozart and Schubert; then came Bruckner, marking a transition to the Germanic strains of the *Hohenfriedberger* march, which led on, in its turn, to the Wagnerian motifs of the *Nibelungen* march. And so it continued until finally an announcer said: 'And now the *Horst-Wessel* song.'

Before the news of the seizure of power throughout the country was broadcast, it was known to the people in the Chancellery. Globocznigg had all Austria on the telephone. National Socialists from all the provinces were telling him about their successes and victories. And whenever any government officials or politicians

Friday, 11 March 1938

loyal to the Schuschnigg government rang up Globocznigg unhesitatingly announced that he was a representative of the government. He did this without Seyss-Inquart's knowledge. Not until later did he put Seyss in the picture, telling him: 'You know, I've seized power for you, and took the part of the government, but I didn't tell you anything, because you would have been against it.'

The picture that presented itself shortly before midnight was clear.

Linz: In the capital of Upper Austria after demonstrations in the main square, in the course of which swastika flags were hoisted on the Town hall, the SA and SS occupied the taxation offices, the customs and excise offices, both railway stations, the Workers' Chamber, the District Governor's offices and the Fatherland Front building. The balcony of the Town Hall was now graced with a picture of Hitler, surrounded by Nazi flags.

Graz: That evening in the main square of the 'capital of revolt' the seizure of power was celebrated by sixty to seventy thousand people. After this the National Socialists filled the principal City and Provincial posts with their own people.

The upheaval took place similarly in all the other provinces and municipalities of Austria.

In Villach it was the executive that led the new movement: 'The seizure of power by the National Socialists', the correspondents reported to their papers, 'was accomplished in an action by the Police, the SS and the SA, under the leadership of *Polizeirat* (Police Councillor) Dr Wicke.'

At Innsbruck the SA and SS had already marched past the main police station in the Suedtiroler Platz unhindered. And the seat of the Provincial Government, where two days previously Chancellor Schuschnigg had been cheered as the guest of honour, had been taken over by the SS at 9.10 p.m., since when a swastika flag had flown above it.

While the citizens of Innsbruck were cheering in their thousands, the first of the Nazis' political opponents were arrested. The editorial offices of the *Kärntner Tageblatt* at Klagenfurt were occupied by the SA and SS, and the Town Hall porter was compelled to hoist the swastika flag over the building. In St Pölten people were already looking forward to the arrival of the Austrian Legion. After the seizure of power 'bicycle columns' rode out to Melk to 'be the first to welcome' the Austrian Nazis trained in Germany.

158

In Vienna itself the Nazi flag had been flying over the police headquarters in the Schottenring since 10.31 p.m., on the instructions of the senior officer on duty. By this time there was scarcely a public building in the capital which had not been thus decorated by the National Socialists.

The National Socialists had also taken over some newspapers by now, amongst them the *Wiener Neueste Nachrichten*. After the July putsch of 1934 the paper had been made subject to a government commissioner because it was judged an organ of the Nazi Party. Now the Nazi cell were masters of the situation. Proudly they announced: 'The *Wiener Neueste Nachrichten* is at the service of the National Socialist movement.' The *Telegraf* was also taken over by the SS. This was the paper belonging to Karl Bondy, a supporter of the Schuschnigg government, who had just managed to flee the country in time.

Some Viennese businessmen had a somewhat different inspiration. They sent a letter of thanks, with flowers, to the German Tourist Office opposite the Opera House. The sweet-scented offerings had already arrived in such numbers during the past few days that the actual business of the German Railways had had to be transferred to a different room. Neatly written—though not without mistakes—the letter placed on record the ideological support of the tradesmen of the Gumpendorfer Strasse in the Sixth District of Vienna: 'We, the undersigned, being true German-thinking Aryan small businesspeople in Vienna, beg leave herewith in humble gratitude at this historic moment for Austria (1938), to present a floral tribute to our dearly beloved and only true Führer of all the German people. In *eternal loyalty* to Adolf Hitler, *the protector of German honour, German culture and German blood* we stand, *Austrian National Socialists !*'

Those who had no taste for such hymns of praise gave vent to their fury in the streets. Here the mob had the upper hand. G. E. R. Gedye, the *Daily Telegraph* correspondent, who had observed the developments in Austria for over ten years, was going through the streets that evening on his way to work. This is how he described the inferno: 'As I crossed the Graben to my office, the Brown flood was sweeping through the streets. It was an indescribable witches' sabbath—storm-troopers, lots of them barely out of the schoolroom, with cartridge belts and carbines, the only other evidence of authority being swastika brassards, were marching side by side with police turncoats, men and women shrieking or crying hysterically the name of their leader, embracing the police and dragging them along in the swirling stream of humanity, motor-lorries filled with storm-troopers clutching their long-concealed weapons, hooting furiously, trying to make themselves heard above the din, men and women leaping, shouting and dancing in the light of the smoking torches which soon began to make their appearance, the air filled with a pandemonium of sound in which intermingled screams of: "Down with the Jews! *Heil Hitler! Heil Hitler! Sieg Heil!* Perish the Jews! Hang Schuschnigg! Heil Seyss-Inquart! Heil Planetta! Down with the Catholics! *Ein Volk, ein Reich, ein Führer!*" to which was now added a fourth ready-learned slogan "*Ein Sieg!*" making the whole incantation: "One People, one Reich, one Leader and one Victory!" Fragments of the *Horst Wessel* song struggled above one's head for survival against the strains of *Today we have all Germany, tomorrow we have the world* and *Deutschland über Alles.* . . . As I walked through or drove past the mobs whose faces called for the pencil of a Gustave Doré, one of the many sentimental phrases applied by the Viennese to themselves mockingly halted my brain—"*Das gold'ne Wiener Herz.*" [1]

For many Austrians who attempted to escape the country that evening, their flight was ended before it had properly begun. At the Viennese railway stations, which lay round the city like a necklace, squads of men wearing swastika armbands had already begun to appear about 9.30 p.m. By the harsh light of the station lamps they searched through cases, bags and boxes and removed any objects of value with the laconic observation: 'Confiscated'. Travellers were led away by the swastika men.

At all of the larger Austrian railway stations the picture was the same. Squads of Nazis entered the train compartments and fetched people out of them. The raids carried out by these arm-band-wearers, most of them young men, were so successful that no substantial increase in the traffic was observed at the Swiss frontier that night.

Many Viennese refugees, afraid of the long journey west across Austria, chose the short journey east. The night express to Brno and Prague, which was due to leave the Ostbahnhof at 11.15 p.m., was so full that it had to travel in two parts. None of them knew that the Czech Minister of Security, Dr Czerny, had given strict orders that holders of Austrian passports were not to be admitted.

Shortly before midnight Karl Franz Bondy, the owner of the *Telegraf,* a convinced Zionist; Eugen Lennhoff, the deputy

[1] G. E. R. Gedye, *Fallen Bastions*, London 1939. Tr.

editor of his paper; and Kurt von Strachwitz, a colleague of the latter, arrived at Kittsee, where the road crossed the frontier into Hungary. They had left Vienna in a taxi. They had first of all driven to Marchegg, where the Czechs had not admitted them. They had already noticed that the roads were lined with abandoned cars, whose occupants had struck out into the woods in order to cross the frontier illegally on foot. The three men from the *Telegraf* had decided to try the Hungarian frontier. Now in the traffic jam in front of the turnpike at Kittsee it looked for a moment as if the road was closed there too. But they got through.

Some Austrians were already safe. At the Carlton-Hotel in Bratislava a group of refugees were sitting together: Zernatto and his wife, Stockinger, the ex-Minister of Commerce, Coudenhove-Kalergi and his wife and Frau Dollfuss. They talked little about the future, more about the past.

᙭᙭᙭᙭᙭

Dr Heinrich Hüttl, the section leader of the police detachment at the Opera House, regarded his service as completed. He had made his report at police headquarters about the day's events and was just about to leave the building when a police detective, wearing a swastika armband, came up and told him that he had orders to arrest him in the name of Dr Presser, the Vice-President of Police. Hüttl immediately demanded to speak with the duty official at the First Commissariat. The latter explained that he had been told to take Hüttl into custody. The reason given was to prevent him falling into the hands of the SS. Hüttl, who was still in uniform, was allowed by his colleagues to telephone his wife. 'I shall be coming home late tonight.' It was to be a long night. It lasted six and a half months.

Many other senior officers in the Viennese police force had experiences similar to that of Hüttl. The rapid revolution within the police—in all the streets the policemen were already wearing swastika armbands and giving Nazi salutes to the demonstrators—emphasized the extent to which the Vienna police had been penetrated by the Nazis. Although the majority of the force had no political allegiance, the ten per cent of organized illegal National Socialists had sufficed at this time to effect the revolution without resistance.

᙭᙭᙭᙭᙭

Friday, 11 March 1938

At the school in Mühldorf which served the Eighth Army as its headquarters, the benches had been pushed to one side or put out into the corridors. On the classroom blackboards the children's writing exercises could still be seen. In another room benches pushed together had to serve as a map table. Everything was improvised. The communications network in particular turned out to be faulty. For this reason 'Army Order of the Day Number One' had for the most part to be passed on by telephone so as to reach the units down to battalion level before midnight.

The order began to be transmitted from 10.15 p.m. onwards:

'I have taken command of the army. In accordance with the Führer's wishes the restoration of order in Austria must be carried out without bloodshed, in so far as the safety of the German troops permits it. In general the attempt is to be made, by effecting early contact with the Austrian troops facing us, to win them over to our side. If they come over to us, they are to be treated in accordance with the invasion order. Austrian units or individual soldiers who declare themselves to be 'neutral' are to be disarmed and gathered together, in accordance with the order of the Army Corps Command, for auxiliary service. Daggers and side-arms can be left on them. If the Austrian troops offer resistance it is to be broken by force of arms . . .

Von Bock
General of the Infantry.'

At the same time 'Army Order Number One' was published. In this the dividing lines between the corps and the targets for the day were set out. For four hours past the troop had been receiving news and situation reports:

'1 In Austria there are threats of disorders; the government has apparently not ordered any mobilization. The possibility must be reckoned with that from the frontier onwards resistance will be offered by the police, the customs and parts of the army. It is possible that there will be stronger resistance at Salzburg (Eighth Brigade there) and beyond the Inn. Preparations to blow up bridges on the frontier rivers have probably been made, street barricades have been identified at Salzburg . . .

162

2 The Eighth Army will move into Austria to restore orderly conditions. . . .

4 From midnight onwards the Corps will hold themselves in readiness to occupy the mouth of the Salzach at Hallern and the bridges on the Salzach and Inn between Reichenhall and Passau, as soon as the order is received, and to remain prepared for the further advance. The crossing at the bridges on a broad front is to be prepared for in advance. . . .

5 The Corps will furthermore hold themselves in readiness for the advance so that it can take place from 0600 hours on the morning of 12 March as soon as the order is received . . .'

But the troops who were to march in were, as the situation report showed at 10.30 p.m., very far from being ready for action. The Seventh Division of the Seventh Army Corps was not ready until 8.00 a.m. the following morning. The Twenty-Seventh Division were still mobilizing at their garrisons. So were the Seventeenth Division of the Thirteenth Army Corps. The Second Panzer Division was not present in full strength at the place of assembly. The *General Goering* regiment and the *Adolf Hitler* SS Leibstandarte were still only on the march in Central Germany.

Fifteen minutes after Bock had read this report the First Division of the Army General Staff gave the go-ahead for the invasion and proposed that the frontier bridges over the Saalach, Salzach and Inn should be occupied at once. The Commander-in-Chief of the Eighth Army asked his Corps whether they had the necessary troops ready and available. As he had already been able to perceive from the situation report, this question had to be answered in the negative. And General von Schobert's Seventh Corps also observed that: '. . . the new government's order to offer no resistance has probably not yet penetrated to the outposts of the Front militia. For this reason an immediate occupation tonight could lead to undesirable exchanges of fire.' Thereupon Bock decided that the frontier bridges would not be occupied until the following dawn at 5.30 a.m. The advance of the main bulk of the army would not begin until eight o'clock.

It was only during the last hour of the day that Bock was able to gain an accurate picture of the situation in Austria. The Army High Command sent him by teleprinter a 'situation report compiled over the past eighteen hours'. Amongst other things this contained the following:

Friday, 11 March 1938

'06.30 hrs: German citizen living in Austria reports that before his departure he had been told on the telephone that the militia has been called up in Austria. 10.00 hours: servant from Neustift (Austria) employed on German soil, called back by Austrian Mayor since all Austrian ex-servicemen must return ... 11.45 hrs: Reliable source in Salzburg reports that no one there has any knowledge of mobilization order. Situation is calm. ... 12.10 hrs: Declarations of martial law are just being printed. ... 13.07 hrs: It has just been established in Braunau that only the Army have been alerted. The police and customs are carrying out their duties as usual ... 14.30 hrs: The Viennese garrison has been alerted because increased National Socialist demonstrations are expected. 14.25 hrs: Customs officer Hartmann observed from Laufen at 14.25 hrs the arrival of a lorry containing forty men of the Austrian infantry at Oberndorf on the Salzach. The detachment has taken up position behind the church, five to six hundred metres from the frontier ... 14.20 hrs: Front militia has called up and equipped all available forces. Austrian post buses with large Teutonic crosses are fetching in the Front militiamen from the provinces ... 17.05 hrs. Plebiscite is said to be postponed indefinitely. This evening celebration demonstrations by the National Socialist Party ...'

Shortly after this report on the day's events had come in, the first section of the Army General Staff confirmed the radio announcement that Seyss-Inquart had taken over the government and that he had sent a telegram asking for military help. And two other important communications were received at Mühldorf before midnight. The first was the order concerning the attitude to be adopted in relation to Czech and Italian troops: 'Czechoslovak troops on Austrian soil are to be treated as enemies. With regard to Italy every provocation is to be avoided.' The second important piece of news was that Hitler would be arriving at the Army HQ at Mühldorf at about midday the next day, following which he would be driving up to the foremost troops.

The Command of the Sixteenth Army Corps had been at Passau for the past four hours. At about midnight General Rudolf Veiel, the Commander of the Second Panzer Division, arrived at Passau. When he reported to General Guderian, he complained that there were neither maps of Austria nor sufficient fuel available for the advance. But Guderian had a solution to one of these problems: He told Veiel to use the ordinary *Baedeker* tourist guide. The question of the fuel supply, on the other hand, was more difficult. Guderian drove to a near-by army depot containing fuel which was only supposed to be used in an action against the Western powers. Guderian was obliged to use the threat of force to make the man in charge hand over the petrol.

President Miklas of Austria, who had been willing at 11.00 p.m. to appoint the Minister of the Interior as provisional head of government, saw that there was now no alternative to making Seyss-Inquart Schuschnigg's successor. The ex-Chancellor and and his Foreign Minister, Guido Schmidt, had repeatedly urged Miklas to do so and Seyss-Inquart himself had tried to plead his own cause: he was no revolutionary and wanted to take office in a constitutional manner. Schmidt argued that the power in the provinces was already in the hands of the National Socialists. One could not expose those few people who were willing to resist to a pointless bloodbath. Just before midnight Miklas finally gave up. He was ready to appoint Seyss-Inquart. Miklas, who had rejected the ultimatums of the German Reich, capitulated in the face of the 'political movement within the German-Austrian nation itself'. But at the same time he set Seyss three conditions: '1. Avoid bloodshed. 2. Restore law and order. 3. Secure the peace of the country.'

By this means the President was attempting from the start to exclude the possibility of intervention by foreign powers, which included the marching in of German troops. Even Seyss-Inquart, the nationalist lawyer, was still hoping to be able to preserve the independence of Austria. He went over to the Hall of Columns and brought his National Socialist friends the new: 'I have been appointed Chancellor.'

Dr Friedl Rainer sat down at his typewriter again. He made out the list of Ministers in Seyss-Inquart's cabinet. Since the afternoon hours when the first candidates had been named it had undergone some alterations. Some names had disappeared and others had more recently taken their place. In the third list, which was typed at midnight, there were, at any rate, some names which, even for President Miklas, did not smack of National Socialist revolution: Glaise-Horstenau was envisaged as Vice-Chancellor, Professor Oswald Menghin as Minister of Education, Dr Rudolf

Friday, 11 March 1938

Neumayer as Finance Minister and Dr Michael Skubl as State Secretary for Security. The remainder of the list was more unequivocally Nazi: the Foreign Minister was Dr Wilhelm Wolff, the Minister of Justice Dr Franz Hueber, the Minister for Social Administration Dr Hugo Jury, the Minister for Agriculture and Forestry Anton Reinthaller, the Minister for Trade and Commerce Dr Hans Fischböck.

The die was cast. As the church clocks of Vienna struck midnight, Miklas had not actually approved the new government list in this form, but the end of the clerico-authoritarian regime set up by Dollfuss and continued by Schuschnigg was already an accomplished fact. The question now was whether the Austrian National Socialists having won power with Berlin's help, could defend it against the lust for annexation of the German Reich.

In Vienna and the towns of the Austrian provinces the National Socialists, drunk with victory, had turned night into day. In Vienna alone tens of thousands of people were still up and about. Cafés and bars were full to overflowing. There at midnight people heard Dr Jury's announcement:

'Dr Seyss-Inquart, the Minister appointed by the Federal President to administer government business, is still engaged in talks with the Federal President about his new appointment. When the meeting is finished the Minister will announce the result of it over the radio. The whole population has complied with Minister Seyss-Inquart's appeal to maintain public law and order. National Socialists! Continue to maintain normal discipline at this historic hour!'

For the supporters of the ex-Chancellor Dr Kurt Schuschnigg, for resolute opponents of National Socialism and for the hundreds of thousands of Jewish citizens of Austria, it was a matter of uncertainty whether they would still be free at the end of the new day which was just beginning.

166

SATURDAY, 12 MARCH 1938

At the Chancellery President Miklas was now ready to accept the list of Ministers proposed to him by Seyss-Inquart. After signing the paper, he arranged for the cabinet to be sworn in the following morning. He had one more thing to enjoin upon Seyss-Inquart. He was to talk to Berlin as qucikly as possible, so as to stop the German troops marching in.

The National Socialists had finally triumphed. A reporter from Ravag stood on the balcony of the Chancellery and described the scene at that historic hour to the radio listeners. When it was announced that the new Chancellor was expected on the balcony there was an incident. Above the victory shouts of the crowd suddenly and unmistakably the cry was heard: 'Heil Schuschnigg!' It seemed as if there was a whole group of counter-demonstrators in the square. Through the noise the listeners could tell that a certain amount of confusion reigned on the balcony.

Then at eight minutes past one on the morning of 12 March 1938 Major Klausner, the Leader of the no longer illegal Austrian Nazi Movement, called from the balcony:

'It is with deep emotion that I announce this solemn moment: Austria has been set free! Austria is National Socialist! Borne aloft by the trust of the whole nation, a new government has been formed, which will devote all its strength to the happiness and peace of this country, following the principles of our magnificent National Socialist Movement. Its first task will be to provide work and bread for all our fellow Germans. Once again a National Socialist uprising has taken place with incomparable discipline. If any further proof were needed that the power in this country is our due, then it has been given by this remarkable uprising and seizure of power. Nobody has been hurt. For this I and the whole German people in Austria are grateful, above all, to our comrades of the SA and SS. And at this hour the person we remember in our thoughts with deep gratitude and love is our Führer, Adolf Hitler. Now the swastika flags are flying victoriously over our homeland. In reverence and gratitude we remember the dead of our Movement, who fell in the struggle for Austria. Their sacrifice has now achieved supreme fulfilment. But to you, my fellow-Germans, men and women, goes out my call: To work! We

have reached our goal: One people, one Reich, one Führer!
Heil to our Führer! Heil Hitler!'

Most of the members of the new government had obeyed the
summons to come to the Chancellery. Now they wanted a
pictorial record of the mood of victory. In the Chancellor's
secretary's room all those present, with the exception of Dr
Rudolf Neumayer, the Finance Minister, went and grouped themselves in front of the corner where Dollfuss had been murdered.
Behind them the Madonna with the everlasting flame. In front
of them the door to the Chancellor's office. Thus they stood to
have their photograph taken.

At about two o'clock Radio Vienna announced the government's first edict: 'The German people in Austria called upon, at
this time of historic significance, to display swastika flags and
red-white-red flags together. Chancellor Seyss-Inquart has decreed that today will be a holiday for all primary and secondary
schools.'

All the members of the former government left the Chancellery at
the same time.

The new Chancellor tried to comfort his predecessor: he
would visit him at his house and naturally his car and his adjutant
would continue to remain at his disposal.

In the central districts of Vienna the streets were still bustling
with animation. Everywhere could be seen the faces of people in
from the suburbs, filled with ecstatic delight. Now the looting
and violence were beginning. The English journalist, Gedye,
was driving through the Josefstadt in a taxi. The car caught up
with a group of Nazis. 'Who dares to ride in a taxi tonight when he
should be jubilating with us?' a blonde woman screamed. 'That
must be a Jewish swine.' The crowd began to adopt a menacing
attitude, but at that moment their procession started to move on
and the taxi-driver called out to them in broad Viennese: 'Na, na.
Zuafällig is does a Arier und a Ausländer a no dazua' ('Now, now
this happens to be an Ayrian and a foreigner at that.')

At the Vienna Town Hall the National Socialists were now
well and truly in the saddle. When the Mayor's son, Ernst
Schmitz, arrived home after his spell of duty in the Fatherland
Front militia he was not allowed into the Town Hall. He had to

spend the night at his fiancée's parents' home. His father had already been placed under house arrest. At 12.20 a.m. it had been announced over the radio that ex-Mayor Lahr had been appointed the new Mayor. Now some of the closest associates of the Schmitz family revealed themselves to be National Socialists of long standing. A servant named Masaryk was caught going through the Mayor's desk. The housemaid—a sickly woman—suddenly revealed herself to be both healthy and 'brown'. And one of the detectives responsible for the Mayor's safety also made known his Nazi allegiance. He had already been suspect for a long time because he always lived beyond his means. The Nazis had sent two more detectives to watch Schmitz.

When President Miklas had left the Chancellery—at the same time as Schuschnigg—Lieutenant Birsak, who was in command of the guards at the President's Palace at Number 15 Hainburger-strasse, was informed by telephone. Birsak alerted his men. The Miklas family were waiting for their father. In the course of the evening the children had gradually all come home, bringing with them news of the demonstrations in the city.

All the way from the Chancellery the President's car was followed by another, unknown, car. In it sat the thirty-year-old managing director of a scaffolding construction firm, Otto Skorzeny. He had met up with his fellow Nazis that afternoon at the gymnasium of the German Gymnasts' Club in the Fifteenth District of Vienna, one of the clubs which had long since served as an illegal military base. That evening Skorzeny and his fellow gymnasts were sent to report in front of the Chancellery. Now, after the departure of President Miklas, Skorzeny's great moment was to have come. He received the order from the chairman of the German Gymnasts Clubs to follow the President's car, in the company of other gymnasts. At the same time a troop of SS men was making its way towards the Hainburgerstrasse from Florids-dorf. Skorzeny and a friend of his raced through the night streets of the still animated city in order to carry out their assignment: to mount guard over the President's house.

Lieutenant Birsak was in the cellar at the President's villa, talking to one of the President's sons, when the call came from the entrance: 'The President is coming.' The sentry had heard the car driving up. He opened the door. The President and his detective walked in. The sentry saluted. Suddenly he saw some men in plain clothes forcing their way into the hall behind Miklas. Miklas, who had already started going up the stairs, stopped, turned and

said: 'I do not need any SS in the house. I have my own guard.'
The sentry leaped up the stairs, placed himself in front of Miklas
and pointed his sub-machine gun at the men. He removed the
safety catch on the gun, which was loaded with thirty-two rounds,
and placed a second magazine on the pillar of the staircase. Then
he called out to the plain-clothes men, who had thrust their
hands into the pockets of their wind-jackets: 'If anyone makes a
suspicious move or takes a single pace forward, I shall use this
gun.' Miklas let fly at the Nazis: 'Who are you and what do you
want?' A tall man introduced himself 'Skorzeny, Engineer.' He
was under orders to take over the guard. Miklas: Orders from
whom?' Skorzeny: 'From Minister Jury.' Lieutenant Birsak,
who had emerged from the cellar, leaped in front of Skorzeny with
a drawn pistol. Skorzeny drew his own. Everyone else stood
motionless. Then Miklas shouted out: 'I will speak to Minister
Jury.' Birsak: 'May I speak to the Minister too?' Skorzeny: 'And
me?'

The three of them went to the telephone which was in the
lower hall. Meanwhile the sentry kept the Nazis covered with his
sub-machine gun. Miklas spoke to Jury. Then the officer of the
guard took over. 'This is First Lieutenant Birsak, Commandant
at the Federal President's Villa. There are only two possibilities:
either I receive an order from my military superiors to withdraw
or I order my men to open fire.' Jury cut in: 'What is your
strength? Are you well enough armed? You must be careful
because of the Communists. Can I speak to Engineer Skorzeny?'
Birsak passed on the telephone: 'Here.' The tall engineer repeated
the words 'Yes, sir', a number of times. Then he put down the
receiver and said to Birsak: 'You have won.' Skorzeny and his
men withdrew to the street.

The Miklas family had been following the events since the
President's arrival from the upper hall. Young Karl Miklas had
been so incensed by the conduct of the National Socialists that
he had wanted to hurl himself upon them. To stop him causing
dangerous trouble his brothers and sisters had had to hold on to
him. For safety's sake they had locked him in the bathroom.

Then the President told his family what had been happening at
the government offices. He was dispirited: '*Finis Austriae.*'
Lieutenant-General Muff had consoled him, when he delivered
the ultimatum: 'The Hitler regime won't last for ever.' Then they
all went to bed. Only Franz Miklas went downstairs again to the
cellar to continue talking with Birsak. Outside in the Hainburger-

strasse the SS men stood around shivering. In long stockings, shorts and wind-jackets.

᛭᛭᛭᛭᛭᛭᛭᛭

The official on duty at the Foreign Office in Berlin that night was Günter Altenburg. At 2.10 p.m. the telephone rang. Lieutenant-General Muff, the Military Attaché in Vienna, came on the line and made an urgent plea for the invasion to be called off. Speaking on behalf of Chancellor Seyss-Inquart, Muff explained: 'The troops should remain in readiness at the frontier but should not cross it. If they have already crossed it anywhere they should be withdrawn.'

The more Seyss had thought about the imminent invasion the less he had liked it. He was also disturbed by the thought of the Austrian Legion—the militant formation of Austrian Nazi emigrés, waiting in readiness in Germany. He had asked Keppler, Hitler's Austrian emissary, to hold up the invasion in any way he could. Keppler himself could see little grounds for the military action. Apart from the temporary delay caused by the President's resistance, the seizure of power had ultimately taken place without friction.

When Muff made his request, Altenburg in Berlin could not believe his ears. He asked to speak to Keppler but Keppler had already come on the line and seconded Muff's plea. Altenburg immediately informed the Political Director of the Foreign Office, von Weizsäcker. Weizsäcker told Altenburg to inform SS-Obergruppenführer Wilhelm Brückner at the Reich Chancellery of the appeal. When Brückner heard about the plea from Vienna he was amazed: 'But we have Seyss-Inquart's own appeal for military assistance. The whole thing is under way. It can scarcely be stopped now.' But he proposed to make contact with the armed forces.

Altenburg did the same. He rang up the duty officer at the War Ministry and told him what had happened. He had scarcely put down the receiver when Brückner rang him back. The time by Altenburg's watch was now 2.30 a.m. Brückner told him it was impossible to stop the progress of the invasion. Why had not Lieutenant-General Muff addressed his inquiry direct to the Reich Chancellery? Brückner was unwilling to credit that the appeal was genuine. 'Are you sure this is not a hoax? Are you quite certain Keppler and Muff have really been on the telephone?'

Saturday, 12 March 1938

When Altenburg confirmed this Brückner declared himself ready to wake Hitler and give him the message.

Scarcely ten minutes later they had their answer. Brückner instructed Altenburg: 'Tell Muff the Führer has decided that the invasion can no longer be held up.' When he telephoned the news through to Vienna he found himself speaking to an angry Military Attaché. Muff: 'I very much regret this news and will be writing a memorandum about it.' Altenburg was cool. 'I will do the same.' Muff relented a little: 'What else can be done about it?' But Altenburg had no idea. He merely recommended the Military Attaché to make contact with the High Command of the Armed Forces. All he himself could do was to pass on Brückner's message. The last attempt to stop the invasion had failed.

Independently of Vienna there were some Army officers in Berlin who also wanted to call a halt to the invasion at the last moment. In these hours of the night General Keitel's telephone did not stop ringing. Even Brauchitsch and the head of the operational staff of the Armed Forces, Major-General von Viebahn, urged him to make representations to Hitler about stopping the invasion. Keitel agreed but did nothing. The German troops continued to advance.

While Brückner was receiving Hitler's decision at the Reich Chancellery Goering's telephone directives continued to be issued. At 2.29 a.m. an official at the Air Ministry was giving Chancellor Seyss-Inquart further instructions.

'The Field Marshal considers it expedient for the Austrian troops not simply to withdraw without fighting but to join forces with the German troops.'

Seyss referred to the attempt to stop the invasion: 'There is no need for it.' Goering's official: 'I do not know what the Führer is doing. Haven't you had word of any kind from the Führer? So far no orders cancelling it have been given.' Seyss was not the man to stick to his guns. After a certain amount of humming and hahing he merely said: 'I have a lot of such questions to see to. In my opinion we can leave the matter until the morning.' Then the conversation turned to the question of names. Goering's Air Ministry official: 'The Field Marshal has strong reservations about Wolff. He says it is particularly important. He has leads which count very much against him, conversations and so on, not quite reliable.' Seyss:

'He is a very good man. You can rely on him completely. He is absolutely in order.'

Berlin: 'And then the Field Marshal wanted to ask you particularly to take charge of the telephone monitoring yourself, yes?' Seyss: 'Certainly.' The official: 'Then one more question, he is very sorry that there are a whole crowd of departmental heads who are still, he says, in touch with Schuschnigg.' Seyss: 'But that is not very serious, it can't all be done at once.' The official: 'And Schmitz is no longer Mayor?' Seyss: 'At the moment he is in protective custody.'

They continued to talk about the composition of the new Government. Goering's Air Ministry official: 'And then I have just heard on the radio, the Führer especially wanted Kaltenbrunner to take over the Security Service. He's got that, hasn't he? And what about Skubl?' Seyss: 'Skubl must stay for the time being, otherwise the whole thing will come unstuck.' Berlin: 'And then the Field Marshal says Fischböck is very questionable too. He must go, he says.' Seyss: 'Let us not just at the moment—we won't talk about that on the telephone.'

After the members of the old government had left, things had grown quieter at the Chancellery. Schuschnigg's secretary was stoking the stove in his second office in the Mestasiogasse with government papers. Anything that seemed to him damaging he confined to the flames. Time and again he returned to the government offices to fetch more fuel. He was not alone. Schuschnigg's adjutant was stoking with a will. Suddenly the door opened. A member of the new Nazi regime came in. 'What are you doing there?' The secretary put on his most innocent expression. 'We are burning personal things, *bitteschön*.' The Nazi disappeared again.

Through the streets of Vienna marched squads of the SA and SS wearing pieced together uniforms or civilian clothes. Their targets were the homes of opponents of the Nazis or supporters of the old regime. At about three o'clock in the morning at Number 4 Mayerhofgasse the caretaker knocked on Dr Hornbostel's door. 'There is someone to see you.' Through the door came Mühlmann, the Nazi functionary, and two young SS men with pistols in their belts. Mühlmann announced that Hornbostel was under house arrest and was not to use the telephone.

Saturday, 12 March 1938

At that moment the telephone rang. Mühlmann picked it up. The Netherlands Embassy was inquiring after Hornbostel's health. 'Dr Hornbostel is very well,' said Mühlmann. He had scarcely put down the receiver when it rang again. But this time the caller did not identify himself and Mühlmann did not discover that it was Schuschnigg's secretary ringing Hornbostel to warn him of his arrest. He had overheard the Nazis at the Chancellery talking about it.

Then Mühlmann left the apartment. Hornbostel would be receiving further instructions in due course: meanwhile the two SS men would remain. The diplomat fixed up billets on the floor for the two young men and went to bed himself.

At this time—it was about 3.30 a.m.—three policemen were ringing at the door of Number 11 on the second floor, third staircase, at Number 6 Bauerngasse. Friedrich Hillegeist, the trades-unionist, opened the door. He had no idea that the Nazis had come to power. 'Have you any arms here?' the police asked. Hillegeist said he had not. The next thing he knew the three men were inside his flat. House search. It was only now that Hillegeist noticed they were wearing swastika armbands. They pounced upon a book on socialism in the bookcase. One of them said: 'We are all Socialists, of course, but you are a Bolshevik.' Then Hillegeist knew the score. He had to go along for 'questioning'.

Shortly after four o'clock a police squad turned up on the first floor at Number 59 Schumanngasse. Frau Olah opened the door. Two policemen and a detective were asking for her son: 'Is Franz Olah here? He must come with us.' Olah, the young trades-unionist, was taken off to the police station in the Rötzergasse. On the way the police squad also picked up another socialist, Adolf Schärf.

All that night the Nazi squads made their way through the city arresting people. The police took over the old lists of the Schuschnigg regime's socialist opponents, who could also be reckoned opponents of the Nazis. The SA and SS dragged Schuschnigg supporters and Jews out of their beds at will and imprisoned them in requisitioned houses. Other opponents of the Nazis were placed under guard in their own homes. Amongst the first people to be arrested in Vienna were the Ministers, Ludwig and Pernter, Hofrat Weiser of the state police and Colonel Adam of the press service.

At about three o'clock at Aspern airport Lieutenant-Colonel of Police Oscar von Schmoczer, the Airport Commandant, experienced a small invasion. Wildly costumed SA and SS men had come to wait for the arrival of the Reich Leader of the SS. Schmoczer had been informed of Himmler's departure from Munich through flight control.

Then three cars drove up. Schmoczer knew all the occupants by sight. Klausner, the leader of the Austrian Nazi Party, Globocznigg, Rainer, Kaltenbrunner, Veesenmayer and State Secretary Skubl. They installed themselves in the airport restaurant. Veesenmayer procured saveloy sausage. The Nazis wolfed it down. In their excitement at the seizure of power they had had nothing to eat apart from the ham rolls the soldier had brought them late on Friday evening in the Hall of Columns.

One man seemed ill at ease in this circle of the victors: Skubl. Von Schmoczer went up to him: 'Herr President, if you like we can go to my rooms and perhaps drink a glass of tea. I will arrange for us to be told when the plane comes in.' Skubl went with him into his small official apartment.

At 4.30 a.m. the moment arrived. From flight control came the word that Himmler was about to land. As Skubl, Schmoczer and the Nazi officials hurried out on to the airfield the two planes from Munich flew in. Twenty-seven SS men with sub-machine guns at the ready leaped out of the plane and secured the airstrip. Himmler and his entourage emerged from their plane.

Kaltenbrunner, dressed in knickerbockers, sports jacket and bow tie, went up to Himmler: 'Beg to report, Reichsführer, total victory for the Movement! The SS awaits further orders.' But Himmler merely threw a disparaging glance at the troop of civilians standing to attention. When Skubl saw Lieutenant-Colonel of Police Meissner in Himmler's party he knew the game was up for him. In 1934 Meissner had been a Lieutenant-Colonel of the Austrian Gendarmerie and had had to leave the country because of his part in the July putsch. At that time Skubl had been Vice-President of Police in Vienna. He decided to offer Seyss his resignation the following morning.

Himmler only remained at the airport a few minutes. Together with Klausner and Kaltenbrunner he and his immediate entourage drove to the Hotel Regina in the three government cars. Before Globocznigg and Rainer were aware of it they had been left standing at the airport with no means of transport. They spent an hour telephoning for a taxi, by which time it had become apparent that after their night of triumph they were being thrust firmly back into the second rank.

᭶᭶᭶᭶᭶᭶᭶

Dawn approached over Vienna. At the Belvedere Schuschnigg had erected a makeshift bed on the floor of his study. His brother had not gone home that night and his fiancée had not wanted to leave him. His seventy-three-year-old father and two maids were also in the house. At five o'clock Schuschnigg's chief adjutant arrived from the Chancellery and woke his chief: the garden was still unoccupied, now was the last chance to escape. But the ex-Chancellor did not want to leave.

What the chief adjutant had seen on the Landstrasse Guertl was the SA approaching (the view of the street from Schuschnigg's own house was blocked by a gardener's house). The guard were called upon by the SA troop to hand over to them. The National Socialists were under the command of a Major of the Austrian Army who had been suspended for political reasons. The guard officer in command, who knew the Major, had refused this demand. But the guard found their own freedom of movement obstructed. To be on the safe side Schuschnigg telephoned State Secretary Skubl and asked whether he was free. Skubl: 'Of course.' The order had already been given for a lorry to go and collect the SA men from outside the Belvedere.

Outside the President's house Skorzeny's SS were still at their posts. The cold of the night seemed to have chilled the National Socialists' revolutionary ardour. Lieutenant Birsak told Skorzeny that he should find a base for his men. Across the street in a cellar they found the meeting room of a temperance organization. The stove, which had not been lit for a long time, smoked terribly. While the SS men were warming themselves, Skorzeny chatted with Birsak and Franz Miklas in the President's cellar. They sat together on a bench round the table, drinking coffee and smoking cigarettes. Skorzeny still had a hand in the pocket of his wind-jacket. Finally Birsak said: 'Herr Engineer, do please feel free to take your hand out of your pocket now; my own pistol is not loaded.' Skorzeny: 'Then you were bluffing.' Birsak: 'I was not bluffing. I should have told them to shoot, believe me.' Then Skorzeny invited Birsak to make a return visit to the SS quarters. 'I must go over to my lads now, why don't you come along?' When they got out into the street they were met by the strains floating up from the cellar windows, of the Nazi song: *Es zittern die morschen Knochen.* (The rotten bones tremble.)

An army provision lorry brought hot tea for the guards. Soldiers and SS shared the provisions. A further lorry arrived with arms for the National Socialists. Slowly it grew light. Back in the palace Birsak saw the SS men waving their guns about. 'They can't carry on like that', he said to Skorzeny. 'There could be a major accident. I will send you over an N.C.O. to teach the men how to handle their weapons.' And as dawn was breaking one of the soldiers of the guard was giving the SS troop weapons training by the wall of the premises in the Hainburgerstrasse.

Skorzeny was relieved. His relief, also an engineer, was less aggressive. Birsak asked him: 'What are you here for exactly?' The engineer: 'We are the *Schutzstaffel*—the defence corps. We are here in support of the executive.' The guards officer: 'Excellent. I am the executive here. If you are here to support me I will give you your orders right away.' He made the SS take up positions in a broad circle round the President's house.

卐卐卐卐卐卐

One hour before sunrise, at 5.30 a.m., the troops of the German invasion Army occupied the frontier crossings into Austria. Bridgeheads were formed at Lindau, Mittenwald, Kiefersfelden, Freilassing, Burghausen and Schaerding. Nowhere was resistance encountered.

In Berlin, as in Mühldorf, everybody was relieved that there was no resistance from the Austrian side. They had still been nervous during the night. When Colonel Jodl, the head of the Reich Defence Division at the High Command, had entered the room of Brauchitsch, the Commander-in-Chief of the Army, he had found him in a mood of despair. Brauchitsch still believed that there might be fighting either with Italy or with Czechoslovakia. And indeed there had been one moment during the night when the situation had looked somewhat tricky. An hour before the frontier crossings were due to be occupied a report reached the Mühldorf headquarters that mule columns were approaching the frontier. The German officers' at first thought that they must be bringing up explosives. But the whole thing had turned out to be harmless. The Austrians were simply bringing garlands to to decorate the bridges.

卐卐卐卐卐卐

Saturday, 12 March 1938

The former government newspaper, the *Wiener Zeitung*, appeared that day with a blank space. The whole text of Schuschnigg's farewell speech had been removed shortly before the paper went to press. The Catholic *Reichpost* appeared with an account of the previous day's events, in which the German ultimatums were mentioned. It was therefore seized. Nor could the *Neue Wiener Tagblatt* be bought, for it had contained an appreciation of the previous Chancellor which was headed 'Kurt von Schuschnigg, a noble man'. The clerical *Neuigkeitsweltblatt* put in an appearance. The papers published by the *Telegraf-Verlag* (*Telegraf am Mittag*, *Echo* and *Nachtausgabe*) were on the Nazis' execution list. But preparations were already in hand to bring out the *Telegraf* in the evening as the *NS—Telegraf*. The *Wiener Tag* appeared for the last time. All the papers left on sale that morning welcomed the seizure of power; the most enthusiastic was the Greater German paper, the *Wiener Neuesten Nachrichten*.

The reactions of the foreign press that morning were various. In France the papers lamented the weakness of the French government's policies almost without exception. The moment for the German action against Austria had been well chosen because of the internal political confusion in France. The *Petit Parisien* declared that because of English reservations over the situation in Central Europe there could be no hope at any time of a positive and resolute demonstration against Germany. The association with Rome through the Stresa agreements had borne bitter fruit. A greater blow had now been struck against the Western powers than when the Germans had marched into the Rhineland. Almost all the French papers carried warnings against German expanisionism.

In England it was different. Few papers that morning took a critical line. The leading article in the *Daily Express* was remarkable: 'By a monstrous piece of folly in 1934 the British Government pledged themselves to defend the integrity of Austria in terms as plain as those which brought us to the side of Belgium in 1914. But this time the situation is very different ... Half of Austria wants Hitler. The acting Austrian Government are asking for Hitler to walk in. Britain and France cannot force the Austrians to be independent. A better parallel would be Hitler's reoccupation of the Rhineland just two years ago. The British Government viewed that "gravely" for indeed it was a similar breach of treaty. But there, also, the German inhabitants welcomed the German "invaders". British people asked themselves, "Shall we fight to

Saturday, 12 March 1938

keep Germans apart?" and answered, "No!" They will ask, and answer, now as then.'

In Berlin the newspaper-sellers had a field day. The papers proclaimed the events of the previous day in banner headlines. The *Völkischer Beobachter*: 'GERMAN-AUSTRIA SAVED FROM CHAOS'.

Early in the morning Seyss-Inquart, who had scarcely slept that night, had rung up Hitler at the Reich Chancellery. Following his unsuccessful attempt during the night to have the invasion stopped completely, he now offered to send units of the Austrian Army to Germany. From the Austrian side this could only be in the nature of a gesture, 'To show that from now on the troops of both states would be combined together.' Hitler agreed.

The mass of the first wave of the Eighth Army crossed the frontier into Austria at eight o'clock. Everywhere the soldiers were welcomed by the Austrian population. During the night the order had been received at the Mühldorf GHQ that the invading units were not to cross the frontier in battle order but with bands playing and flags flying. And thus in brilliant sunlight began the *Blumenkorso*, the 'battle of the flowers', as the soldiers at once dubbed it. In spite of this, however, fire protection and some security measures were not dispensed with.

As had been proposed from Mühldorf, before the advance many officers made contact with the commandants of the Austrian garrisons ahead of them, so as to be on the safe side. The officer commanding the Sixty-First Infantry Regiment even spoke to the District Governor of Kufstein in advance. As a result, when the troops arrived, the population were cheering and from the fortress the German anthem was being played.

Nevertheless there were some difficulties. As a result of traffic jams and delays caused by refuelling at ordinary roadside petrol stations, the advance of the Second Panzer Division was held up. They were not able to enter Austrian territory until nine o'clock, an hour late. The vanguard was formed by the Fifth and Seventh Tank Reconnaissance Battalions, and the Second Motor-Cycle Rifle Battalion. At the head was General Guderian. The SS Leibstandarte *Adolf Hitler*, which had only arrived from Berlin during the night, was still assembling at Straubing.

At nine o'clock two *Luftwaffe* transport formations took off

179

from Berlin, carrying two companies of the *General Goering* Guard Battalion. With an escort of DO17 planes. Their destination: Aspern airport, Vienna.

The first division of the Army High Command gave orders that an officer of the invading army should push on at once as far as the Brenner frontier to greet the Italian troops. The lieutenant-colonel chosen set off at once, with a detachment of light machine guns, motor-cycle riflemen and anti-tank defence, via Matrai, Steinach and Gries.

The Commander-in-Chief of the Eighth Army, General von Bock, ordered the following: '1. Immediate dispatch of an advanced party from Army GHQ to Vienna. 2. Mechanized forces of the Panzer Corps are to thrust on as far as Vienna today. 3. Seventeenth and Twenty-seventh Divisions (second wave) to be transported by rail from their peace-time stations direct to Vienna.'

The Panzer troops advancing from Passau had a distance of 275 kilometres to cover: they received the following order from Bock: 'Panzer Corps arrives today, Saturday, Vienna. The units which will lead the advance are the Reconnaissance Section and parts of the Rifle Brigade under General Guderian. Before entering Vienna contact is to be made with the Military Attaché, General Muff. Telegraph hourly the objectives reached.' That was the best Bock could hope to achieve that day. But he must try to have some result ready to report to Hitler, who could be at Mühldorf in a few hours' time. The propaganda exploitation of the advance was Goebbels's responsibility. He had provided each advancing unit with a propaganda vehicle from his Ministry.

When Seyss-Inquart came into the Chancellery he was still wearing the red-white-red emblem of the Fatherland Front in his buttonhole. Seyss briefly addressed the civil servants presented to him: they were all to return to their desks. The Front officials would be assigned to other posts. There would naturally be close contact with the Party. No one need have any anxiety who had not incurred personal guilt.

At this moment Himmler's assistant, Daluege, was announced. Seyss asked the officials to wait outside. Daluege did not stay long with Seyss. When he had left again with his SS escort Seyss looked changed, paler. Seyss to the officials: 'I can say nothing further now. I intend to retain Austria. God grant that I succeed. Go home for the moment and wait for further instructions.'

Hantschk still had one worry. When the rest had left he went in again to see Seyss. Zernatto had entrusted him with the winding up of the Fatherland Front. Could Seyss give him written confirmation of this, to serve as an entry pass to the occupied Fatherland Front building? The new Chancellor complied with this request.

After their night of victory the new masters in Austria allowed the losers to feel their power that Saturday morning, at government offices and factories, at boarding houses and in the streets. Jews and political opponents of National Socialism were seized and forced to clear away the last traces of Schuschnigg's cancelled plebiscite. With brushes and very strong caustic solution they were made to scrub off the portraits of Schuschnigg, the countless 'Ja' slogans and the Teutonic Crosses which had been painted on the pavements. As the men and women knelt on the ground to do this, the crowds howled with pleasure. G. E. R. Gedye of the *Daily Telegraph* saw the first 'cleaning squad' at the Praterstern:

'It was employed on trying to wash off the stencilled portrait of Schuschnigg from the pediment of a statue. Through the delighted crowds storm-troopers dragged an aged Jewish working-man and his wife. With tears rolling silently down her cheeks, looking straight ahead and through her tormentors, the woman held her old husband's arm, and I could see her trying to pat his hand. "Work for the Jews at last, work for the Jews" the mob howled. "We thank our Führer for finding work for the Jews".'

The first major looting began. Jewish businesses and department stores were raided, mostly by youths. The favourite targets were clothing and delicatessen shops. The synagogue in the Seitenstättengasse was occupied by the SS.

The search continued for refugees. The trains bound for the east were held up near Kagran on an open stretch of line, searched by the SA and then sent back to Vienna. In other places the Hitler Youth also took part in these raids.

Saturday, 12 March 1938

The tidal wave of arrests was only just beginning. Following their arrival at five o'clock that morning Himmler and his staff had 'at once taken all measures needed to uphold law and order in consultation with Austrian police authorities, before the actual entry of the German troops began.' In this the SA, SS and Gestapo were able to make use of the thousands of pages of files which represented the Austrian police dossiers on all persons who had been politically prominent during the Christian-authoritarian regime. The names of the five-thousand-odd active socialists also fell into the Nazis' hands. This made their task a simple one.

At Viennese newspaper offices power was mostly seized by junior employees. When the editor of the *Neue Freie Presse* arrived that morning several of the senior staff had already fled. A clerk and an advertisement space seller were playing at being the new bosses. It was similar on other papers. At the radio station in the Johannesgasse the duty officer had slept overnight in his office for safety's sake. He planned to remain there until the first flush of revolution was past. A Dr Franz Pesendorfer had been functioning as provisional director since Friday evening: two technicians were laying down the law. The head of the cultural and scientific departments only learned about these changes when he arrived at the building in the morning. Outside in the street was a guard of SS men. Henz found a strange young man in his office who told him he should report to the technical director. But all the latter could tell Henz was that he had been suspended. The head of the music department had a similar experience. When he saw his office desk was occupied he simply closed the door and went home.

Just after Ernst Lothar, the director of the Theater in der Josefstadt, had arrived at his office that morning, two actors appeared. They said they were representatives of the National Socialist cell at the theatre and wanted to discuss matters with him. One thing, they began, was certain: Zuckmayer's play *Bellman*, which was due to open next, could not now be presented. Lothar informed the two young Nazi-activists that he had decided to resign. He had considered this step during the night, after listening to the news on the wireless about the seizure of power. The Nazi actors were opposed to this: No, they said, he must stay, at least for a certain amount of time. Nothing would happen to him. But Lothar remained firm in his decision to leave the country. He mentioned that he had a brother living in Switzerland.

182

Saturday, 12 March 1938

The true masters in the city now were the caretakers. They denounced all the tenants with whom they had had rows in the past. Particularly Jews. And maids were also a source of terror now to Fatherland Front families. Over the years these girls—who often had boy friends in the Party or one of the Party formations—had heard all their table talk and knew their employers' political views inside out. There was now capital to be made out of this.

Property owners were quick to make known their true allegiance. In a special edition of the *Zeitschrift für den Oesterreichischen Hausbesitz* (the Austrian Property Owners' Gazette) they proclaimed: 'Fellow Germans! German house owners! It is no coincidence that the last word in the short article "Orientation" in our last issue was "Fellow Germans" (*Volksgenossen!*). Today, thanks to the most unparalleled reversal in the fortunes of any country, we can begin with this word and call upon you to make sure that the outward appearance of Vienna reflects the boundless joy which fills the hearts of all German Austrians. During the coming week every house and every window in our city must testify to the unreserved support of the native Viennese for the National Socialist State. Heil Hitler!'

Nobody wanted to miss out on the celebration of the *Anschluss*. The Austro-German *Volksbund* (a Pan-German association) at Number 3 Trattnerhof, Vienna 1, had lists 'available for signature from 9.00 a.m. to 1.00 p.m. and from 3.00 p.m. to 6.00 p.m.' by those who wanted to congratulate its committee members, Seyss, Jury and Menghin. Four Ministers of the Protestant church, Beyer, Eder, Heinzelmann and Zwernemann, strove to make up for the pro-Schuschnigg stand taken by their church on Thursday by adopting a militant line: 'The Protestant Church of German-Austria stands united and resolved at this historic hour, which sees the return of the German people of Austria into the community of the German Reich, to share its life and destiny. We believe that this hour is blessed by God . . .'

Hitler landed at the Oberwiesenfeld airport at Munich at 10.10 a.m. After a short stop he drove on to Mühldorf. He had brought a complete staff with him. Apart from Wilhelm Keitel, the Chief of the High Command, there were Dr Otto Dietrich, the German Press Chief, Martin Bormann, the administrative head of the

183

Saturday, 12 March 1938

National Socialist Party, Philipp Bouhler, the head of the Führer's office staff, and Josef Bürckel, the Saar Gauleiter. And so that the triumphant journey could be recorded in all its details, Hitler had brought along his personal photographer, Heinrich Hoffmann. As it advanced to Mühldorf on the Inn, Hitler's convoy drove past formations of marching troops of the Eighth Army.

꧁꧂꧁꧂꧁꧂

At about eleven o'clock the former Fatherland Front official, Dr Maximilian Pammer, arrived back home at Number 29 Löwengasse in Vienna. He told his wife about the presentation in Seyss-Inquart's office at the Chancellery. He saw no more hope for the future. 'They will probably lock me up in a concentration camp.' Pammer did not have to wait long. At 11.30 a.m. two detectives arrived. They took away his passport and searched his home for Fatherland Front papers and funds. Then they arrested him and took him to the prison in the Rossauer Lände.

At the prison a man was brought in wearing the uniform of a police officer: Dr Heinrich Hüttl, who twenty-four hours previously had been in charge of the police in the Opera House sector. A continuous stream of new prisoners was brought in.

Meanwhile in Vienna Mary (Muriel E. Gardiner) was sitting alone in her apartment in the Rummelhardtgasse. Her socialist friend, Josef Buttinger, alias Richter, had left Vienna on the Paris express that morning, together with Mary's daughter, the governess, Finni Wodak, and Tony Hyndman, her English friend. Buttinger had been carrying a forged Czech passport.

Mary was busy procuring more such passports for other socialists in danger. They could only be obtained through the Socialists' Foreign Bureau in Brno. There genuine passports belonging to Czech comrades were transformed into false passports for Austrians by swapping the photographs. But for this purpose photographs and personal descriptions had to be brought to Brno. Mary, who possessed genuine British and American passports, took this task upon herself. One of her customers was Manfred Ackermann, the Youth Secretary.

Ackermann, who had been hiding since the previous night at the home of his friend, Karl Ehrental, in the Heimhof in the Thirteenth District, already had proof of the fact that he was in danger. The police had turned up to arrest him at his home in the Brigittaplatz that morning at seven o'clock. After searching the

184

house the police had gone away. The passport photos which had been prepared at Ehrental's house early in the morning showed an altered Ackermann. In place of his curls he had a shaven head and he was no longer wearing his glasses.

卐卐卐卐卐卐卐

Chancellor Seyss-Inquart told his office at noon that he could be reached at the Hotel Meissl & Schaden in the Neuer Markt. The elated National Socialists were to hold a victory celebration there.

This time when the Chancellor walked out of his office he was leaving it equipped with all the legal qualifications for his position; that morning the swearing-in of the cabinet had taken place. The formal act had not taken long. President Miklas had only spoken a few words: 'Herr Chancellor and Ministers, you are appointed on the basis of the Austrian Constitution and you are bound to fulfil all rights and duties in accordance with this Constitution.' Then the members of the cabinet had taken the oath on the 1934 Constitution.

But the power in Seyss's own hands was at most only the tip of the iceberg. The composition of his cabinet had already to a great extent been dictated by Goering. Only a few hours previously Heinrich Himmler, the Reichsführer SS, had also gone to work and had demanded the removal from the government of Skubl, the State Secretary for Security. Skubl was himself ready to resign. When Glaise-Horstenau had told him of Himmler's demands Skubl's answer had been: 'He can have my resignation right away.' He had gone to Seyss immediately and handed in his resignation, not forgetting to refer to Himmler. The Chancellor had flared up: 'I will not be dictated to.' But Skubl had stood by his resignation.

Germany had also demanded the resignation of the President. For this reason Seyss had first sent his constitutional expert, Dr Wimmer, to see Miklas. Then Seyss had gone himself. But Miklas's defiant instincts were roused: 'This time I am going to stay.' Seyss had taken note of this and given the President two pieces of news. Firstly he had agreed with Hitler that morning that, to coincide with the advance of the German Army, units of the Austrian Army would be sent into German towns. Furthermore he was planning to meet the Reich Chancellor in Linz some time that afternoon.

卐卐卐卐卐卐卐

Saturday, 12 March 1938

At the Foreign Office in Berlin Günter Altenburg was writing a memorandum about the situation.

The German Foreign Office had no idea that Germany had presented the sovereign state of Austria with ultimatums and had therefore asked von Stein, the German Chargé d'Affaires in Vienna, what all the talk of 'alleged German ultimatums', was about. Altenburg now noted down the answer from Vienna:

'In reply to the question about the alleged ultimatums delivered from the German side, Legation Councillor von Stein reports that two ultimatums were referred to in today's *Reichpost*. The first ultimatum is alleged to have been delivered to the Federal President by State Secretary Keppler. Herr Keppler has explained to Legation Councillor von Stein that he by no means talked to the President in terms of an ultimatum. Herr Keppler simply explained to the President that it was the wish of the German government that the plebiscite in Austria should be postponed and that, perhaps, certain changes in the government of Austria might be considered . . .'

But while Keppler had watered down his ultimatum of the previous evening, Muff had told von Stein the full truth. He had received the order from Goering at 5.45 p.m. on 11 March to present the following ultimatum to President Miklas: 'If Field Marshal Goering has not heard by 7.30 p.m. that Seyss-Inquart has been made Chancellor, then two hundred thousand men, who are waiting ready at the frontier, will march into Austria. The President will bear full responsibility for the consequences of his refusal.'

Altenburg noted: 'Legation Councillor von Stein transmitted Lieutenant-General Muff's report by telephone and commented that he had not been present at the events described, otherwise he would have attempted to prevent the step. Furthermore the attempt must be made to induce the Austrian government to deny that any ultimatum whatever was delivered from the German side. State Secretary Keppler will discuss this today with Chancellor Seyss-Inquart.'

At the Reich Propaganda Ministry Dr Joseph Goebbels, the Minister, sat down behind a small oval table. On a lace tablecloth lay the 'Proclamation by the Führer and Reich Chancellor'. Goebbels had already given the text to the foreign correspondents in Berlin at 11.30 a.m. Now the German people were to hear it.

All German and Austrian radio stations transmitted Hitler's proclamation:

'Germans! For many years we have witnessed with sorrow the fate of our fellow Germans in Austria ... The sufferings to which this country has been subjected, first from without and later from within, we experienced as our own ... A regime lacking all legal title attempted to maintain its existence, which was rejected by the overwhelming majority of the Austrian people, through the most brutal use of terror and of physical and economic reprisal and annihilation ...

'Germans! During the past few years I tried to warn the previous rulers in Austria against this, their chosen course. ... I tried, further, to convince these rulers that in the long run, even for a great nation, it is impossible—because it is unworthy —for us to continue to look on while people who belong to the same nation as ourselves are oppressed, persecuted and imprisoned simply because of their origins, or their allegiance to this nation, or because of their loyalty to an idea. Germany alone has had to take in over forty thousand refugees. Another ten thousand in this little country have travelled a weary road through prisons and detention camps. Hundreds of thousands have been reduced to beggary, to poverty and misery ... A country which for many years has had no elections of any kind, lacking all the means to assess who is entitled to vote, announces a ballot which is to be held within three and a half days ... Against this unprecedented attempt at election-rigging the German people in Austria themselves rose up ... The German Reich will no longer tolerate the persecution of Germans in this territory ... I have therefore resolved to place the assistance of the German Reich at the disposal of the millions of Germans in Austria. Since this morning the soldiers of the German Armed Forces have been marching across the entire frontier of German-Austria ... Speaking for myself, as Führer and Chancellor of the German people, I shall be happy to be able to set foot once again in this land which is also my homeland, as a free and German citizen. And I shall convince the world that in these days the German nation in Austria is living through an hour of the most blessed joy and emotion ... Long live the National Socialist Reich! Long live National Socialist German-Austria! Signed: Adolf Hitler. Berlin, 12 March 1938.'

Saturday, 12 March 1938

In the arcade courtyard at the Vienna Town Hall the attendants heard the 'Proclamation by the Führer and Reich Chancellor' at a staff reception. In the hall of the First Criminal Court the court officials and judges listened to it and then sang the *Horst Wessel* song, with their right hands raised in salute. The radios were switched on in offices, inns, factories and homes throughout the country, and in the streets Goebbels' voice rang out over the loudspeakers. The people stood stock still. In Vienna the traffic ground to a halt. Then columns of people formed up, singing: *Die Fahne hoch.* At Aspern airport the aeroplanes were coming in from the Reich in an endless stream. From the sky the leaflets rained down upon the land: 'National Socialist Germany greets National Socialist Austria and the new National Socialist Government with true and inalienable affection.'

While Goebbels was reading out Hitler's proclamation Goering was rung up by Prince Philip of Hessen from the Italian Foreign Ministry in Rome.

Hessen: 'It is important to make contact with the Führer.'

Goering: 'That can't be done at the moment.'

Hessen: 'This is what it is about: Mussolini wishes to know if he could publish the Führer's letter. He says it is very important for him here because of his own position and *vis-à-vis* public opinion and secondly in connection with the forthcoming visit from the Führer.'

Goering: 'Tell him the following: he will realize that I must naturally ask the Führer, you understand? It is such a vital matter. But I shall definitely have made contact with the Führer within two hours.'

Hessen: 'Made contact in two hours?'

Goering: 'I think so, definitely. I fully understand Mussolini's request but this is something which naturally only the Führer himself can decide.'

Hessen: 'There is one point about this: the Fascist Grand Council is meeting at the moment and he would also like to make it known to them.'

Goering: 'Very well, then please tell Mussolini I earnestly beg him to be patient with me for two or three hours until I have caught the Führer.'

The conversation finished at 12.22 p.m.

Eight minutes later Hitler arrived at Mühldorf on the Inn. He drove without stopping, between the cordons formed by the inhabitants of the little Bavarian town, to the headquarters of the Eighth Army at the central school. After being greeted by General von Bock, Hitler disappeared into the schoolhouse. The square immediately outside the entrance was fenced off by soldiers and SS men. A small man pushed his way through the barrier. The guards let him pass. In the corridor of the school he met Hitler: 'I am the Mayor of Mühldorf, Gollwitzer. We are happy to be able to welcome you here.'

Of the Party dignitaries who were standing around in front of the school, Gollwitzer only knew Gauleiter Bürckel. He saw the Führer's pennant removed from the black Mercedes in which Hitler had arrived and fixed on to a high-standing army field truck. The mayor was puzzled as to where the Führer could be going. Then one of the entourage told him: 'The Führer is going to Braunau.'

In a small room at the school General von Bock gave a talk about the position. Hitler was in the best of moods when he heard that the troops had not encountered resistance anywhere. Bock reported further that the formations of the *Luftwaffe* had landed at Aspern late that morning, as planned. The Guards regiment and transports had been flown into Vienna. The foremost units of the Eighth Army had reached Linz. Everywhere they had been received with enthusiasm.

But the advance was nevertheless giving the military considerable headaches because of the overloading and blocking of all the roads. Furthermore not even the Army GHQ was fully manned yet.

Hitler asked Bock whether he thought it necessary to establish a theatre of operations for the Eighth Army. The General said he did not because cooperation with the civilian authorities was functioning smoothly. Hitler emphasized the necessity for a rapid amalgamation of the Austrian troops into the German Armed Forces. He also underlined that military units were to move into Carinthia and Styria as quickly as possible, 'so that those provinces to which the German and National Socialist cause is particularly indebted may soon have reason to rejoice'. Departing from his invasion order, Hitler refused to assign to Bock the 'executive power'. He said it was undesirable 'to intervene in the process of reshaping the land of Austria through the executive power'.

While Hitler was still in the map room at Mühldorf school Goering had the text of Hitler's long letter to Mussolini

Saturday, 12 March 1938

transmitted to the Eighth Army headquarters from Berlin, so that the Führer could delete those parts that he did not wish to have published.

Meanwhile Goering's telephone had rung once again in Berlin.

Goering answered peevishly: 'Yes, what do you want?' It was Prince Philip of Hessen in Rome.

Goering: 'Yes, what's the matter?'

Hessen: 'I thought you were going to ring me up.'

Goering: 'No, no, not at all. Listen, Prince, I have spoken to the Führer ... He says the whole letter, as it stands, may not be suitable for publication because there are some passages in it that could perhaps create new difficulties. So he is going to look through the letter quickly now and then give the Duce the passages that are best left out ... So altogether it will take another hour, hour and a half.'

Hessen: 'An hour, hour and a half. Very good. May I pass on this interim message?'

Goering: 'Yes, but do tell him expressly that the Führer asks him to wait. He wants to prevent new difficulties cropping up ...'

Hessen: 'Very good I will pass that on right away.'

Goering: 'And then ... will you tell the Duce what I told Magistrati yesterday: the German troops who have moved into Innsbruck have strict orders to go no further than Innsbruck. Only the commanding officer, a colonel, will be going on to make a courtesy call on the gentlemen. ...'

Hessen: '... and then may I add just one thing more, that the British Ambassador here has been to see Count Ciano and they got the same reply as the French. If you would tell the Führer that.'

Goering: 'Very good. Now then, the Führer will already have spoken to you yesterday.'

Hessen: 'The Führer was marvellous yesterday evening on the telephone.'

Goering: '... The Führer simply said that he is so tremendously happy that he has never for a moment doubted the greatness of the Duce's personality. ... I congratulate you on having had such a wonderful mission to perform.'

Hessen: 'Yes, I am very proud of it.'

Goering: 'It is your finest yet.'

Hessen: 'Yes, fantastic, I am tremendously proud of it.'

The conversation ended at 1.04 p.m.

Meanwhile at Mühldorf Hitler had finished editing his letter to Mussolini for publication and had ordered its transmission to Berlin. Then he went with his entourage to the Gasthof Dinhuber at Number 3 in the town square for lunch. At the Post Office, during this time, the journalists were telephoning back enthusiastic reports to their papers and to the German News Agency: '. . . Into this town which is filled with unspeakable joy . . . We stop for two hours amidst the jubilation of all Mühldorf. Nobody has stayed away—neither the oldest nor the youngest. All of them have crowded into the town square and above it all the flags of the eternal victory of the German people are flying at this hour of rest. . . .'

By 2.00 p.m. Hitler had rested long enough. The journey was resumed in the direction of the Austrian frontier—on to Braunau.

In the cipher department at the Chancellery in the early afternoon three telegrams for transmission landed on the desk of the cipher clerk, Karl Mauler. The new Austrian Foreign Minister was sending them to his colleagues in Germany, Italy and Hungary: Wolff expressed his delight at the co-operation between the friendly states.

On the outside of the Fatherland Front building in the Platz Am Hof there was already a brand-new sign which said: 'Führer's Office' and a portrait of Hitler. Inside Dr Albert Hantschk, the former administrative head of the Front, was attempting to carry out the final instructions given him by Zernatto, his ex-chief in exile. He was drafting circulars to the external branches of the Fatherland Front, so as to set in motion the winding up of the organization. Outside the door stood National Socialists, wearing swastika armbands, and SA stormtroopers. It had transpired that even within the Front building, the citadel of the regime, illegal Nazis had been active. Now in the great black office building, where he had worked daily as an official for several years, Hantschk felt like a prisoner.

Then several men came in at the door who were happy to relieve Hantschk of his chief worry, the Front's campaign fund, which Zernatto had handed over to him. The National Socialists took the millions of schillings without ceremony. All Hantschk's protests were of no avail. He appealed to Count Czernin, a

National Socialist: 'The cash and notes handed over to me in trust have been taken away.' Czernin: 'C'est la guerre.'

ᛉᚱᛉᚱᛉᚱᛉᚱᛉᚱ

In Braunau people had already been awaiting Adolf Hitler for hours. The news had quickly got round: 'The Führer is coming this afternoon.' For the little town on the Inn, directly on the Austro-German border, the visit had a particular significance: it was there that Hitler had been born forty-nine years before.

It was 3.50 p.m. when the officer commanding the Seventh Army Corps, General von Schobert, who had set up his headquarters in the Braunau *Zur Post* hotel, welcomed Hitler on the bridge. Then the car drove on to Austrian soil. The leader of the Braunau National Socialist Party thrust his way forward to the car: 'My Führer! The great honour has fallen to me to be the first to greet you on the soil of your homeland. The few hours of freedom we have enjoyed have made it impossible to prepare a reception appropriate to the historic significance of this moment. But you can be assured, my Führer, that nowhere in Germany do our hearts go out to you more joyfully than here in your homeland. My Führer, your homeland thanks you for the fact that you have made her free. Your homeland wishes you every conceivable blessing. Your homeland, my Führer, greets you with a threefold Sieg Heil!' Hitler replied: 'No power in the world will tear this country from me now.' The motorized caravan drove on until it reached the house at Number 15 Salzburger Vorstadt where Hitler had been born. It was now an inn. But the room on the first floor where Hitler was born was furnished as a memorial.

Hitler set off on his triumphal drive to Linz. The streets were crammed with Austrians and marching troops. Abandoned tanks and other vehicles lay along the roadsides. In the narrow streets of the towns heavy vehicles had torn the corners off the houses.

At 3.20 p.m. in Berlin Hitler's temporary deputy, Hermann Goering, was holding his third conversation that day with Prince Philip of Hessen in Rome. He was now able, as promised, to tell Hessen which passages should be deleted from Hitler's letter before publication. They were, in particular, the sentences which dealt with Czechoslovakia and which argued a threat to Germany from a rapprochement between Austria and Czechoslovakia. Goering had a copy of the letter in front of him, in which he had crossed out with his fountain pen the paragraphs and sentences not destined for publication.

Goering: 'So just tell the Duce, in short, that the Führer simply asks for this business with Czechoslovakia to be left out, because, as he will understand, . . . that could lead to something stupid.'

Hessen: 'Is that all, then?'

Goering: 'Yes, then that's all fine. I don't think the Duce himself would want it. It could be unpleasant for him as well. Tell the Duce we have been able to let the Czechs off very lightly. We have managed this with complete success; so far Czechoslovakia has declared itself completely reassured—there would only be fresh trouble.'

For this reason there must be no hitches.

Goering: 'That would only give France the opportunity to intervene.'

Hessen must 'cross out very heavily' the passages in the text. After this job was done Goering became the art-collector.

'Perhaps if you have time you could have a look and see if this Augusta, you know, if it has been brought out for me. . . .'

At 3.00 p.m. Colonel Georg von Majewski—a fifty-year-old engineer officer from the staff of the Eighth Army GHQ—called on Lieutenant-General Muff, the German Military Attaché in Vienna. Majewski had been sent by Bock, the Commander-in-Chief of the invasion army. He handed Muff a letter, calling upon him to make arrangements for the quartering of the Panzer Corps advancing into Austria under Lieutenant-General Guderian. Bock continued: 'I ask you also to make arrangements for a joint parade of the above, and perhaps other German troops, together with the Austrian garrison. Looking at it from here, it seems expedient to bring the leaders of the Austrian Army in on the preparations, while leaving no doubt, in the friendliest possible manner, that the will of the German High Command is decisive and must be carried out.'

There was a letter enclosed, which Muff and Majewski took to the Commander-in Chief of the Austrian Army, Schilhawsky. Bock had written to him:

Saturday, 12 March 1938

'Herr General! With our entry on to Austrian soil I have the honour to greet you as a former brother officer and to express my delight and my thanks to you for the comradely attitude which your troops have shown today to their German comrades. I hope very soon to have the opportunity to greet you in person. . . . In comradely affection, Heil Hitler! von Bock, General of Infantry.'

꿀꿀꿀꿀꿀꿀

In Linz, the capital of Upper Austria, tens of thousands of people had been waiting in the square in front of the Town Hall for an hour and a half. At 3.30 p.m. the local Nazi Party loudspeaker van had driven through the streets and announced: 'In half an hour the Führer, Adolf Hitler, will speak in the town square.' But there was no sign of Hitler. The Linz radio station on the Freinberg—it had been occupied by the SS on Friday evening—was told about Hitler's impending arrival. Captain Ziebland, a former illegal Nazi who ran a music and radio shop, had taken over the radio station.

But still Hitler did not come. At 5.07 p.m., therefore, a number of people made an appearance at the front of the Town Hall: the new Chancellor, Arthur Seyss-Inquart; Heinrich Himmler, the Reich Leader of the SS: Goering's brother-in-law, Franz Hueber, the Minister of Justice; Edmund Glaise von Horstenau, the Vice-Chancellor; State Secretary Wilhelm Keppler and other National Socialists. They had hurried over from Vienna by plane. They were called to Ziebland's microphone.

Hueber spoke first. A historic process was taking place, said the Minister, the shaping of the German nation into unity. His cabinet colleague, Glaise-Horstenau, found this to say:

'Never have I experienced such magic in this town as today, when the Führer of the German Reich and of the German people is once more, after so long, treading this soil. This soil, so well known to him from his youth and so dear to his heart.' And, addressing himself to the German troops present: 'We greet our German comrades as we greet their Supreme Commander, the Führer and Reich Chancellor!'

But Hitler still had not arrived, so Himmler had to spring into the breach for him:

194

'In the course of my life I have often been in this town and in earlier years I have often spoken here. But I have never dreamed that I should one day live to see this supreme day of celebration here in this town. I want to say to you all, in the name of all of us Germans from the Reich, who have the honour, the pride and the joy to be able to come here to Austria as your guests and friends, how happy and proud we are that this piece of German soil, which bore us our Führer, Adolf Hitler, has become free and is returning again, after centuries, to the great German homeland.' When the applause had died down Himmler concluded: 'And so will it be: one Führer, one people, one Reich!'

Only a few hundred yards away, at Numbers 6/10 Mozartstrasse, the Nazis were showing another side of their character. At the main Linz Police Station the Chief Inspector of Police suddenly heard a noise in the next room, which was the office of the Police President, Dr Viktor Bentz. He hurried next door and found the whole room full of SS, most of them men from Linz whom he knew. Their attitude was menacing, but Bentz was not intimidated. He reprimanded the intruders, who had already hurled themselves in blind rage at the Fatherland Front emblems hanging on the walls of the office. The Nazis withdrew. Another police official, Police Inspector Dr Ludwig Bernegger, had only avoided the Nazi storm-troop by taking the advice of friends and leaving his office earlier than usual. Apart from Bentz and Bernegger, two other police officials stood high on the Nazis' list for revenge. But the settling of accounts with these men, who during the past few years had watched and waged war on the activities of the illegal National Socialists, was still to come. While the people of Linz continued their long wait for Hitler in the main square, Police President Bentz drove out of the city to his summer residence at Schloss Haus. He believed he would be safe there for the time being. He was never to see the city again.

At the Berlin home of Baron von Neurath, acting Foreign Minister, words of reassurance were being spoken to the Czech Ambassador, Dr Mastny: the Austrian affair was simply a family matter between Germans. Czechoslovakia had no grounds for alarm. On the contrary, Germany wanted improved relations with her. Neurath repeated the assurance that the German troops would stop short at a distance of thirty kilometres from the Czech frontier. Schuschnigg had himself been responsible for the dramatic turn of events in Austria: he had been too confident of his own power. 'God deserted him. Otherwise what must happen now would not have been necessary,' said Neurath.

Mastny explained that he was glad to be able to discuss relations between the two countries with Neurath. 'We will never give Germany grounds for any kind of attack, but if such a thing should come about we know how to defend ourselves. We are not afraid. We have our allies and our friends and our outstanding Army.'

Before Neurath had left the Foreign Office for home he had signed a long letter to Nevile Henderson, the British Ambassador, in which the London protest of 11 March was characterized as inadmissible and the fact of the German ultimatum was flatly disputed:

'Monsieur L'Ambassadeur! In your letter of 11 March Your Excellency stated that news had reached the British Government that a German ultimatum had been delivered in Vienna. . . . In the name of the German Government I must state in reply that the British Government is not within its right in claiming the role of a protector of the independence of Austria . . . the German Government must from the outset reject as inadmissible the protest lodged by the British Government, even though only conditional. . . . there ensued a Cabinet crisis in Vienna, which in the course of the 11th of March led to the resignation of the former Federal Chancellor and the formation of a new Government. It is not true that forcible pressure on the course of these developments was exercised by the Reich. In particular the statement subsequently spread by the former Federal Chancellor to the effect that the German Government had delivered an ultimatum with a time-limit to the Federal President, in accordance with which he was to appoint as Federal Chancellor one of certain proposed candidates and construct the government in conformity with the proposals of the German Government, failing which the entry of German troops into Austria would have to be contemplated—is pure imagination. As a matter of fact the question of the dispatch of military and police forces from the Reich was first raised by the fact that the newly formed Austrian Government addressed to the Government of the Reich, in a telegram which has already been published in the press, an urgent request that, for the re-establishment of peace and order and for the prevention of bloodshed, German troops should be dispatched as soon as possible. . . .'

At 7.25 p.m. Prince Philip of Hessen telephoned Goering once again:

'I only wanted to report once more that I have been with the Duce once more this afternoon. I told him everything you instructed me to. He was enormously pleased with the greetings from the Führer and from yourself. . . . Then he said that he was in absolute agreement with the deletions. They were just what he envisaged. He had had the same reservations. I asked him to show me. It was exactly the same. The thing will be published this evening. He will read out the letter in the Assembly and will speak at the Grand Council about Italy's attitude, so as to have the country's approval in his dealings.'

Goering: 'Excellent.'

Hessen: 'Then England has again made an approach here. Again they wanted a statement of Italy's attitude to Austria. This was refused. . . .'

Goering: 'Splendid news. . . . I can only repeat to you that the Führer is really inexpressibly happy about the attitude down there . . .'

Hessen: '. . . Before I rang up I have just been with the King again, and I have reported it all to him, and he is very, very much in agreement with everything as well and sends his very best wishes . . .'

Goering: 'Well in Austria the rejoicing is unbelievable. We did not ourselves believe that the sympathy would be so great.'

Hessen: 'It is so massive.'

Goering: 'The people are howling and sobbing with joy . . . in fact they say it's so moving that our people are in tears themselves. . . . And as for this great Fatherland Front—they have crawled away into their mouseholes. All the Fatherland Front offices are already flying swastika flags today. And the joke is that most of them have put them up themselves because they were Nazis all the time.'

Hessen: 'The swastika flag is already flying on the Consulate and the Embassy here.'

Goering: 'Very good.'

Hessen: 'Then the King told me another interesting thing. Beck [The Polish Foreign Minister] told him that in one day just after the Berchtesgaden business 25,000 Jews from Vienna applied for passports to go abroad. People say it would be a good thing to open the frontiers for a bit so that the whole brood could get out.'

Goering: 'But not with their currency, otherwise we'll have them all slipping off abroad. The Jews can go but they must be so good as to leave their money behind: it was stolen in the first place.'

The conversation ended at 7.31 p.m.

General Guderian, who had been in Linz with units of the Second Panzer Division since noon that day, had taken over the closing of the roads in the Inner City. Austrian troops as well had been placed at his disposal. The crowd was still waiting. Loudspeaker vans drove round the square, throwing little swastika flags amongst the people. This caused scuffles as everyone wanted to have a victory souvenir. Soon the cheering could be heard in the distance, sweeping closer, like a tidal wave. In front of the Town Hall the new Mayor and the Provincial Governor had taken up position to welcome the Führer. Searchlights shone down from the Town Hall into the crowd. Slowly the column of cars made its way towards the gates. At 7.30 Hitler entered the Town Hall.

The honour of the Führer's visit to the capital of Upper Austria was already a source of envy. Graz, in particular, the 'capital of revolt', was unwilling that Linz should be the only town to be visited. The Nazi Provincial Governor of Styria sent the following message by telegram: 'To the Führer and Reich Chancellor Adolf Hitler, Linz an der Donau. Graz greets its beloved Führer in ancient loyalty and awaits him with a longing heart and asks for a visit from him. Sieg Heil! The Provincial Government of Styria.' The Mayor of Vienna, Major Lahr, also put in a word for himself. He and Karl Gratzenberger, the National Socialist promoted to Deputy Mayor, who had played a part in the surrender of the Town Hall the previous evening, telegraphed: 'In order to give visible expression to the eternal memory of this day and of the spirit which now inspires the city of Vienna, the new National Socialist leadership of the second largest German city has given the square in front of the gothic Town Hall the name of "Adolf-Hitler-Platz" . . . Heil Hitler! Lahr. Gratzenberger.'

Hitler appeared on the balcony of the Linz Town Hall. Beside and behind him were top Austrian and German Nazis. General Daluege, who was responsible for security measures, was never far from Hitler's side.

Federal Chancellor Seyss-Inquart gave his first speech as head of the Austrian Government:

'My Führer! At a moment of significance for the German people and, in its long-term effects, for the whole course of European history, I welcome you, and with me our whole homeland welcomes you back, my Führer and Reich Chancellor, for the first time to Austria.' Tumultuous applause. 'We Austrians have now declared our allegiance to this leadership, freely and openly, proudly and independently and for all time, while at the same time solemnly declaring that Article 88 of the peace treaty is null and void. The mighty forces of the Reich are moving into our land to the delight of Austria. Austria's soldiers are going out to greet regions of Germany, not as an act of defiance but in a clear and conclusive confirmation of the fact that the German nation in its entirety is standing by to safeguard German right before all the world and to defend it for all time! Our goal is the German-national Reich with order, peace and freedom of the peoples, and we are standing on the threshold of its opening up and Adolf Hitler is its Führer!'

Article 88 of the Treaty of St Germain, which Seyss-Inquart had declared to be null and void, laid down: 'The independence of Austria is inalterable, unless the Council of the League of Nations agrees that it shall be changed . . .'

Then Hitler spoke. It was the first speech he had made on Austrian soil as the German Reich Chancellor:

'Germans! Fellow Germans! Herr Chancellor, I thank you for your words of welcome. But above all I thank all of you who have come here today to bear witness to the fact that it is not merely the will and the desire of a few people to found this great German-National Reich: it is the desire and the will of the whole German nation! Let us also hope that some of our well-known international truth seekers are not only here tonight to see the reality, but will also admit it later on. When I once set forth from this city I carried within myself the same faith that fills me today. After the many years during which I have clung to this faith, you can judge my feelings now that I have brought it to fulfilment.'

Already every sentence had been punctuated with cries of 'Sieg Heil!' and cheering, but now the roaring crowd prevented Hitler from speaking for several minutes. Then Hitler went on:

'If it was Providence that once called me forth from this city to the leadership of the Reich, then it must also have given me the mission—and it can only have been a mission—to restore my homeland to the German Reich!'

Once again the cheering interrupted Hitler's speech.

'I have believed in this mission. I have lived for it and fought for it. And I believe that now I have fulfilled it! Every one of you bears witness and stands surety for this! On what day you will be called I do not know. I hope it will not be long delayed. For on that day you must stand up and be counted. And I am confident that before the whole German nation I will be able to point with pride to my own Homeland.'

'Yes, yes, yes' came the shouts from the main square for several minutes.

'This result must show the world that any future attempt to tear this nation apart will be a vain one. And just as it will then be your duty to make your contribution to this German future, so all Germany is ready to make her contribution and she is already making it, this very day. You must look on the German soldiers, who are marching into Austria at this time, from every district in the Reich, as fighting men who are ready and willing to sacrifice themselves for the unity of the whole great German nation, for the might of the Reich, for its greatness and its majesty, now and for evermore! Germany, Sieg Heil!'

When the cheering had subsided the crowd sang the German anthem and the *Horst Wessel* song.

Following this welcome, Hitler drove to the Hotel Weinzinger at Number 1, Zollamtstrasse: the former Erzherzog Karl Inn stood at the corner of the square, right on the bank of the Danube. For the next hours and days this hotel was to be the command headquarters of the German Reich.

🔲🔲🔲🔲🔲🔲🔲

That evening Wels became the seat of the GHQ of the Eighth Army. The transfer along the 125 kilometres of road from Mühldorf had begun in the late afternoon. The Commander of the Army, General von Bock, had gone on ahead to have a look at the advance of units of the Seventh Division through the difficult and mountainous Hausruck district. Bock was dissatisfied. The chaos on the approach roads was increasing.

At 7.30 p.m. the reconnaissance troop of the Seventh Reconnaissance Battalion crossed the city boundary of Vienna. An endless column of private cars had tagged on behind and now stretched back almost as far as the eye could see. Before them lay the city of over a million. To the young man in the black uniform with the death's heads on his lapels it was an unknown city. At the roadsides the people stood and shouted; 'One people, one Reich, one Führer!'

🔲🔲🔲🔲🔲🔲🔲

Since 7.00 p.m. endless columns of people had been marching through the streets of Vienna. For hours the radio had been repeating statements calling upon people to take part in demonstrations that evening. Along the Ringstrasse streamed a torchlight procession. It was directed by the new organizational head of the Viennese Party. In the Schwarzenbergplatz the members of the new government who were not with Hitler in Linz took the salute from the march past of the torch-bearers. German soldiers who had come to Vienna by train as a billet party were carried on the shoulders of the cheering crowd. Torchlight processions demonstrating Nazi enthusiasm were under way all over Austria.

🔲🔲🔲🔲🔲🔲🔲

At about midnight the advance command of the Eighth Army reached Vienna. The picture of the situation which presented itself to General von Bock, the Commander-in-Chief, at the end of the first day of the invasion was as follows: the Tenth Army Depot had established their headquarters at Innsbruck, the Seventh Army Corps at Ried, the Thirteenth Corps at Schaerding. The reinforced Ninety-Eighth Mountain Rifle Regiment had reached Innsbruck; the reinforced Sixty-First Infantry Regiment, Wörgel; the SS-Standarte *Deutschland*, Kufstein; the Fourteenth Infantry Regiment, Bregenz. The Mountain Rifle Brigade was between Strasswalchen and Salzburg, the SS-Standarte *Germania* at Salzburg; the Seventh Division was between Ried and Braunau. The Twenty-Seventh Division had boarded transport at their peace-time garrisons to go to Vienna, as had the Seventeenth Division. The Tenth Division was in the region of Grieskirchen; the SS-Standarte *Adolf Hitler* to the west of Linz; the *General Goering* Regiment was scattered between Straubing and St Polten. The German police had been more sucessful in reaching their objectives: they were now present in almost all the provinces of Austria.

SUNDAY, 13 MARCH 1938

That Sunday morning the sun rose at 6.19 a.m. over Vienna. The day was dawning on which Schuschnigg had planned celebrate his great victory at the polls. As trains and planes arrived, a stream of Party and State officials from the German Reich poured out of them. Everyone wanted to be in Vienna as quickly as possible.

At about nine o'clock four thousand children assembled at the Westbahnhof. Boys and girls with flags and pennants. Many of them still wore the uniform of the *Jungvolk*, the Fatherland Front's youth organization. But they all wore swastikas—either pin-on badges or armbands. Not all of them were Viennese. Reinforcements had come in from several of the provinces. On Friday they had still been under the command of Count Thurn-Valsassina, the leader of the *Jungvolk*. The Count had resigned. Now an excited young man named Schoas was rushing round giving out orders. The young people called him *Bannführer*.

The children were waiting for a member of Hitler's cabinet, Baldur von Schirach, the thirty-one-year-old Reich Youth Leader. He arrived on the 9.40 train. Schirach had learned about the events in Austria when making a tour of inspection of the Youth Leadership Academy in Brunswick. He had returned to Berlin at once. But there he had learned that there was no possibility of getting a plane to Vienna. All the available planes had already been taken. So Schirach had caught the night express to go and organize the Austrian youth.

At the Vienna Westbahnhof the children and adolescents shouted 'Heil!' Schirach made a speech:

'Over long years you have proven your loyalty to Germany and have held fast to National Socialism. When times were hard you still had faith in the Führer and in Germany—and we in you! Youth of German-Austria! I bring you the greetings of seven million boys and girls who owe their allegiance to Adolf Hitler. Through me they send you word of their happiness and joy at your joy and courage ... This is the most wonderful day in our lives because we can again stand face to face. Now, too, we can march all shoulder to shoulder behind the same flag and feel the undying pulse of our great community ...'

Sunday, 13 March 1938

Then the boys and girls shouted out loud and long: 'Sieg Heil!'

卐卐卐卐卐卐卐

At the Austrian President's home, at Number 15 Hainburger-strasse, the situation had not altered. Lieutenant Birsak still occupied the house with his Guards and the National Socialist sentries were still standing out in the street. Early that morning Miklas had driven to the Rochuskirche, as he did every Sunday, then to the Chancellery. Miklas had come only grudgingly at the government's request. For him Sunday was a holy day. But the government, which he had sworn in only the day before, was to be reshuffled and augmented. In place of State Secretary Skubl, who had tendered his resignation—Seyss-Inquart had received it in writing that morning—the Austrian head of the SS, Kalten-brunner, was to be put in charge of Security. Further additions to the government were: Major Hubert Klausner as Minister for Political Education, Ministerial Secretary Dr Friedrich Wimmer as State Secretary at the Chancellery and Colonel Maximilian de Angelis as State Secretary at the Ministry of Defence. With these men the cabinet had gained a marked preponderance of Nazis.

Miklas, who could no longer exercise any influence over the situation, appointed the Ministers proposed by Seyss and swore them in. Then he drove home again. For the rest of the day he hoped to be left in peace.

卐卐卐卐卐卐卐

Nobody was allowed to see Schuschnigg, the ex-Chancellor, with the exception of his secretary, who was given special leave by the State Police to bring him various personal items from the Chancellery. The secretary also brought news: Schuschnigg's departure abroad was being considered; Seyss had promised cars and financial help. Now he had resigned Schuschnigg had no source of income. The only material security he had for his future was a promise given him in 1934 that after leaving office he would receive the usual pension and would be appointed head of one of the Supreme Courts. The fulfilment of this promise now seemed unlikely.

The secretary also told him that several embassies would

offer him asylum and protection. The offer seemed frankly hypothetical. Although the Chancellery guards were still at their posts in the garden Schuschnigg could no longer leave the house if the Nazis did not wish him to.

In Berlin Reich Field Marshal Goering considered the time had come to inform Ribbentrop about the situation. At 9.15 a.m. he telephoned the Foreign Minister in London, where he had had long since finished making his calls on the British Government. Goering assumed that his call to England would be overheard and therefore told the Foreign Minister that all the reports about a German ultimatum to Austria were lies. The ultimatum had been delivered by the National Socialist Ministers, Seyss-Inquart, Glaise-Horstenau and Jury. It was only at the request of Seyss-Inquart that the German Military Attaché had gone with them when the ultimatum was delivered to Miklas.

Goering also told how Seyss-Inquart had sent a request to Berlin for German troops. After a long monologue by the Field Marshal, Ribbentrop asked: 'Tell me, Herr Goering, how exactly are things in Vienna, is it all clear now?'

Goering: 'Yes. Yesterday hundreds of my planes landed with some companies to secure the airfield, and they were received with enthusiasm. . . . Furthermore I should like to tell you that the Austrian troops have not withdrawn: everywhere—in the field and in their garrisons—they have at once fraternized with the German troops.'

When Ribbentrop expressed a wish to go to Vienna himself Goering said:

'I am in Berlin today. I am here for Heroes' Day but I want to say straight away that you must first stay in Berlin for a bit. I have had specific orders from the Führer that every Minister must remain here, you know, otherwise we should end up with a migration on our hands. Yesterday there were no Ministers or civil servants at home. I could have used a thousand planes. Naturally they all want to take part in this joyful celebration. So I have to be draconian and hold the gentlemen back.'

꿢꿢꿢꿢꿢

Since the early hours of the morning enthusiastic citizens of Linz had been standing in front of the Hotel Weinzinger, hoping to see

Hitler. They blocked the route of the trams coming across the bridge from the Urfahr district. In the hall of the hotel leading Party figures, men from Hitler's entourage and senior officers were standing together. The German seat of government, having moved to Linz, was operating on an improvised basis.

The situation kept changing all the time. There had already been five drafts for a law establishing an Austro-German Federation, all of them having been overtaken by events. The plan for a union embodied in the office of one supreme head of state had been abandoned. Instead, a complete *Anschluss* was envisaged. The previous afternoon, in his speech from the balcony of Linz Town Hall, Hitler had indicated that first a plebiscite must take place and that further developments could then follow. But the enthusiasm in Linz and the other cities in Austria made him change his mind. He now wanted to go the whole hog. Already that morning when Dr Dietrich had put before him the press folder containing extracts from foreign newspapers, Hitler's comment had been: 'If they are already rebuking me for something I have not done, then I might as well do it.'

Now, late in the morning, Hitler told State Secretary Keppler in Vienna about the new situation: he must sound out the feelings of the Austrian government on the subject of an immediate *Anschluss*. The political situation abroad was favourable. Ribbentrop had reported from London that a calm view of the situation was taken there: they would agree to any development by legal means.

Shortly before noon one of the Führer's orderlies brought the text of a telegram into the hotel room of the Press Chief, Dr Dietrich. The text: 'To His Excellency, the Italian Prime Minister and Duce of Fascist Italy, Benito Mussolini. Mussolini, I will never forget you for this. Adolf Hitler.' When the telegram reached him in Rome Mussolini remarked to Ciano, the Foreign Minister, who was standing beside him: 'Maledetto tedesco!' There was nothing left for Rome to do but to grin and bear it. The same view was also expressed in a report on the session of the Fascist Grand Council. The events in Austria, it said, were regarded as 'the product of an existing situation, and as a clear expression of the feelings and will of the Austrian people.'

At midday Hitler went to Leonding to visit his parents' grave. Meanwhile in the small dining-room at the Hotel Weinzinger Josef Bürckel, the Gauleiter of the Saar-Palatinate district, met the Reich Press Chief's chief-of-staff, Helmut Sündermann.

Bürckel showed the young man a sheet of paper, not yet folded, which bore Hitler's signature. Sündermann read: '1. I entrust Gauleiter Bürckel, Saar-Palatinate, with the task of reorganizing the National Socialist Party in Austria. 2. In this capacity Gauleiter Bürckel is charged, as provisional head of the National Socialist Party in Austria, with the preparation of the plebiscite. 3. Gauleiter Bürckel is fully empowered by me to take or to order to be taken all measures which are necessary for the proper fulfilment of the mission entrusted to him.' The victor of the Saar plebiscite now had the job of ensuring that a large percentage voted 'Yes' in Austria. He wanted to get his propaganda drive started as quickly as possible.

Shortly before 3.00 p.m. the first German unit arrived in Vienna by rail.

In the former Fatherland Front building in the Platz Am Hof the leadership of the Austrian Nazi Party was being reorganized. New jobs and titles were being allocated. The former Racial-Political Councils were dissolved. The former Councillors were given the task of 'organizing reparations for the damages suffered by the National Socialists.'

At Vienna's grandiose Imperial Hotel the Reich Youth Leader, Baldur von Schirach, was holding a meeting. He founded the 'Hitler Youth Super-Region of Austria'. The Nazi 'German Students Union of Austria' took over leadership of Austrian academic youth. The churches, too, swam with the new tide. The Protestants had already addressed declarations of allegiance to the Nazi leadership the previous day. Now the Catholic Church came into line. Because of the all-too-close association of Church and State during the past few years, the head of the Catholic Church in Vienna, Cardinal Innitzer, was bound to be apprehensive now that he would be held responsible for a good deal. He still found incomprehensible the failure of Schuschnigg's Austria—conceived as a Catholic state and governed more in accordance with the maxims of the Pope's Social Encyclical than with political principles—to weather the storm. In order to save his Church the Cardinal had a declaration inserted in the *Reichspost*: 'The Catholics of the Archdiocese of Vienna are called upon to thank God in their prayers on Sunday for the bloodless course taken by the great political upheaval and to pray for a happy

Sunday, 13 March 1938

future for Austria. Naturally all instructions issued by the
authorities must be readily and willingly complied with.' The
paper added the following commentary:

'In the love of our nation we see the best possible service we
can give to the Creator. We render gladly to our nation what is
our nation's and faithfully unto God that which is God's. The
supreme prince of the Church in our country has given his
blessing to the long-awaited hour of German unification. So
let us now fix our eyes upon the Führer and say: Shoulder to
shoulder we Germans of Austria are today entering the
German community of destiny.'

Otto of Habsburg had arrived in Paris the previous day. Until
Saturday morning he had been attempting to make telephone
contact with his friends in Austria from Steenockerzeel. Then
the lines had been cut. Now he was trying to persuade the Austrian
Embassy in Paris and the missions in other European capitals not
to recognize the demise of Austria. They should preserve their
independence. But his proposals met with no success. He was
therefore pressing on with a second undertaking: together with
the Press Attaché at the Austrian Embassy he was founding a
reception organization for refugees from Austria. As its temporary
headquarters they chose the Austrian Consulate-General, the
head of which was a Frenchman, who was ignoring instructions
from Vienna.

In Vienna Theodor Hornbostel was collected from his home by
SS men in uniform. In the van that carried him there were
already two other prisoners, Eduard Ludwig, the President of the
Press Chamber and Walter Adam, Schuschnigg's press chief.
Hornbostel, Ludwig and Adam were taken to a house in the
Konkordiaplatz. Here the Eighty-Ninth SS Standarte had
established their headquarters.

At the Vienna Town Hall police arrived to take away Richard
Schmitz, the Mayor, who had so far been under house arrest.
'Remain good Austrians', Schmitz said, taking his leave of his
family. Schmitz was taken by taxi to the police gaol in the
Rossauer Lände.

Ex-State Secretary Dr Michael Skubl went to the police head-quarters to collect his personal belongings. There he learned that the head of the state police, Ludwig Weiser, had been arrested. Skubl rang up Seyss-Inquart. But the latter gave an evasive answer. It was Skubl's turn next. When he got back home the SS guards were lining up outside. The ex-State Secretary was under house arrest.

Thousands of people strayed from hiding place to hiding place, were on the run, or remained at home as if hypnotized, waiting for the knock at the door. Funder, the publisher of the *Reichspost*, drove with his family to Carinthia. The Nazis remained on his trail and caught him. Albert Hantschk, the Fatherland Front official, took up lodgings with friends. The Youth Secretary of the Revolutionary Socialists, Manfred Ackermann, was taken in by Muriel (Mary) Gardiner at her home in the Lammgasse.

Towards midday Wilhelm Stuckart, from the Berlin Ministry of the Interior, and Karl Clodius, from the Berlin Foreign Office, had arrived in Vienna from Linz by plane. They discussed the draft law with the German State Secretary, Keppler, and the Austrian State Secretary, Dr Wimmer. Their job was to translate into legal phraseology Hitler's demand for an immediate *Anschluss*. Then all of them, except Clodius, went to see Seyss-Inquart at the Chancellery. After about an hour Clodius was summoned as well: for in the drafting of the German law the question had arisen of whether and in what circumstances Austrian trade and financial agreements as well as Austria's foreign loan arrange-ments were to be honoured. In Article 2 of the law there was a provision that the rights and obligations derived from agreements made by Austria should continue to be valid. Clodius declared himself opposed to this. As Keppler agreed with him, the offending passage was deleted.

Seyss-Inquart had called a cabinet meeting for the early after-noon in the Cabinet Room at the Chancellery. There was only one item on the agenda: the passing of the *Anschluss* law. But at three o'clock the circle was still not quite complete. Seyss-Inquart told the Ministers that Stuckart had informed him of Hitler's wish that the law should be passed as quickly as possible. The 'great moment of the *Anschluss*' had arrived. As he took it that all agreed, or were forced to agree, he did not even read out the text of the 'Law about the reunification of Austria with the German Reich.' No note of those present was made and no minutes were taken. Seyss-Inquart merely noted: carried unanimously. According to the constitution of 1934 the cabinet was empowered to amend the constitution in this way. However, it still required the counter-signature of the Federal President.

Thus, at this moment, Seyss-Inquart could only give the waiting Keppler an interim decision. He added that he had asked the former Foreign Minister, Dr Guido Schmidt, to sound out Miklas on the subject of putting his signature to the law or some other constitutional settlement. Schmidt was already at the Hainburgerstrasse. He had begun by explaining to the President that he had come as a private individual to say good-bye. He was planning to go to Germany. But then he came to the real reason for his visit: the government had passed a law uniting Austria with the Reich. Now they needed the Federal President's signature. What Schmidt thought about this he did not say.

When the ex-Minister had left the Hainburgerstrasse, Seyss-Inquart appeared in his turn with two of his Ministers, Menghin and Wolff. Miklas received the trio in the conference room next to the lower hall. Seyss-Inquart could not even show Miklas a final text of the law: all he had was a draft. The President refused to sign. Not only for political, but also for constitutional reasons, as he said. First of all he was unable at that moment to verify whether the law had been passed in a manner that conformed with the constitution. Furthermore he was of the opinion that in such a case there must first be a plebiscite. But then he gave in. He did not know whether this development would be to the benefit of the Austrian people, but he did not wish to stand in its way and would therefore resign.

At the desk in front of the fireplace President Miklas and Chancellor Seyss-Inquart each prepared written documents, which they then exchanged. They comprised the resignation procedure. Wolff and Menghin stood by. Miklas wrote by hand on a double sheet of paper:

'Herr Chancellor, in reply to your letter of the 13th inst. I ask you to take note that as from today I resign from my functions as Federal President and hereby transfer them to the Federal Chancellor, in accordance with Article 77, Clause 1, of the Constitution of 1934. I have reached this decision because of pressing circumstances in the situation of the Federal Republic of Austria which appear to make it urgently necessary for all the supreme functions to be concentrated into the Federal Chancellor's hands. May the Austrian people, to whom, until I draw my last breath, all my senses, my aspirations and my heart belong, with God's help enjoy a happier future. Miklas.'

Then the ex-President said good-bye to Seyss-Inquart, who now combined in his person the offices of Chancellor and President—but only in order to renounce both offices immediately, and with them the independence of Austria. Miklas's parting words to Seyss expressed a pious plea: 'Protect my Austria!' Then the ex-President went back upstairs to his family and said: 'Thank God, I am a private citizen at last.'

When Seyss-Inquart entered the room at the Chancellery where Keppler, Stuckart and Clodius were waiting, he had Miklas's resignation document in his hand. He showed it to Keppler, remarking that it had passed off 'easily and smoothly'. Once again the members of the cabinet who were present came together 'in order to approve individual additions caused by the altered situation' and in order to authenticate the law. Seyss-Inquart, Glaise-Horstenau, Wolff, Hueber, Menghin, Neumayer, Reinthaller and Fischböck signed a supplementary clause that the law had been passed in accordance with the constitution. Meanwhile Keppler was informing Hitler by telephone. The Reich Chancellor told Keppler to come to Linz with Seyss-Inquart the same day.

Hermann Goering, who had remained in Berlin as Hitler's deputy, knew nothing until this moment about the way the political situation had developed. Nobody had informed him about the *Anschluss* law. Since Saturday he had been following the enthusiasm of the Austrians over the radio. Then the realization had come to him, independently of Hitler, that the moment had arrived for a complete *Anschluss*. He sent a message to Milch, his deputy, in Vienna. Milch was to fly to see Hitler in Linz immediately and draw his attention to the possibility of an *Anschluss*. At 5.09 p.m. Milch landed at Linz. His conversation with Hitler and been brief. Hitler had treated the suggestion as self-evident and then said to Milch: 'Give Goering my warmest greetings and tell him I am glad about his proposal.'

At the Weinzinger Hitler gave an interview to Ward Price of

the *Daily Mail*. He assured him 'in all sincerity' that four days before he had had 'no idea at all that I should be here today, or that Austria would have been embodied, as she is from tonight, with the rest of Germany on exactly the same basis as Bavaria or Saxony.' He spoke of Schuschnigg's 'betrayal' as something which he could not tolerate. 'I am a realist. Look at my relations with Poland. I am entirely ready to admit that Poland . . . needs an outlet to the sea. It is a bitter thing to us that this has to be obtained at the expense of a corridor through German territory, but we realize what it means for the Poles.' Price asked Hitler about his attitude towards the Anglo-French note of protest. Hitler: 'I cannot understand it. These people here are German.'

At 7.30 p.m. a press conference for the foreign correspondents was held at the Chancellery in Vienna. The government spokes-man was a gentleman with a monocle who twenty-four hours previously had been working in Berlin: this was Lazar, the Press Attaché from the Austrian Embassy. First he announced the President's resignation. Then he asked the correspondents to be patient for a few minutes. At 8.00 p.m. he would have an important announcement to give them. Then, he read out the 'Federal Constitutional Law about the reunification of the German Reich'. It consisted of five articles:

'Article 1: Austria is a province of the German Reich. Article 2: A free and secret plebiscite will take place on Sunday 10 April 1938 to ratify the reunification with the German Reich. Article 3: The result of the plebiscite be decided by the majority of votes cast. Article 4: The necessary preparations for the execution and completion of this Federal Constitu-tional Law will be made by ordinance. Article 5: (1) This Federal Constitutional Law takes effect on the day of its proclamation. (2) The Federal Government is charged with executing this Federal Constitutional Law.'

The press in Berlin were also told. At 8.00 p.m. a speaker read out the text of the Austrian *Anschluss* law. Then the text of the corresponding German law was announced:

'Article 1. The Federal Constitutional Law passed by the Austrian Federal Government concerning the reunification of Austria with the German Reich on 13 March 1938 hereby becomes a law of the German Reich . . .'

Under Article 2 it was specified that:

'The body of law at present existing in Austria will remain in
force until further notice. The introduction of the law of the
Reich into Austria will be effected by the Führer and Reich
Chancellor or by the Minister of the Reich empowered by him
to do so. Article 3: The Reich Minister of the Interior is
empowered to issue the legal and administrative regulations
necessary for the execution and completion of this Law, in
consultation with the appropriate Ministers of the Reich.
Article 4: The Law takes effect on the day of the proclamation.
Linz, 13 March 1938. The Führer and Reich Chancellor, the
Reich Minister of the Interior, the Reich Minister of External
Affairs, the Deputy Führer.'

The Austrian Ambassador in Berlin, Tauschitz, was told on
the telephone about the *Anschluss* by the head of the German
Department in the Vienna Foreign Office. Tauschitz was also
requested to bring the Embassy under the authority of the
German Foreign Office. After this conversation Tauschitz had
informed Prince Bismarck of the Berlin Foreign Office. And it was
from Bismarck that Ribbentrop, the Foreign Minister, learned
the news only a few hours after his return from London. Ribbentrop was with Goering at the Villa Karinhall: they had been
astonished and checked back with Tauschitz. But the Austrian
Ambassador had confirmed the news.

By 9.00 p.m. everyone knew. The Austrian radio announced
the *Anschluss*, which was now an accomplished fact. The GHQ of
the invasion army heard the news at Wels. In Vienna loudspeakers
in the streets broadcast the news. There were demonstrations in
the streets: the cry of the demonstrators was: 'One people, one
Reich, one Führer!'

The powers pledged to defend Austria—Britain, France and
Italy—had reconciled themselves to a situation which they
believed to be irrevocable. Britain had only sent paper protests to
Berlin and the French had followed suit once they had realized
that in taking any military counter-measures they would have
been left on their own. Now both countries had only one thing in
mind: to safeguard the integrity of Czechoslovakia. If Hitler
were to lay a finger on this country then they would go to war. The

213

Sunday, 13 March 1938

British Foreign Secretary, Lord Halifax, informed Nevile Henderson that Czechoslovakia had passed on to London all the assurances that Goering had given to Mastny, the Czech Ambassador in Berlin, in the course of the past forty-eight hours. Goering's word of honour was, as it were, being deposited in the political Bank of England. Henderson was instructed: 'You should inform the German Government that these undertakings have been communicated to us by the Czechoslovak Government and that His Majesty's Government are glad to take note of these repeated and solemn assurances.'

In Rome Mussolini and Ciano received a large number of anonymous letters strongly criticizing Italy's conduct over the Austrian situation. But Ciano noted in his diary: 'Destiny has fulfilled itself. It is certainly no pleasure for us. But one day the world will understand that it was all inevitable. The Duce says that one ambiguity has been removed from the map of Europe. And he listed three others that still remain and that must be resolved in the same way and in the following order: Czechoslovakia, Switzerland and Belgium.'

Reich Field Marshal Goering's assessment of the political situation abroad had proved correct. In a telephone conversation on Sunday evening with General Bodenschatz, his adjutant, who was with Hitler in Linz, the theme he kept returning to was that of England's temporising role in the Austrian coup. When Bodenschatz quoted a remark of Hitler's—'The British Ambassador in Austria tried to back up Schuschnigg till the very last'—Goering interrupted:

'Hullo, tell the Führer that reports have come in, brown reports, that are all quite clear because they were intercepted. From them it is absolutely certain that the action only failed because England declined.' Bodenschatz: 'Very good, because England declined.'

Goering: 'So, the Führer will receive this tomorrow morning. This was the situation: the French were certainly intending to embark on an action without any reservations and the English have therefore come under heavy fire from them. I can show you all the decoded dispatches. And it was only because England backed out that the action was called off.'

Bodenschatz: 'Very good, the action was called off.'

Goering went on: 'The situation now is that the great powers —that France is telling its ambassadors in the various countries that it can do nothing because England has failed and above all because England simply refused.'

Again Bodenschatz echoed from Linz: 'England simply refused to make any move at all . . .'

Then Goering again: '. . . to support Schuschnigg in his resistance. If the Ambassador in Vienna did this . . .

Bodenschatz finished the sentence: '. . . then it was off his own bat.'

Goering: 'Then he was doing it off his own bat. I must say in the interests of fairness—and the Führer will have the evidence of this by tomorrow morning—that England did not encourage him to resist, but clearly refused to give any guarantee.'

Bodenschatz: 'Very good, I will tell him that.'

Goering did not want to disturb Hitler, who had just finished his dinner at the Hotel Weinzinger, with his political insights.

Bodenschatz: '. . . he is going up now. I can put a call through to you, Herr Field Marshal.'

Goering: 'Then it had better be later, the best thing would be before he goes to bed.'

Bodenschatz: 'How much longer will you be up, sir?'

Goering: 'Two or three hours more.'

Bodenschatz: 'He is just going up to his room now.'

Goering: 'Yes. Perhaps he can do it later.'

Bodenschatz: 'There is radiant enthusiasm everywhere, Herr Field Marshal. No one has ever experienced anything like it.'

Goering (who would have liked to be in Linz, but was not allowed to come): 'Yes, I'm sure. I can believe it all. Well, auf Wiedersehen!'

Bodenschatz: 'Heil Hitler, Herr Field Marshal.'

During the course of the evening Franz von Papen, the former German Envoy in Vienna, received a telegram from Hitler at his Berlin home. He was required in the Austrian capital on Monday. At the same time the radio gave a Party announcement: 'The Führer has received Minister Franz von Papen into the National Socialist German Workers' Party in appreciation of his valuable services and has awarded him the Gold Medal.'

Sunday, 13 March 1938

The German Legation in the Metternichgasse in Vienna, for years Papen's centre of operations, had become entangled, thanks to Lieutenant-General Muff, the Military Attaché, in the events of the last days. What role had been played by the young men from the foreign organization of the Nazi Party, who had been put up in rooms at the Legation some time previously, remained obscure. But while Papen in Berlin—infected with the general *Anschluss* fever—was preparing for his flight the next day, Wilhelm von Ketteler, one of his closest collaborators at the Vienna Legation, disappeared for good. He had spent the evening with Fräulein Rose, Papen's secretary who lived near the Legation. When he left the house late that evening she saw him walking down the fairly dark street to the Embassy. Some way behind him three men were following him. . . .

Ketteler was hated by the Nazis. An old associate of Papen's, he had had to go into hiding temporarily at the time of the Roehm Putsch on 30 June 1934. After the Berchtesgaden agreement in February 1938 Ketteler, foreseeing the outcome, had taken a number of important papers from the Legation to Switzerland in a box. This fact, and the current rumours that he had intended to shoot Hitler when a suitable opportunity occurred, had written his death warrant.

꒱꒱꒱꒱꒱

Shortly before midnight Seyss-Inquart arrived in Linz—together with Keppler and Wimmer, as well as the author of the *Anschluss* Law, State Secretary Stuckart—in order to report officially to Hitler the 'passing of the Reunification Law'. They sat together at the Hotel Weinzinger. After Seyss had made his report Hitler was silent for a long time. Finally he said that he was happy to have brought his homeland into the Reich without bloodshed. Seyss-Inquart asked whether the Austrian Party might retain 'a relative independence . . . under an Austrian leader.' Hitler, who had at noon that day already given Bürckel the job of running the Party, replied evasively: 'Possibly'. Then Seyss-Inquart asked that Austria, too, should be granted 'a degree of independence, as an administrative province'. Hitler replied that Austria would indeed have its own governor appointed. Then the Chancellor of forty hours' standing rose to his feet and solemnly asked his Führer if he might be allowed 'to return to my private profession as a lawyer'. Hitler deferred making a decision on this. Now Seyss raised a point of detail: the 'incorrect exchange rate of two schillings to the mark.' The Reich Chancellor agreed to a more favourable rate. Then he signed the German pendant to the Austrian *Anschluss* Law, which Stuckart and Keppler had brought. With this act Austria ceased to exist as an independent state.

Three hours previously, at about 9.00 p.m. the Commander-in-Chief of the Eighth Army, General von Bock, had arrived in Vienna. In the late afternoon he had again discussed with Hitler in Linz the question of the final troop dispositions. Hitler had ordered a parade for Tuesday, 15 March, which Bock was to arrange.

The actual HQ of the Eighth Army had remained in Wels with Major-General Ruoff. Bock believed he could absent himself from his HQ without risk and there was no longer any expectation of fighting taking place. The tactical task of the officers consisted now only in directing the advancing troops. For Bock the position that evening was as follows: once again the day's objectives had not been achieved. Half the Panzer Corps was in Vienna, units of the Seventeenth and Twenty-Seventh Divisions which were brought into Austria by train had been unloaded in Linz and Vienna.

Shortly before midnight General von Bock was officially given the news of the political events of the day. From the Linz headquarters the Führer and Supreme Commander of the Armed Forces sent him the following directive:

'1 The Austrian Federal Government has just effected by law the reunification of Austria with the German Reich. The Government of the German Reich has recognized this decree by means of a law passed today.
2 On the basis of this I now ordain that the Austrian Army today comes under my command as a part of the German Armed Forces.
3 I invest General von Bock, Commander-in-Chief of the Eighth Army, with the command of the present German Army within the Austrian frontiers.
4 All members of the former Austrian Army are to take the oath of allegiance to me as their Supreme Commander imimediately. General von Bock will issue the necessary instruc-

tions at once. Note: Officers who do not consider they can take the oath are to be discharged immediately. Signed Adolf Hitler.'

The Schuschnigg regime, which three days previously had determined the whole life and outlook of the country, seemed forgotten. At this hour the tidings of victory in the Fatherland Front plebiscite should have been pouring into Vienna. Schuschnigg and his supporters had reckoned on an overwhelming success. But everything had changed overnight. 'Heil Schuschnigg' had given way to 'Heil Hitler'. Only one municipality remained true to the old regime—not out of obstinacy but from ignorance of recent events. In the commune of Innervillgraten in the jurisdiction of Lienz in the East Tyrol, which had been cut off from the outside world by very heavy snow, all of the 817 inhabitants entitled to vote had been to the ballot that Sunday to vote 'for a free and German, independent and social, for a Christian and united Austria'. The result was a 95 per cent vote for Schuschnigg.

MONDAY, 14 MARCH 1938

That morning the Vienna *Montagsblatt* published a declaration to the effect that it was now 'totally cleansed of Jews'. The Aryans of the *Montagsblatt* also proclaimed 'their dearest wish'. It was as follows: 'That the Führer should become aware of the bonds of the homeland that bind him to us and that these feelings may cause him to decide to take up residence on Austrian soil as often as possible in the future and to conduct the business of the Reich from Vienna during a part of each year. We salute the founder of the Greater German Reich.' All the newspapers published the *Anschluss* law, and under it the names of Hitler, Frick, Ribbentrop and Hess appeared. Then, when the papers were already on sale, the editorial offices were told that on 15 March Goering be added as co-signatory. At the larger post offices in the city all letters were stamped with a special postmark that bore the words: 'The Führer in Vienna'.

At nine o'clock that morning a civil servant of the Austrian Foreign Office was refused admission to the Chancellery. Another member of the Foreign Office staff, who had also fallen out of favour, received a telephone message from Dr Wolff, the Foreign Minister, telling him it would be better for him not to come in to the office any more. But most of the officials of the previous government were now serving the new regime. Although Austria's rulers were so busy with greetings and demonstrations of enthusiasm, they still found time to get down to business. A decree appeared in the name of the Minister of Justice which removed from office 'all judges and public prosecutors who are Jews or half-Jews'. With equally lapidary brevity the 'admission of Jews or half-Jews into the legal profession' was banned. That morning the first Austrian court, in Graz, passed a sentence 'in the name of the German people'. In Vienna the Austrian government passed a law to stop the flight of capital. The Minister of Finance ordered a limit on withdrawals of a thousand schillings per week. People leaving the country were not allowed to take more than fifty schillings with them. The Stock Exchange and the schools remained closed until further notice.

At nine o'clock in the ceremonial hall of the Lower Austrian Provincial Government in Vienna the officials were sworn in, as they were at all other offices.

Meanwhile the Nazi leaders were becoming worried about the

countless acts of wild looting that had taken place during the last few days. There was an official announcement: 'It appears that individual departments or offices are requisitioning private cars without prior authority. This is to cease immediately, failing which the SS will proceed with the greatest severity against every infringement.' The Gauleiter's office announced: 'Confiscations of goods, expropriations and arrests by members of the Party or the SA are strictly forbidden unless carried out with the express permission of either the Gauleiter or the SA Gruppenführer of Vienna. Contraventions of this order by unauthorized individuals will be punished.' Seidler, the head of the Vienna SA, decided that the thieves would be best suited to catching the thieves: 'Irresponsible elements are taking advantage of the time of upheaval to appropriate property that does not belong to them. The SA Group Vienna hereby orders all sections to take the severest possible action against this rabble and if necessary to arrest them and transfer them to the Teinfalt SA barracks.' Lest the Party's reputation should suffer, the looting was blamed on to Communists dressed in Nazi uniforms.

Aspern airport now saw the arrival of a man who intended to organize the Austrian SA on the German pattern. This was the Berlin Chief of Staff of the SA, Viktor Lutze. He brought with him the name of the man appointed to be Austria's chief SA leader, Hermann Reschny, the head of the 'Austrian Legion'.

Two opponents of the Nazis, police detectives Josef Schmirl and Josef Feldmann, were murdered in Linz prison. Schmirl was strangled in his cell by Nazi intruders. Feldmann was shot. The Nazis already had two senior police officials on their consciences. Dr Viktor Bentz, the Linz Police President, had been taken from his summer residence at Schloss Haus by a squad of Nazis. On the drive throught the woods near Praegarten there were shots in the car. Dr Bentz had shouted for help a few times. But he was beyond help. Police Inspector Dr Ludwig Bernegger had also been concerned with the underground Nazi movement in the days before 11 March. In the early hours of Monday morning a troop of Nazis had arrested him at his home in Linz. They had taken him out into the street and killed him. Immediately after these murders the covering-up process began. In the cases of Bentz and Bernegger death certificates were produced on which no cause of death was shown. In Schmirl's case the story was spread that he had hanged himself in prison. The newly instituted Gestapo office in Linz took charge of the cases.

The bodies were burned. Bent's and Bernegger's widows were presented with urns containing the ashes.

In Vienna the humiliation of Jewish citizens continued. The religious community was closed down; its committee members, Friedmann, Stricker and Löwenherz, were arrested. Out of some three hundred thousand Jews in Austria two-thirds lived in Vienna. Of all the cities in Europe Vienna contained the most Jewish doctors and lawyers. Austrian Jews occupied leading positions in banking, in industry, in commerce, in literature, in the theatre and the press. Now all this was changed. Austria's latent anti-semitism came to the boil.

Since two o'clock that morning Theodor Hornbostel, the former Political Director of the Foreign Office, had been washing the new masters' requisitioned cars at the illegal Nazis' prison in the Konkordiaplatz. After this he was taken to the official prison, the Vienna city gaol in the Hahngasse.

In Bratislava Guido Zernatto and his wife received false passports from the French Consulate in the names of 'Gustave and Renée Rapp', booksellers from Silina. The ex-Foreign Minister, Guido Schmidt, was flown to Berlin on the order of Goering, who guaranteed his safety.

In Linz the crowds were cheering again. At 10.40 a.m. Adolf Hitler showed himself once more outside the Hotel Weinzinger. Shouts of 'Sieg Heil!' and chanted slogans accompanied Hitler's procession as it made its way out of the Upper Austrian capital in the direction of Vienna. A long journey of 189 kilometres along the old Niebelungenstrasse lay ahead of them. Cheering crowds everywhere. The children were on holiday, the shops closed.

Shortly after 1.00 p.m. the procession reached the Abbey at Melk. Here a detachment of the Austrian Army was drawn up. Their commanding officer reported to Hitler. For the first time Austrian troops presented arms to the German Chancellor, to whom they had sworn allegiance a few hours previously. Bells rang, cannon fired a salute. At 1.45 the cavalcade halted at St Pölten. At an inn owned by a veteran Party member lunch was laid for the local Nazi aces and the Chancellor's entourage.

During the meal there was a telephone call from Vienna. It was a message from Cardinal Innitzer, bidding Hitler welcome to Austria. The Cardinal had ordered that the bells of Vienna should

Monday, 14 March 1938

be rung when the Reich Chancellor entered the city. After stopping for an hour, Hitler set out once more, to drive the last 66 kilometres to Vienna. On the road as far as St Pölten it had still been possible to drive at 40 kilometres per hour. Now the speedometer needle in Hitler's Mercedes hovered at a little over 20 kilometres per hour. The cheering Austrians would not let him drive by any faster.

At noon that day in Berlin Josef Goebbels, Minister of Propaganda, was busy getting the *Anschluss*-fever into top gear at his so-called 'eleven o'clock press conference'. All the papers were full of German News Agency reports or stories from their own staff reporters in Austria. There was much enthusiasm and little hard information. At about the same time Nevile Henderson, the British Ambassador in Berlin, was coming to the end of a meeting with Baron von Neurath. Earlier on that morning Goering had assured Henderson that the plebiscite to be held on 10 April would be free and secret. If fifty-one per cent of the Austrians voted against the *Anschluss* law then it would cease to be valid. Henderson had asked Neurath if such assurances would be kept even though the Austrian and German armies had been amalgamated. Neurath assured him that this could be relied on. But the German government was counting on a vote of eighty per cent for the *Anschluss*. As it turned out even this estimate was too low.

Winston Churchill had no doubt that the German Invasion of Austria meant the beginning of the end for Europe:

'The gravity of the event of March 12 cannot be exaggerated. Europe is confronted with a programme of aggression, nicely calculated and timed, unfolding stage by stage, and there is only one choice open, not only to us but to other countries, either to submit, like Austria, or else to take effective measures while time remains to ward off the danger and, if it cannot be warded off, to cope with it. . . . If we were to go on waiting upon events . . . how much should we throw away of resources which are now available for our security and for the maintenance of peace? How many friends would be alienated, how many potential allies should we see go, one by one, down the grisly gulf? How many times will bluff succeed until behind bluff ever gathering forces have accumulated reality? Where are we going to be two years hence, for instance, when the German Army will certainly be much larger than the French Army and when all the small nations will have fled from Geneva to pay homage to the ever waxing power of the Nazi system, and to make the best terms that they can for themselves?'

Three hours after leaving St Pölten Hitler's cavalcade drove on to the Ringstrasse in Vienna. It was 5.40 p.m. A journey through flag-decked villages lay behind them. The people had often been packed so tight that the outrider escort vehicles driving behind Hitler were forced to squeeze right into the main convoy.

Hitler entered Vienna to the sound of cheering and the ringing of all the church bells. At the Riederberg, just outside Vienna, the Austrian Chancellor, Seyss-Inquart, and Frick, the German Minister of the Interior, had joined Hitler's cavalcade. Standing up in his car, his right hand raised in the Hitler salute, the Führer and Chancellor of the German Reich drove into the city where almost thirty years previously he had lived on an allowance, and as a painter of postcards. His escort of security guards had a hard job on their hands. Not only were the streets lined with people. There were people at every window and even enthusiastic supporters sitting on the rooftops. The SS men on the running boards of the cars were on the alert for would-be assassins. But everywhere there were only jubilant crowds to be seen.

At the Hotel Imperial the whole Austrian cabinet was assembled. Seyss-Inquart presented the individual members.

A telegram had arrived for Hitler. It contained Mussolini's reply to the telegram Hitler had sent him, thanking him for his approval of the invasion. It was addressed to: 'Hitler/Vienna'. The text read: 'My attitude is determined by the friendship between our two countries sealed in the Axis pact. Mussolini.'

There was no end to the aircraft landing at Aspern airport. The Ministers, government officials and Party men were flocking into Austria from Berlin. That morning Franz von Papen, Hitler's one-time Envoy in Vienna, had arrived in response to the Reich Chancellor's summons by telegram. The Austrian Foreign

Monday, 14 March 1938

Minister, Dr Wolff, now handed over his Ministry to Ribbentrop. Since Austria had ceased to exist it no longer needed a Minister to direct its foreign policies. Wolff: 'As the last Austrian Foreign Minister, it is with deeply felt joy that I transfer the business of the Austrian Minister into your hands. We Austrians have only one Fatherland. That is Germany.'

By early afternoon Colonel de Angelis, the State Secretary at the Ministry of Defence, had been given a preliminary review of the swearing-in of the Austrian Army ordered by General von Bock. Almost every one of the 50,000 in the Austrian Army had sworn the oath: 'I swear by God this sacred oath that I will give absolute obedience to the Führer of the German Reich and people, Adolf Hitler, the Supreme Commander of the *Wehrmacht*, and will be ready at all times, as a brave soldier, to lay down my life for this oath.' Only 126 had refused to speak the words. Out of these, 123 were men who counted as Jews by the terms of the Nuremberg Laws of 1935.

The Eighth Army GHQ was trying to act with tactical finesse: it sent liaison officers both to Gauleiter Bürckel, the reorganizer of the Austrian Nazi Party appointed by Hitler, and to Chancellor Seyss-Inquart, who still held office. The objectives for the advance that day had once again not been achieved. Traffic conditions had proved to be catastrophic. Particularly disturbing had been the flow of new formations—particularly from the rear—which had been set in motion by Army authorities in Germany in accordance with the original plan. Not even the police formations under the command of the Eighth Army GHQ had been able to prevent this advance.

The roads had been blocked by civilian vehicles driving out from Vienna to meet Hitler and the German soldiers. The Eighth Army Command's proposal that the German-Austrian frontier should be temporarily closed to all civilian traffic had indeed been approved, but it had only been possible to carry it out to a limited extent.

Other difficulties had also cropped up: Party authorities in South Germany had in some cases held back men reporting for military service to use them for their own purposes. Then there had been shortages of transport equipment. The SS Standarte *Deutschland* had simply appropriated horses designated by the

Eighth Army for its own use; and in the race to Vienna the undisciplined behaviour of units of police, SS and Air Force had repeatedly caused chaos on the roads.

The Austrian troops who might have resisted the invasion had by now long since been amalgamated into the German *Wehrmacht*. Colonel-General von Brauchitsch and General von Manstein, the man who had worked out the invasion plan, were holding talks in Vienna with State Secretary de Angelis of the Defence Ministry, about the reorganization of the Austrian Army into a new series of military districts.

That evening found the Viennese still on their feet. Thousands were standing in the street, particularly outside the Hotel Imperial, where Hitler was staying. The chanting rang out over the broad Ringstrasse: 'We want to see our Führer!' At 7.10 p.m. the Viennese were asked over the loudspeakers to moderate their enthusiasm. 'At this time the Führer has urgent work and urgent meetings to attend to. The Führer will make one more appearance on the balcony. After this I must call upon you all to go home, so as not to disturb the Führer at his work. Sieg Heil!' Then the military and Party vehicles parked near the hotel directed their lights towards the balcony of the Imperial. Hitler showed himself to the crowd. He was scarcely able to speak one complete sentence. Again and again he was interrupted by cheering. Hitler:

'My fellow Germans, men and women! What you are feeling now I have shared with you at the most profound level during these last days. Our German nation has experienced a great historical turning point. What you are experiencing now is being experienced with you by the whole German nation.' For several minutes the shouts of 'Sieg Heil!' interrupted his speech. 'Not only two million people in this city but the seventy-five million people within the Reich. They are all deeply stirred and moved by this historical turning point and all of them now make a solemn vow: that whatever may happen no one will ever again destroy and no one will ever again divide the German Reich, as it exists today. No hardship, no threat and no force can break this vow! And today this vow is being made by all Germans from Königsberg to Cologne, and from Hamburg to Vienna!'

It seemed as if the cheering in the streets would never die down.

TUESDAY, 15 MARCH 1938

On the morning of 15 March the sun rose over Vienna at 6.15 a.m. It was five years to the day since Chancellor Engelbert Dollfuss had used the police to prevent the National Assembly meeting. Now the clerico-fascist regime had been replaced by a Nazi dictatorship.

A continuous stream of aircraft from the Reich was still landing at Aspern airport, Vienna. Government and Party functionaries from Germany poured in. The President of the Reichsbank, Dr Hjalmar Schacht, was received by the Austrian Ministers, Neumayer and Fischböck. Schacht wanted to concern himself with the Austrian National Bank and technical financial questions. In speaking to Kienböck, the President of the National Bank, whom he had known since 1933, Schacht did not mince his words. 'The National Bank will be incorporated. You cannot become a director of the Reichsbank. What do you want? A retirement pension or compensation?' Kienböck chose compensation. The rate of exchange was fixed at two schillings to the Reichsmark. It was not until later that the general exchange rate of 1.5 schillings came in.

꧁꧁꧁꧁꧁꧁

Almost all those dismissed were regimental officers. Apart from Zehner and Schilhawsky there was no one from the Defence Ministry. A personnel commission was meanwhile hard at work at the Ministry investigating the 'political reliability' of further officers.

In the city of Linz the directors of the Kraus und Schober department store were thrown into prison. The business was taken over by the Nazi members of the staff and a sign to this effect was at once displayed at the entrance. All the Jewish businesses in the city had already been labelled as such, all Jewish associations had been disbanded.

An epidemic was rife in Austria: denunciation. Everyone blackened his neighbour to the new masters. Personal grievances were paid off in this way but for the most part it was simply a question of jobs. The denunciations swelled to such massive proportions that even Gauleiter Josef Bürckel's office issued statements condemning the accusers: 'Anyone who demands that the holder of a given post be removed can in no circumstances be a candidate for that post himself . . .'

And now the 1.8 million Viennese were to be treated to the spectacle most of them had been awaiting for days. Berlin policemen were controlling traffic and crowds in the congested streets. Many of the spectators had come in from the surrounding districts by car and bus. The staffs of firms and businesses marched in close order into the Inner City. Slowly individual blocks formed in the Heldenplatz. Separate from one another stood the SA, SS, Hitler Youth and BDM. The 'Deutschland' motorized loudspeaker convoy had twenty-five mobile transmission vans parked in the side streets, so as to bring the enjoyment of the forthcoming speeches to as many as possible. In front of the Hofburg bands of the armed forces and police were drawn up.

More than a quarter of a million people were standing in the Heldenplatz, and hundreds of thousands more stood in the streets through which Hitler was to come. A gigantic swastika flag bellied above the first guests of honour, who were assembled on the terrace at the Hofburg. By the Ringstrasse, where early in the afternoon the parade of German and Austrian troops was to march past, a hundred workmen were still busy erecting a platform.

Chancellor Seyss-Inquart arrived at the Hotel Imperial to collect Hitler. The Reich Chancellor had still not answered Seyss-Inquart's plea to be allowed to return to his private profession. Hitler demanded to see the text of Seyss-Inquart's speech. Then he returned the paper. He approved.

Shortly before eleven o'clock Hitler's procession crossed the Heldenplatz. On the balcony of the Hofburg Hitler first turned to the radio announcer. 'You must announce that Reich Governor Seyss-Inquart is to speak.' While the cheering rang out across the square for several minutes the Führer's standard was flown above the balcony. Seyss-Inquart went up to the microphone:

'My Führer! As the last head of the Austrian Federal State I report to the Führer and Reich Chancellor that the law has been passed according to the will of the German people and their Führer. Austria is a province of the German Reich.'

Thunderous applause.

'To the German people and the whole world I proclaim that Adolf Hitler at this hour has entered as Führer and Reich

Chancellor the citadel of the old capital of the Empire, the guardian of the crown of the Empire.'

Renewed cheering.

'That goal towards which centuries of German history have striven, for which untold millions of the best Germans have bled and died, their goal in the heat of battle, their comfort in the bitterest hours—today has been achieved. The Ostmark has come home.'

Through the applause came the chanted choruses:

'We thank our Führer!'

Seyss-Inquart's next sentences were interrupted repeatedly by cheering and chanting.

'My Führer! The forces of all past generations of the German people are summoned up in your will, and you, my Führer, have done this for the sake of all future generations of Germans. Today the Germans of all ages, past and future, salute the Führer as the perfector of the task; today the Führer salutes the new, the eternal Germany! . . . My Führer! Wherever the road leads we will follow! Heil, my Führer!'

Then Hitler attempted to make himself heard:

'Germans! Men and women! In the space of a few days a transformation has taken place within the German national community, the extent of which we can see today but the full significance of which only future generations will be able to appreciate . . . I now proclaim this country's new mission. It corresponds to the command which once brought the German settlers here from all the regions of the old Reich. The most ancient Ostmark of the German people shall henceforth be the newest bulwark of the German nation and the German Reich.'

Loud prolonged applause.

'This land is German, it has recognized its mission, it will fulfil it and will never be surpassed by anyone in loyalty to the great German national community.'

Hitler was prevented from continuing by the shouts of 'Sieg Heil!' After thanking the Party functionaries who alone had made this transformation possible, Hitler shouted out over the Heldenplatz:

'And thus it is that I can at this time proclaim to the German people the greatest act of fulfilment of my life. As Führer and Chancellor of the German nation and Reich I now proclaim before German history the entry of my homeland into the German Reich.'

Applause for several minutes. Then:

'Germany and her new organ, the National Socialist Party and the *Wehrmacht* of our Reich, Sieg Heil!'

As Hitler's column left the Heldenplatz a new surge of cheering swept across the square. Hitler drove back to the Hotel Imperial down streets lined with people shouting 'Sieg Heil!'

In front of the outer Burghof gate of the Hofburg in the Heldenplatz the guards of honour marched up. There was also a company in Austrian uniforms with German eagle emblems sewn on to them. On both sides of the gate flames burned in shallow dishes. Then the command rang out: 'Guard! Guard, present arms!' Accompanied by the shouts of the crowds, Hitler drove past the Burghof gate and took the salute from the guards of honour. It was 1.30 p.m.

With Hitler came almost two dozen German and Austrian officers. Only Keitel and Reich Governor Seyss-Inquart followed Hitler inside the Heroes' Monument, which was dedicated 'to the memory of the glorious Imperial Army 1618–1918'. Hitler laid a wreath before the memorial tablet. The ribbon was decorated with Hitler's standard. After this ceremony Hitler went to the saluting base opposite the Burgtor. The parade could begin. It was shortly before 2.00 p.m.

The parade began with a fly-past of 378 German and 27 Austrian planes. At 2.15 p.m. the military band struck up in front of the Heroes' Monument. At the head of the parade came the motorized troops; then followed artillery, anti-tank defence and the Thirty-Eighth Intelligence Section. All the German troops that had reached Vienna were on parade and so were all available Austrian units.

Tuesday, 15 March 1938

The parade was over shortly before four o'clock. Hitler returned to his hotel. Accompanied by Father Johann von Jauner and his secretary Cardinal Innitzer drove up in front of the Hotel Imperial. As the three priests got out of their car jeers and raucous whistling broke out across the Ring. Papen was standing at the door to welcome the prelate: he declared himself extremely glad 'that Eminence has decided to make this visit.' The crowd behind him cursed and spat, but the SS sentries at the door presented arms. As the Cardinal walked up the steps to Hitler's suite, the crowd outside could be heard shouting: 'To Dachau! To Dachau!' and 'Chuck the Cardinal in the Canal!' Innitzer was smiling. He was still smiling as he walked up to Hitler.

The German Chancellor made the *Anschluss* sound appetizing to the prelate. He would, he said, welcome the cooperation of the two great German churches. And: 'If the Church is loyal to the State it will not regret it. If there is good cooperation in Austria then this religious springtime here may also have its effect in the old Reich.' Innitzer replied that the Catholics in Austria were ready to give their loyalty to the State. The conversation was a brief one. Innitzer left the hotel contented.

Arthur Seyss-Inquart, the newly minted Reich Governor of Austria, was discussing with the German Minister of the Interior 'the decree of the next measures to be taken', which had already been prepared by German State Secretary Stuckart. The man who had only been Chancellor of Austria for a matter of hours had no alternative but to sign the statutory documents. Seyss had also been given the rank of SS-Gruppenführer. The role he was to play now was indicated in the 'decree of the Führer and Reich Chancellor about the government of the province of Austria', which Hitler and Frick had signed:

'Article 1. The Austrian Federal Government is designated "Austrian Provincial Government". I appoint the Reich Governor in Austria to be responsible for the Austrian Provincial Government. His seat is in Vienna. Article 2. The Reich Governor is empowered to regulate the division of duties within the Provincial Government, subject to the approval of the Reich Minister of the Interior. . . .'

At the same time various German laws were declared to be valid also for Austria. This was the case with the Reich flag law, the law about the formation of new parties, the law securing the unity of Party and State and the ordinance for the implementation of the Four-Year Plan. The consequences of Austria's being brought into line were already evident in the first regulations decreed by the Reich Governor for the plebiscite of 10 April. Amongst them: 'Jews do not have the right to vote . . .'

Hitler took off for Germany with most of the people who had gone with him to Munich, Linz and Vienna. He had been in Austria for some seventy-two hours. As the D2600 had left Aspern and was flying over Austria Keitel noticed that the Führer was weeping. By way of explanation Hitler indicated the view from the cabin window: 'All that is German soil now.'

Vienna was still in a victory mood. The opponents of National Socialism did not show themselves in the streets and the others, in their enthusiasm, did not see—or did not choose to see—what was happening before their eyes: arrests, suicides, the persecution of Jews and political opponents, the looting of shops and private houses.

The National Socialists employed both brute force and psychological pressure against their enemies, even against dyed-in-the-wool representatives of 'Austro-fascism'. Emil Fey, former Vice-Chancellor, major and leader of the *Heimwehr*, was hounded to death. The fact that he had been present at the Chancellery on 25 July 1934, when the National Socialists had seized the building and murdered Dollfuss, was Fey's undoing. For the Nazis were now looking for someone on to whom they could pin the Chancellor's murder. A war of nerves began. Fey and his family were threatened by letter and telephone. On Sunday, 13 March Fey had asked two close friends to visit him at his home. Fey feared a show trial. When his friends tried to reassure him by saying that there were enough witnesses to prove his innocence, Fey said: 'But do you think that would stop them finding hundreds of people, who, in their enthusiasm for National Socialism, would be willing to swear they saw me shooting Dollfuss?'

Only a few hours previously Fey had addressed a desperate letter to Glaise-Horstenau, the Vice-Chancellor. The two were on good terms. Fey had written:

'Dear friend! As I hinted to you on the telephone on Saturday and reminded you today, through Section Councillor Barek, people seem to have something against me. .... The wildest rumours are being circulated, by quite responsible people, claiming that I have been arrested, or will be, for the wildest of reasons. There does seem to be some foundation for these rumours and in any case at times of upheaval such as these even rumours can suffice in some circumstances to lead to disaster. I therefore beg you most urgently, if it is at all possible, to intercede today with the powers that be, for me to be left in peace and for an instruction to this effect to be passed on to those under them. .... I, for my part, have been helpful when I could. Believe me the matter is serious and extremely pressing. Very best wishes, Yours, Fey.'

But the one-time Vice-Chancellor had not waited for an intervention. He had summoned his son, Herbert, from the Military Academy in Wiener Neustadt. Friends who had offered to get Fey out of the country were met with a refusal. Fey had decided to commit suicide with his family. Once more, late in the night, a friend came and tried to dissuade him. But there was only one thing he could do for Fey: take charge of his letters of farewell: 'After mature consideration I am entering the ranks of the great army ...'

The doctor's report noted that father and son had shot themselves. The death certificate for Fey's wife read: 'Two shots through the skull. Killed by another hand. Family suicide.'

꙰꙰꙰꙰꙰꙰꙰

At the Archduke Franz Ferdinand's artist's studio at the southern edge of the Belvedere Gardens the former Chancellor of the Austrian Republic, Kurt von Schuschnigg, had been living for four days as a prisoner. His guards still patrolled the house, but they had themselves long since been under surveillance by the victory-intoxicated SA. Schuschnigg's short-lived successor, Seyss-Inquart, had broken all the promises he had made to his predecessor in the early hours of Saturday morning. He had not been to see Schuschnigg, he had not made a car available to him, and, as for Schuschnigg's adjutants, not even Lieutenant-Colonel Bartl was allowed into the house. What Schuschnigg could not know was that over many questions Seyss's own hands were tied. Schuschnigg had tried to offer resistance to Hitler at the wrong point in time and with insufficient means. For him there was to be a seven-year journey through the prisons and concentration camps of the Third Reich.

卐卐卐卐卐卐

Seven days, which had failed to shake the world, were coming to an end. The week had begun on 9 March 1938 with Schuschnigg's optimistic proposal for a vote on an independent Austria. But by then even the upper echelons of the government contained opponents of Austrian independence: fanatics with dreams of a Greater Germany, Party activists, men who did not hesitate to betray both government and country. In the other countries of Europe independent Austria had had few friends. Britain was prepared to appease Hitler's Germany, Italy was already within Berlin's sphere of influence, France alone was too weak. The past few days had shown all this clearly enough. And the very people who could have supported Schuschnigg, the Austrian Socialists, were called in by him too late and too half-heartedly. Furthermore Schuschnigg had dared to challenge Hitler without himself being prepared to resist to the last. He had conceded the game as lost before it was begun.

In these seven days Schuschnigg's Austria, organized on a 'corporative' basis and ruled as a Catholic dictatorship, had first been turned into a Nazi satellite under Seyss-Inquart and then into the Ostmark, the German Reich's eastern territory. After their original protests the Western powers had gone back to business as usual. But Hitler's expansionist urge had been clearly brought to their attention. Czechoslovakia seemed to be the next target. The Western powers were preparing accordingly. The German Ambassador in Paris, Count Welczack, reported on 15 March that the Czechoslovak Ambassador had been given a binding promise that in the case of conflict with Germany, if the Czechoslovak government sent word that they considered themselves to be attacked without provocation, 'France would regard herself as being at war with Germany.' The British Ambassador in Paris had made a similar report. But the British government was unwilling at this stage to let itself be tied down quite so firmly.

Even the reports from other British missions could not persuade the Foreign Office. The British Minister in Moscow cabled to Lord Halifax: 'In a conversation I had with M. Litvinov [the Foreign Minister] today, he said he was sure that Herr Hitler, having now annexed Austria, was not going to stop there and would soon proceed to deal with Czechoslovakia.' From Prague the British Ambassador reported: 'Having liquidated Austria, the Government of the Reich will doubtless soon tackle the next item on their programme, Czechoslovakia.'

From Czechoslovakia Hitler's Fifth Column spoke up. Konrad Henlein, the leader of the 'Sudeten-German Party', drew up a statement which was to be published on 16 March:

'Sudeten Germans! In these days decisions of great significance for the German people have been taken. There must scarcely be a single German who has not, wherever he lives, shared in the jubilation of our brothers and sisters in Austria. The Sudeten German community have witnessed the return home of the Alpine German community with the greatest joy, just as they had previously felt the deepest sympathy for their sufferings. ... Let us all fight on under the banner of the Sudeten-German Party for the rights and honour of our people.'

Hitler had once described his foreign policy in a conversation with Hermann Rauschning, the President of the Danzig Senate, in these terms:

'If I go to war then I will one day, in the midst of peace, simply send troops into, let us say, Paris. ... Everything is prepared down to the smallest detail. ... They occupy the ministries, Parliament. Within a few minutes France, Poland, Austria or Czechoslovakia is robbed of her leading men. ... But I have long been in contact with men who will form a new government.'

The Czechoslovak case had not yet become acute. For this case the German military had drawn its lessons from 'Case Otto', which had just been concluded. Thus the Commander-in-Chief of the Eighth Army: 'There is no doubt whatever that in the case of enemy resistance, especially from the air, the events on the Passau-Linz-Vienna road could have led to a catastrophe.' And: 'Faced with a frontier defended according to plan, the Army would not have been able to enter the country before the morning of 13 March.' If there had been fighting, the defects and losses which appeared would have been intensified. Bock's list of defects:

the Army staff revealed shortcomings, the officers were in part unqualified, the auxiliary equipment of the GHQ was inadequate and was brought up too late, the discipline on the advance left much to be desired. Bock: 'The inevitable blockages were caused by a considerable number of vehicles from the Panzer Division, left standing on the roads, broken down and unusable troop carriers and numbers of military, police and civilian vehicles, which were multiplied by fuelling at public filling stations.'

Although the advance met no resistance, twenty-five German soldiers were killed in the traffic chaos and nineteen were seriously injured. The number of Austrians thus killed was not recorded.

After three days of National Socialism in Austria the enthusiasm of the Austrian Party leaders began to wear off. In a great many cases the Party men who had managed to get jobs after long years in the illegal Party had them taken away again. Repeated re-shuffles reflected the backstage in-fighting. An additional factor was the hordes of Germans from the Reich who poured into the country, on orders from Berlin, to take up jobs. The Ostmark was to be thrust into the front rank. What was in store for the Austrians, even while they were still enjoying their first flush of enthusiasm, was prophesied by the SS journal *Das Schwarze Korps:* 'It is certain that the wind of resistance to Prussia which emanates from the old-world abbey gardens as well as from the stuffy parlours and stifling wine taverns, will soon be swept away by a fresh breeze... Soon every active—and inactive—Austrian will have a Prussian standing behind him and every fault will be unsparingly criticized with biting accuracy.'

In seven days Schuschnigg's Austria had become Hitler's Ostmark. And for seven years the slogan would hold good: 'Ein Volk, ein Reich, ein Führer!'

On 1 April 1938 the first transport carrying Austrians arrived at Dachau concentration camp. Amongst the prisoners were: Colonel Walter Adam; Richard Alexander, the Chief of Staff of the *Schutzkorps;* Hans Becker, the Fatherland Front propaganda chief; Dr Robert Danneberg, the Socialist; Dr Desider Friedmann, the head of the Jewish religious community; Theodor Hornbostel, of the Foreign Office; Dr Maximilian Pammer, the head of the political department of the Fatherland Front; Alexander Eifler, the Chief of Staff of the Republican *Schutzbund;*

Tuesday, 15 March 1938

Franz Olah, the Socialist; Richard Schmitz, the Mayor of Vienna.

In March and April 1938 SS-Untersturmbannführer Adolf Eichmann became the head of the Vienna central office for the emigration of Jews out of Austria. By the end of the year Eichmann's methods of compulsion had succeeded in driving 45,000 Austrian Jews out of the country. His principle was that rich Jews willing to emigrate must pay the emigration costs for their poorer fellow sufferers.

On 10 April 1938, out of 4,484,000 Austrians entitled to vote, 4,453,000 voted 'Yes' in Hitler's plebiscite. This was 99.73 per cent. 5776 ballot papers were spoiled. 11,929 Austrians voted 'No'.

On 29 September, at the Munich Conference, Britain, France and Italy agreed to Hitler's demand that Czechoslovakia should cede the border territories of Bohemia and Moravia, which were inhabited by Sudeten Germans, to the Reich. The integrity of the remainder of Czechoslovakia was to be guaranteed by the great powers.

On 1 October 1938 the German troops marched into the Sudetenland.

On 15 March 1939 Czechoslovakia was occupied by German troops. Bohemia and Moravia were incorporated into the German Reich as a protectorate. The Western powers again looked on.

On 1 September 1939 German troops attacked Poland. Two days later Britain and France declared war on Germany. The Second World War began, in which Austrians in German uniform fought on the German side.

On 13 April 1945 the Red Army occupied Vienna.

On 27 April 1945 Dr Karl Renner formed a provisional Austrian government, composed of Social Democrats, Christian Socialists and Communists. On the same day the three parties signed a 'Declaration of Independence'. In Article Two it stated: 'The *Anschluss* imposed on the Austrian people by force in 1938 is null and void.'

LIST OF SOURCES

The authors wish to express their thanks to all individuals and institutions without whose help in supplying information and making material available this work would not have been possible. Particular thanks are due to the participants in and witnesses of the events described in this book who gave oral and written information to bridge the frequent gaps in the written sources.

The following institutes, libraries and archives have been most generous in placing their collections at our disposal or in giving information:

The Vienna City Archive
The Bavarian State Library, Munich
The Central Index of the German Federal Archives, Kornelimünster
The Documentation Archive of Austrian Resistance, Vienna
The Institute of Contemporary History, Munich
The Institute of Contemporary History, Vienna
The Linz City Archive
The Tagblatt Archive, Vienna

In addition to these, the archives of the following newspapers have been consulted:

The *Arbeiter-Zeitung*, Vienna
The *Süddeutsche Zeitung*, Munich
The *Volkesstimme*, Vienna

I ORAL INFORMATION WAS SUPPLIED BY THE FOLLOWING:

Manfred Ackermann; Friedrich Birsak; Dr Fritz Bock; Adele Bumbik; Dr Alfred Detig; Dr Erich Führer; Hans Gollwitzer; Dr Otto von Habsburg; Ludwig Hahne; Prof. Lambert Haiböck; Dr Albert Hantschk; Fritz Haynisch; Prof. Dr Rudolf Henz; Dr Ludwig Hift; Friedrich Hillegeist; Rudolf Hiller; Dr Wilhelm Höttl; Theodor Hornbostel; Dr Heinrich Hüttl; Heinrich Kodré; Franz Koudelka; Dr Franz Krisch; Hellmuth Laegeler; Ernst August Lassen; Alice Lillie; Dr Viktor Matejka; Karl Mauler; Walter Mehring; Dr Karl Melchard; Dr Josef Miklas; Erhard Milch; Hermann Miltzow; Franz Olah; Dr Maximilian Pammer; Dr Hermann Pfaundler; Georg

List of Sources

Radotic; Dr Franz Sobek; Karl Sobolak; Dr Hjalmar Schacht; Count Siegfried Schack; Dr Friedrich Scheu; Baldur von Schirach; Dr Gertrud Schmitz; Martha Schmitz; Oskar von Schmoczer; Dr Arthur von Schuschnigg; Dr Kurt von Schuschnigg; Josef Strabl; Dr Walter Sturminger; Dr Leopold Tavs; Friedrich Vogl; Alois Vollgruber; Hans Weigel; Karl Zöllner; Riccarda Zernatto.

II WRITTEN INFORMATION WAS SUPPLIED, AMONGST OTHERS, BY THE FOLLOWING:

Maximilian de Angelis; Dr Erich Bielka; Dr Christian Broda; Muriel M. Buttinger; Count Richard Coudenhove-Kalergi; Gabriele Eichelberg; Gerhard Engel; André François-Poncet; Dr Viktor Fröhlichsthal; Max Gilbert; Dr Johann Granichstädten-Czerva; Max Gruber; Willibald Hauser; Franz Hofbauer; Dr Franz Huebert; Dr Ludwig Kleinwächter; Philipp Knab; Emanuel Krivinka; Thomas Lebersorg; Dr Albin Lennkh; Dr Max Löwenthal; Erich von Manstein; Dr Jonny Moser; Franz Penka; Anton Pohl; Josef H. Pregartbauer; Gabriel Puaux; Annelise von Ribbentrop; Leopold Schlager; Alois Schulz; Dr Johannes Schwarzenberg; Count Lutz Schwerin von Krosigk; Otto Skorzeny; Roman Sohn; Albert Speer; Dr Otto Stein; Lilly Stepanek; Heinrich Stümpfl; Fritz Wiedemann; Dr Paul Wilhelm-Heininger; Paul Winterstein; Dr Karl Zechenter; Adele Zeilinger; Dr Rudolf Zoffal.

III SOURCES

(1) In addition to the documents drawn up for the Nuremberg War Criminals Trials and the Schmidt Trial, as well as microfilm of the relevant German documents, the following archive documents were consulted:

Akten betr. Land Österreich. Aus Reichs- und Preussisches Ministerium des Inneren Reg. Vc Bd. 1, Nr. 3700 v. 13. März 1938 bis 31 Dezember 1940 (Copy in Austrian Resistance Archive, Vienna)

Der Einsatz der 8. Armee im März 1938 zur Wiedervereinigung Österreichs mit dem Deutschen Reich. Bericht des Oberbefehlshabers der Heeresgruppe 3 an den Oberbefehlshaber des Heeres vom 18. Juli 1938 (Copy in Austrian Resistance Archive, Vienna)

Erster Österreichischer Transport nach Dachau am 1. April 1938 (Austrian Resistance Archive, Vienna)

Jansa, Alfred, Erinnerungen, Masch. MS (Copy in Austrian Resistance Archive, Vienna)

Hillegeist, Friedrich, Manuskript eines Vortrags, gehalten am 12. März 1963 in der Wiener Urania (Institute of Contemporary History, Vienna)

(Miklas-Dokumente), Verschiedene Niederschriften von Bundes-
präsident Wilhelm Miklas aus den Jahren 1938 bis 1945 (Miklas
Family, Private Collection)
(Wilhelmstrassen-Prozess), Hektographierte Akten des Falles XI vor
dem Militärgerichtshof IV in Nürnberg (Institute of Contemporary
History, Munich)

(2) *Documentary Publications, Manuals*
Akten zur Deutschen Auswärtigen Politik 1918–1945, Archiv des
Auswärtigen Amtes, Serie D (1937–1945), Bd. 1
Almanach der österreichischen Eisenbahnen XIV. Jahrgang 1938,
herausgegeben v.d. Generaldirektion der Österreichischen Bundes-
bahnen nach dem Stand vom 1. Jänner 1938
(Amtskalender), Oberösterreichischer Amtskalender. Der Oberöster-
reicher, Auskunfts- und Geschäftsbuch für das Jahr 1938, Linz,
Dezember 1937.
(Amtskalender), Österreichischer Amtskalender für das Jahr 1937, 16.
Jahrgang, Vienna 1937
Aus Goerings Schreibtisch, Ein Dokumentenfund. Bearbeitet von
T. R. Emessen, Berlin 1947
Berber, Fritz (Hrsg.), Deutschland–England 1933–1939. Die Doku-
mente des deutschen Friedenswillens, Essen 1940
Berber, Fritz, Europäesche Politik 1933–1938 im Spiegel der Prager
Akten Essen 1941
Dienstbuch der Vaterländischen Front, Vienna n.d. (=1937)
Documents on British Foreign Policy 1919–1939, ed. by E. L.
Woodward, Rohan Butler, Third Series, Vol. 1 (1938), London 1949
(Erhebung), Die Erhebung der österreichischen Nationalsozialisten im
Juli 1934. Akten der Historischen Kommission des Reichsführers
SS, Vienna-Frankfurt 1965
Groner, Richard, Wien wie es war. Ein Nachschlagewerk für Freunde
des alten und neuen Wien, Vienna-Munich 1956
Handbuch der bewaffneten Macht, Vienna 1938
Handbuch der bundesunmittelbaren Stadt Wien, 62. amtlich redigier-
ter Jahrgang, Vienna 1937
(IMT), Dr Prozess gegen die Hauptkriegsverbrecher vor dem
Internationalen Militärgerichtshof in Nürnberg, Bde. 1–42, Nurem-
berg 1947–1949
Jahrbuch der deutschen Luftwaffe, Leipzig 1939
Jahrbuch des deutschen Heeres, Leipzig 1939
Rot-Weiss-Rot-Buch, Gerechtigkeit für Österreich. Darstellungen,
Dokumente und Nachweise zur Vorgeschichte der Okkuptation
Österreichs, 1. Teil, Vienna 1946
Rühle, Gerd, Das Dritte Reich. Dokumentar. Darstellung des Aufbaus
der Nation, (6) Das sechste Jahr 1938, Berlin 1939
Rüehle, Gerd, Das Dritte Reich, Sonderband: Die österreichischen
Kampfjahre 1918–1938, Berlin 1940

List of Sources

Schematismus für das österreichische Bundesheer und die Bundes-
heeresverwaltung, bearbeitet im Bundesministerium f. Landes-
verteidigung, Vienna 1936
(Schmidt-Prozess), Der Hochverratsprozess gegen Dr Guido Schmidt
vor dem Wiener Volksgericht, Vienna 1947
Sperlings Zeitschriften- und Zeitungsadressbuch, Handbuch der
deutschen Presse, 60. Ausgabe 1937, Leipzig
Stockhorst, Erich, Fünftausend Köpfe. Wer war was im Dritten
Reich, Velbert 1967
Vienne et ses environs, Guides Gruben Vol. 206, 3. Edition, Berlin
1937
(Wehrmacht), Des Führers Wehrmacht half Grossdeutschland
schaffen. Berichte deutscher Soldaten von der Befreiung der Ost-
mark und des Sudetenlandes, herausgegeben vom OKW, Berlin 1939
Weltgeschichte der Gegenwart in Dokumenten, hrsg. von Michael
Freund und Werner Frauendienst, Bd. 5, Essen 1940

(3) *Newspapers and periodicals*
(especial use was made of issues for the year 1938)

(a) German publications
Das Schwarze Korps
Illustrierter Beobachter
Münchner Neueste Nachrichten
Völkischer Beobachter, Munich edition

(b) Austrian publications
Linzer Volksblatt
Neue Freie Presse, Vienna
NS-Telegraf, Vienna
Reichspost, Vienna
Tagblatt, Linz
Tagepost, Linz
Tages-Post, Graz
Telegraf, Vienna
Völkischer Beobachter, Vienna edition
Wiener Neueste Nachrichten
Wiener Zeitung

(c) Other publications
Das Neue Tagebuch, Paris
The Times, London

(d) Particular issues of various newspapers and periodicals, amongst
others:
Berliner Illustrierte, special edition 2 April 1938
Neue Zeitschrift für den österr. Hausbesitz, Vienna, special edition 12
March 1938

'Reichskanzler Hitler in seiner Geburtsstadt Braunau', in: *Neue Warte am Inn*, 16 March 1938

'Zwölf Zeitgenossen geben Rechenschaft', in: *Die Presse*, 9–10 March 1963

Glaise-Horstenau, Edmund, 'Persönliche Erinnerungen an die Märztage 1938', in: *Neues Wiener Tagblatt*, 12 March 1939

Hüttl, Heinrich, 'März 1938—letzter Dienst für Österreich', in: *Das Kleine Volksblatt*, 12 March 1946

Jury, Hugo, 'So kam es zum 11. März 1938', in: *Völkischer Beobachter*, Vienna Edition, 12–13 March 1939

Kubena, Johann, 'Konnte Österreich 1938 Widerstand leisten?', in: *Die Presse*, 19 March 1947

Pauli, Herta, 'Wien 1938: Anruf aus Berlin', in: *Die Weltwoche*, 8 March 1968

Sailer, John, 'Gespräche fünf Minuten vor zwölf', in: *Arbeiter-Zeitung*, 10 March 1963

Sailer, Karl Hans, 'Am 11. März 1938', in: *Arbeiter-Zeitung*, 9 March 1947

IV THESES

Bärnthaler, Irmgard, *Geschichte und Organisation der Vaterländischen Front*. Ein Beitrag zum Verständnis totalitärer Organisationen, Phil. Diss. Vienna 1964

Botz, Gerhard, *Das politische Geschehen in Wien 1938–1940*, Phil. Diss. Vienna 1965

Deutsch, Heidrun, *Franziska Fürstin Starhemberg—eine Biographie*. Phil. Diss. Vienna 1967

Edlinger, Günther, *Friedrich Funder und die Reichspost in ihrer Stellungnahme zur Politik des Nationalsozialismus gegenuber Österreich von 1930 bis zum Anchluss 1938*. Phil. Diss. 1964

Fessl, Christine, *Die Innenpolitsche Entwicklung in Österreich in den Jahren 1934 bis 1938*. Phil. Diss. Vienna 1967

Gschaider, Peter, *Das Österreichische Bundesheer 1938 und seine Überführung in die deutsche Wehrmacht*. Phil. Diss. Vienna 1967

Haage, Peter, *Egon Friedell und der Journalismus*. Phil. Diss. Vienna 1964

Oswald, Franz, *Die Stellung von Major a. D. Emil Fey in der Politik der Ersten Republik und des Ständestaates*. Phil. Diss. Vienna 1964

Polanz, Ingeborg, *Die Bedeutung der Boulevard-Zeitung als meinungsbildendes Instrument, nachgewiesen am Telegraf/Nachtausgabe*. Phil. Diss. Vienna 1964

Tober, Helmut, *Alexander Eifler. Vom Monarchisten zum Republikaner*. Phil. Diss. Vienna 1966

List of Sources

Wagner, Friedrich, *Der österreichische Legitimismus 1918–1938. Seine Politik und Publizistik.* Phil. Diss. Vienna 1956

V ACCOUNTS, MONOGRAPHS, MEMOIRS

Abshagen, Karl Heinz, *Canaris, Patriot und Weltbürger*, Stuttgart 1955
Achtzig Jahre Wiener Sicherheitswache, herausgegeben v.d. Bundespolizeidirektion Wien, Vienna 1949
Alberti, Enno Maria, *Die deutch-österreichischen Beziehungen in den Jahren von 1936 bis 1938*, Wolfsburg 1954
Auclères, Dominique, *Mes quatre vérités. Mémoires d'une envoyée spéciale*, Paris n.d.
Andics, Hellmuth, *Der Staat, den keiner wolte*, Freiburg 1962
(Bartz, Karl), *Grossdeutschlands Wiedergeburt. Weltgeschichtliche Stunden an der Donau* (Geleitworte: H. Goering, Text: K. Bartz, Bild: H. Hoffmann), Vienna 1938
Baur, Hans, *Ich flog Mächtige der Erde*, Kempten 1956
Benedikt, Heinrich (Hrsg.), *Geschichte der Republik Österreich*, Vienna 1954
Bermann-Fischer, Gottfried, *Bedroht—Bewahrt. Der Weg eines Verlegers*, Frankfurt 1967
Berndt, Alfred Ingemar, *Meilensteine des Dritten Reiches. Erlebnisschilderungen grosser Tage; Der Marsch ins Grossdeutsche Reich*, Munich 1942
Bibl, Viktor, *Österreich 1806–1938*, Zurich-Leipzig-Vienna 1939
Bleyer-Härtl, Hans, *Ringen um Reich und Recht. Zwei Jahrzehnte politischer Anwalt in Österreich*, Berlin 1939
Bochow, Martin, *So wurde Grossdeutschland. Ein Bildebericht aus den entscheidenden Frühjahrstagen des Jahres 1938. Das Gedenkbuch für Kinder und Kindeskinder*, Berlin 1938
Bokisch, Otto und Zirbs, Gustav, A., *Der Österreichische Legionär. Aus Erinnerungen und Archiv, aus Tagebächern und Blättern*, Dresden 1940
Braunthaul, Julius, *The Tragedy of Austria*, London, 1948
Brook-Shepherd, Gordon, *The Austrian Odyssey*, London, 1957
Brook-Shepherd, Gordon, *Anschluss: The Rape of Austria*, London, 1963
Buttinger, Joseph, *Am Beispiel Österreichs. Ein geschichtlicher Beitrag zur Krise der sozialistischen Bewegung*, Cologne 1953
Churchill, Winston S., *The Second World War*, Vol. I, London 1948
Ciano, G., *Tagebücher 1937/38*, Hamburg 1949
Coudenhove-Kalergi, Richard, *Ein Leben für Europa*, Cologne-Berlin 1966
Dachauer, Max, *Das Ende Österreichs. Aus der k. u k.-Monarchie ins Dritte Reich*, Berlin 1939

Danimann, Franz, *War Österreichs Untergang 1938 unvermeidlich?*, als MS gedruckt, Vienna 1962

Detig, Alfred, *Wie der Führer Oesterreich heimbrachte. Die historischen Tage vom 12. März bis zum 10. April 1938*, Leipzig 1938

Deutsch, Julius, *Alexander Eifler—Ein Soldat der Freiheit*, Vienna 1947

Deutsch, Julius, *Ein weiter Weg. Lebenserinnerungen*, Zurich-Leipzig-Vienna 1960

Dietrich, Otto, *12 Jahre mit Hitler*, Munich 1955

Dodd, William E., *Ambassador Dodd's Diary 1933–38*, New York 1941

Dutch, Oswald, *Thus died Austria*, London 1938

Eckinger, Josef, *Front im Frieden. Das Buch der deutschen Waffenträger Österreichs*, Linz 1938

Ehrenbuch der nationalsozialistischen Rebellen der ehemals österr. Post, Vienna 1938

Eichstädt, Ulrich, *Von Dollfuss zu Hitler, Geschichte des Anschlusses Österreichs 1933–1938*, Wiesbaden 1955

Esebeck, Hans Gert Frh. von (Hrsg.), *Marsch für Grossdeutschland, mit 76 Abb. vom Marsch der bayerischen Ostmark-Division nach Wien*, Bayreuth 1938

Fahrensteiner, Franz, *Das war sein Kampf*, Bd. 1: *Von den Anfängen bis 1939*, Vienna/Munich 1963

Foerster, Wolfgang, *Generaloberst Ludwig Beck. Sein Kampt gegen den Krieg*, Munich 1953

Foertsch, Hermann, *Schuld und Verhängnis. Die Fritsch-Krise im Frühjahr 1938 als Wendepunkt in der Geschichte der nationalsozialistischen Zeit*, Stuttgart 1951

François-Poncet, André, *Souvenir d'une ambassade à Berlin*, Paris, 1946

Fuchs, Martin, *Un pacte avec Hitler. Le drama autrichien 1936–1938*, Paris 1938

Funder, Friedrich, *Als Österreich den Sturm bestand*, Vienna 1957

Galéra, Dr Karl Siegmar Baron von, *Österreichs Rückkehr ins Deutsche Reich, von Kaiser Karl zu Adolf Hitler*, Leipzig 1938

Gedye, George Eric Rowe, *Fallen Bastions*, London, 1939

Gehl, Jürgen, *Austria, Germany and the Anschluss*, London-New York-Toronto 1963

Goldinger, Walter, *Geschichte der Republik Österreich*, Vienna 1962

Goerlitz, Walter, *Generalfeldmarschall Keitel, Verbrecher oder Offizier?*, Göttingen 1961

Graz, die Stadt der Volkserhebung, hrsg. v. Gaupropagandaamt Steirmark, Graz 1938

Gschoepf, Rudolf, *Mein Weg mit der 45. Infanterie-Division*, Linz 1955

Guderian, Heinz, *Erinnerungen eines Soldaten*, Heidelberg 1951

Gulick, Charles, *Oesterreich von Habsburg zu Hitler*, Bd. 5, Vienna 1950

Gunther, John, *Die vorlorene Stadt*, Vienna-Munich 1964

Hadamovsky, Eugen, *Weltgeschichte im Sturmschritt. Hitlers Marsch nach Wien, Prag und Memel*, Munich 1941

List of Sources

Hagen, Walter (di.i Welhelm Höttl), *Die Geheime Front. Organisation, Personen und Aktionen des dt. Geheimdienstes*, Linz-Vienna 1950

Hammerstein-Equord, Kunrat Freiherr von, *Spähtrupp*, Stuttgart 1963

Hannak, Jacques, *Der Fürst, der sein Land verkaufte. Aus den Erinnerungen Ernst Rüdiger Starhembergs*, Vienna 1949

Hansen, Henrich (Hrsg;) *Volk will zu Volk*, Dortmund 1938

Hartlieb, Wladimir von, *Parole das Reich. Eine historische Darstellung der politischen Entwicklung in Österreich von März 1933 bis 1938*, Vienna-Leipzig 1939

Hartmann, Mitzi, *Austria still lives*, London, 1938

Helmer, Oskar, *50 Jahre erlebte Zeitgeschichte*, Vienna 1957

Henderson, Nevile, *Failure of a Mission*, London 1945

Heusinger, Adolf, *Befehl im Widerstreit. Schicksalsstunden der deutschen Armee 1923-1945*, Tübingen-Stuttgart 1950

Hillgruber, Andreas, 'Der Anschluss Österreichs 1938', in: *Neue Politische Literatur*, (9) 1964

Hitler, Adolf, *Mein Kampf*, Munich 1941

Hofer, Dr Josef Theodor, *Weggefährten. Vom Österr. Freiheitskampf 1933 bis 1945*, Vienna 1946

Holldack, Heinz, *Was wirklich geschah. Die diplomatischen Hintergründe der deutschen Kriegspolitik*, Munich 1949

Hossback, Friedrich, *Zwischen Wehrmacht und Hitler 1934-1938*, Wolfenbüttel-Hanover 1949

Huebmer, Hans, *Österreich 1933-1938*, Vienna 1949

In der Mauer, Wolf, Zernatto, Vienna 1966

Ingrim, Robert, *Der Griff nach Österreich*, Zurich 1938

Itzinger, Karl, *Tagebuch vom 10. Februar bis 14. März 1938*, Linz 1938

Jedlicka, Ludwig, *Ein Heer im Schatten der Parteiein*, Graz-Cologne 1955

Jedlicka, Ludwig, 'Verfassungs- und Verwaltungsprobleme 1938-1955', in: *Entwicklung der Verfassung Österreichs vom Mittelalter bis zur Gegenwart*, Vienna 1963

Jedlicka, Ludwig, 'Ernst Ruediger Starhemberg und die politische Entwicklung in Österreich im Frühjahr 1938', in: *Österreich und Europa, Festgabe f. Hugo Hantsch zum 70. Geburtstag*, Graz-Vienna-Cologne 1965

Kerekes, L., *Allianz Hitler-Horthy-Mussolini. Dokumente der ungarischen Aussenpolitik (1938-1944)*, Budapest 1966

Klusacek, Christine, *Österreichs Wissenschaftler und Künstler unter dem NS-Regime. Monographien zur Zeitgeschichte, Schriftenreihe des Dokumentationsarchivs des österr. Widerstandes*, Vienna-Frankfurt-Zurich 1966

Koerner, Ralf Richard, *Die publizistische Behandlung der Österreich-Frage und die Anschlussvorbereitungen in der Tagespresse des Dritten Reiches (1933-1938)*, Münster 1956

List of Sources

Koerner, Ralf Richard, *So haben sie es damals gemacht . . . Die Propagandavorbereitungen zum Österreich-Anschluss durch das Hitlerregime 1933 bis 1938*, Vienna 1958

Körber, Robert, *Rassesieg in Wien, der Grenzfeste des Reiches*, Vienna 1939

Kordt, Erich, *Wahn und Wirklichkeit. Die Aussenpolitik des Dritten Reiches, Versuch einer Darstellung*, Stuttgart 1948

Kordt, Erich, *Nicht aus den Akten. Die Wilhelmstrasse in Frieden und Krieg. Erlebnisse, Begegnungen und Eindrücke 1928–1945*, Stuttgart 1950

Krauss, Helene, *Wir danken unserem Führer!*, Vienna-Leipzig 1940

Langoth, Franz, *Kampf um Österreich. Erinnerungen eines Politikers*, Wels 1951

Leichter, Otto, *Glanz und Elend der Ersten Republik*, Vienna 1965

Leichter, Otto, *Österreichs freie Gewerkschaften im Untergrund*, Vienna-Cologne-Zurich 1963

Leichter, Otto, *Zwischen zwei Diktaturen. Österreichs Revolutionäre Sozialisten 1934–1938*, Vienna-Frankfurt-Zurich 1968

Lennhoff, Eugene, *The last five Hours of Austria*, London, 1938

Lorenz, Reinhold, *Der Staat wider Willen. Österreich von 1918–1938*, Berlin 1940

Lother, Ernst, *Das Wunder des Überlebens. Erinnerungen und Ergebnisse*, Vienna 1961

Ludwig, Eduard, *Österreichs Sendung im Donauraum. Die letzten Dezennien österreichischer Innen- und Aussenpolitik*, Vienna 1954

Mader, Julius, *Jagd nach dem Narbengesicht. Ein Dokumentar-Bericht über Hitlers SS-Geheimdienstchef Otto Skorzeny*, (Ost-) Berlin 1963

Mahler-Werfel, Alma, *Mein Leben*, Frankfurt 1963

Manstein, Erich von, *Aus einem Soldatenleben 1887–1939*, Wels 1958

Melzer, Frithjof (Hrsg.), *Weltgeschichte miterlebt! 7 Tage Österreich. DNB- Berichte aus Österreich vom 9. bis 15. März 1938*, Berlin 1938

Meysels, Th. F., *Die erste Woche*, Jerusalem, n.d.

Mikoletzky, Hans Leo, *Österreichische Zeitgeschichte*, Vienna 1962

Molden, Otto, *Der Ruf des Gewissens. Der österr. Freiheitskampf 1938–1945*, Vienna-Munich 1958

Morton, Frederic, *Die Rothschilds. Porträt einer Familie*, Munich 1965

Moser, Jonny, *Die Judenverfolgung in Österreich 1938–1945. Monographien zur Zeitgeschichte*, Vienna-Frankfurt-Zurich 1966

Mueller-Hillebrand, Burkhart, *Das Heer 1933–1945, Entwicklung des organisatorischen Aufbas*, Bd. 1: *Das Heer bis zum Kriegsbeginn*, Darmstadt 1954

Neufeldt, Hans-Joachim (Jürgen Huck, Georg Tessin), *Zur Geschichte der Ordnungspolizei 1936–1945*. Teil II: Georg Tessin, *Die Stäbe und Truppeneinheiten der Ordnungspolizei*, Coblenz 1957

Österreich unter dem Reichskommissariat, Bilanz eines Jahres Fremdherrschaft, Paris 1939

List of Sources

(*Ostmark*), *Wie die Ostmark ihre Befreiung erlebte*, (no place of publication) 1940

Papen, Franz von, *Der Wahrheit eine Gasse*, Munich 1952

Pembaur, Walter, *Im letzten Kampf um Österreich*, Vienna-Leipzig 1939

Raab, Herbert, *Widerstand, Tagebuch eines Sturmführers*, Vienna 1942

Reich von Rohrwig, Otto, *Der Freiheitskampf der Ostmark-Deutschen*, Graz-Vienna-Leipzig 1942

Reimann, Viktor, *Innitzer, Kardinal zwischen Hitler und Rom*, Vienna 1967

Rendulic, Lothar, *Soldat in stürzenden Reichen*, Munich 1965

Renner, Karl, *Österreich von der Ersten zur Zweiten Republik*, Bd. 2, *Nachgelassene Werke*, Vienna 1953

Ribbentrop, Anneliese von, *Verschwörung gegen den Frieden*, Leoni 1962

Ribbentrop, Joachim von, *Zwischen London und Moskau*, Leoni 1953

Rieser, Max, *Österreichs Sterbeweg*, Vienna 1953

Rintelen, Anton, *Erinnerungen an Österreichs Weg, Versailles, Berchtesgaden, Grossdeutschland*, Munich 1941

Rintelen, Enno von, *Mussolini als Bundesgenosse. Erinnerungen eines Militärattachés in Rom 1936–1943*, Tübingen-Stuttgart 1951

Robertson, E. M., *Hitler's prewar Policy and Military Plans 1933–1939*, London, 1963

Romanik, Felix, *Der Leidensweg der österreichischen Wirtschaft, Monographien zur Zeitgeschichte*, Vienna-Frankfurt-Zurich 1957

Schacht, Hjalmar, *76 Jahre meines Lebens*, Bad Wörishofen 1953

Schellenberg, Walter, *Memoiren*, Cologne 1959

Schlabrendorff, Fabian von, *Offiziere gegen Hitler*, Frankfurt 1959

Schmidt, Paul, *Statist auf diplomatischer Bühne 1923–1945*, Bonn 1951

Schmitz, Trude, 'Dr Wilhelm Miklas', in: *Die österr. Bundespraesidenten*, Vienna 1963

Schopper, Hans, *Presse im Kampf, Geschichte der Presse während der Kampfjahre der NSDAP (1933–1938)*, Brünn (Brno)-Vienna-Leipzig 1941

Schuschnigg, Kurt von, *Ein Requiem in Rot-Weiss-Rot*, Zurich 1946

Seabury, Paul, *Die Wilhelmstrasse*, Frankfurt 1956

Sheridon, R. K., *Kurt von Schuschnigg*, London 1947

Shirer, William L., *The Rise and Fall of the Third Reich*, London 1960

Skorzeny, Otto, *Geheimkommando Skorzeny*, Hamburg 1950

Stadler, Karl, *Österreich 1938–1945 im Spiegel der NS-Akten*, Vienna, Munich 1966

Starhemberg, Ernst Rüdiger, *Between Hitler and Mussolini*, London 1941

Steinbauer, Gustav, *Ich war Verteidiger in Nurnberg*, Klagenfurt 1950

Steininger, Anton, *Augbruch ins Reich*, Graz-Leipzig-Vienna 1941

List of Sources

Strauch, Rudi, *Sir Nevile Henderson, Britischer Botschafter in Berlin von 1937 bis 1939. Ein Beitrag zur diplomatischen Vorgeschichte des Zweiten Weltkrieges*, Bonn 1959

Sündermann, Helmut, *Die Grenzen fallen. Von der Ostmark zum Sudetenland*, Munich 1939

Völker, Heinz, *Die Deutsche Luftwaffe 1933–1939. Aufbau, Führung und Rüstung der Luftwaffe sowie die Entwicklung der deutschen Luftkriegstheorie*, Stuttgart 1967

Wache, Karl (Hrsg.), *Deutscher Geist in Österreich. Ein Handbuch des völkischen Lebens der Ostmark*, Dornbirn 1933

Wathen, Mary Antonia, *The Policy of England and France toward the 'Anschluss' of 1938*, Washington 1954

Weber-Stumfohl, Herta, *Ostmarkmädel, Ein Erlebnisbuch aus den Anfangsjahren und der illegalen Kampfzeit des BDM in der Ostmark*, Berlin 1939

Weidt, Kurt, 'Hat Hitler Österreich überfallen? Der Anschluss in zehn Stationen', in: *Politische Studien* 14, 1963

Weinberger, Lois, *Tatsachen, Begegnungen und Gespräche, Ein Buch um Österreich*, Vienna 1948

Weizssäcker, Ernst von, *Erinnerungen*, Munich 1950

Welchert, H. H., *Österreichs Weg ins Reich 1917–1938*, Hamburg 1938 to 1941

Wels in den Tagen der Befreiung, Wels 1938

(*Wien*), *Die nationalsozialistische Revolution in Wien, Bildbericht über die Ereignisse vom 11. März bis 10 April 1938*, Geleitwort Dr. Ing. Neubacher, Vienna 1938

(*Wiener Zeitung*), *250 Jahre Wiener Zeitung. Eine Festschrift*, Vienna 1963

Wieser, Georg, *Ein Staat stirbt. Österreich 1934–1938*, Paris 1938

Wildner, Clemens, *Von Wien nach Wien. Erinnerungen eines Diplomaten*, Vienna-Munich 1961

Wimmer, Lothar, *Zwischen Ballhausplatz und Downingstreet*, Vienna-Munich 1958

Winkler, F., *Die Dikatur in Österreich*, Zurich 1935

Wisshaupt, Walter, *Wir kommen wieder! Eine Geschichte der Revolutionären Sozialen Österreichs 1934–1938*, Vienna 1967

Wolters, Rudolf and Wolf, Heinrich, *Die neue Reichskanzlei*, Berlin n.d.

Zernatto, Guido, *Die Wahrheit über Österreich*, New York 1938

Zernatto, Guido, *Vom Wesen der Nation*, Vienna 1966

Zöllner, Erich, *Geschichte Österreichs von den Anfängen bis zur Gegenwart*, Vienna 1961

Zuckmayer, Carl, *Als wärs ein Stück von mir*, Frankfurt 1966

INDEX

Index

Index

Index

Index